How to Catch
MORE TROUT

by Charles R. Meck

Illustrations by
William Frangos and Sabrina Heep

(handwritten inscription: To Jenny, I hope you have a great meeting at ... you find fly. Sport. June 25, 2007)

A Beaver Pond Publication
Greenville, Pennsylvania

How to Catch MORE TROUT

©*2001 Charles R. Meck*

To contact Charles Meck:
www.charlesmeck.com

Beaver Pond Publishing

P.O. Box 224
Greenville, PA 16125
Phone: (724) 588-3492
Fax: (724) 588-2486
Email: beaverpond@pathway.net

TABLE OF CONTENTS

DEDICATION

T his book on *How to Catch More Trout* is dedicated to Peter Kunis of Mine Hill, New Jersey. Peter died on June 1, 1999. The evening before he died he had fished the Lackawanna River in northeastern Pennsylvania, and had his best event ever of matching a hatch. Peter caught five trout that evening during a sulphur hatch and all were over 18 inches long. Peter went out to the Lackawanna River the next day, June 1, with his best reel and bamboo fly rod in search of some more big trout. Several hours later one of his friends, Howard Sweeny, saw Peter's car parked along the river and looked for him. Howard found Peter's rod and reel in the water and finally found Peter's body along the river. When Howard retrieved Peter's fly rod he found that the fly had been broken off the leader. Evidently Peter died of a heart attack attempting to land that last big brown trout. What a way to go!

Peter, your friends like Howard Sweeny and Jim Misiura, and many others in the Northeast will forever miss you, but we're all certain that you're now fishing that big river in the sky and catching a lunker on every cast.

ACKNOWLEDGMENTS

Over the past couple years much of what I've included in this book has been presented at various conferences, workshops and conclaves. As a result of those talks and encouragement from the audience for more information, I wrote this book. Thanks to Chuck Furimsky and Barry Serviente who conduct Fly Fishing Shows in Marlboro, Massachusetts; Somerset, New Jersey; Charlotte, North Carolina; and Annapolis, Maryland. For nine years they've been kind enough to include me in their great programs.

Thanks also to New Mexico Trout and to their president Dick Newman and members Mike Maurer. This is probably the best trout organization in the entire United States. They really know how to conduct their annual program which is usually held in January. It was with the encouragement of many of the registrants at their Conclave 2000 that I decided to complete this book.

Thanks also to Jody Howell of the Lynx Creek Unlimited Shop in Prescott, Arizona, and to the group that attended a recent talk in that great city. They gave me plenty of ideas for the book.

Thanks also to Jake and Donna McDonald who run the Upper Canyon Outfitters just outside of Alder, Montana. Recently Jerry Armstrong, a fishing guide, and I ran a fly fishing workshop at the lodge. I learned a lot from Jerry at that program.

Thanks also to Gary Hitterman of Casa Grande, Arizona, for sharing patterns like the Zebra Midge with me. Gary's one of the finest fly tiers I've had the pleasure of meeting.

Thanks also to Bill Frangos. Bill is a member of New Mexico Trout and lives in Albuquerque, New Mexico. He recently showed me one of his illustrations on knot tying and I immediately knew who I wanted to illustrate knots in the book. Thanks also to Sabrina Heep a student at Al Collins School in Tempe, Arizona, who also made the casting illustrations for the book.

Strategies for *How to Catch More Trout* work on a wide spectrum of waters, such as the Ruby River in southwestern Montana (top), the Willowemoc in New York (center), and the Ausable in Michigan (bottom).

– 1 –
INTRODUCTION

A re you just beginning to fly fish? Have you been fly-fishing for several years? Or, maybe you consider yourself an expert and have been casting that fly for decades. No matter what you are you'd like to catch more trout. I've been fly fishing for more than 50 years and I can still look back at those early days when I came home skunked more often than I care to remember. After all these years those barren days have become fewer and fewer. Why? I've watched and observed—and above all—I've learned.

Much of what I learn about fly fishing—the feeding habits of trout,

You'll find that these tactics help you catch more trout on southwestern waters like the Verde River near Cottonwood, Arizona.

and what works and doesn't—I've done by sitting down on a stream bank and watch action unfold in front of me. I often sit and watch other anglers fish; I watch insects emerge and trout feed on them; and above all I see what works and what doesn't work. I learn a lot by just sitting and watching. I've been doing this for years. While I worked on *Meeting and Fishing the Hatches* in 1975 I sat back for hours and studied the emergence of the yellow drake.

These non-events have helped me in my 50 years of fly-fishing. From these observations I have developed a series of strategies that I follow closely if I want to catch more trout. These ingredients important to a more successful fishing trip are pattern selection, where you fish that pattern, drag or lack of it on the fly, what tippet you use to connect the fly, and how you detect strikes. These five ingredients, plus fishing when hatches appear and when conditions are terrible, will increase appreciably the number of trout you catch. We'll cover all of these and other important ingredients thoroughly in this book.

Let me give you an example how the information in this book will help you. Ron Dorula is a skilled fly fisher and fly tier from southwestern Pennsylvania. I recently had an opportunity to fly fish with him for several hours during a trico spinner fall. I sat back and watched while Ron cast over more than a dozen trout rising to the spinner fall. The stream was extremely low and the trout skittish. Every cast seemed to scatter a few trout. Ron used the same size 24 Trico pattern for more than a half-hour and had only a couple trout look at it. He sat down with me and we discussed why he wasn't catching any trout. Yes, he had covered the trout with drag free drifts. Second he fished at the level where the trout were feeding—on the surface. We then looked at two other important ingredients to catching trout—pattern and leader. Ron added a piece of 8X-fluorocarbon tippet and began casting again. Now the trout showed more interest. Dozens of trout drifted with the pattern but most refused it. Next he changed the pattern from a size 24 spent spinner to a size 26-parachute pattern. After switching to the smaller pattern Ron immediately began to catch trout. He landed a dozen fish on that new pattern before the hatch had ended. Why? He had followed all the rules for catching more trout. He switched the pattern to a smaller one; he had no drag when he drifted the pattern over rising fish; he added a piece of finer leader; and he fished a floating fly over rising trout. These are all things you'll learn more about in this book.

What won't you learn about in this book? You won't learn how to cast for distance. Many fly casters would argue that you've got to be an expert fly caster to catch more trout. I've seen many of these professional fly casters throw a 100-foot line and then ask those who have watched

Following the five ingredients in this book, you'll catch more trout on the San Juan River in New Mexico on a late winter day.

The Yakima in eastern Washington can produce many fine trout for the person using the right techniques. While you're there, why not have fun catching more trout?

Henry's Fork in Idaho is an insect factory. What better place to find trout in numbers to test the easy techniques on the following pages?

The Eglinton River on New Zealand's South Island races to the ocean. Its length is full of trout. Around the globe, the right strategies will produce.

them to try to do the same. How many times have you had to cast a hundred feet to reach a trout? In my more than 50 years of fly fishing I've found that most trout can be reached with a cast of 30 to 40 feet. A required cast much farther than that is a real exception rather than the rule.

You also won't learn about equipment selection. You can buy a balanced outfit from Orvis, Sage or Winston that will cost 400 to 500 dollars and that outfit will last you a lifetime. Many anglers ask me what length of rod I prefer and I usually tell them a nine-foot-five weight. I've found that size rod to work well on streams and rivers across the United States.

What will you learn in this book? You'll learn about some new strategies, tactics and techniques that I've experimented with over the past decade or two. You'll learn about using sunken spinners. I'll never forget that time more than two decades ago when I saw an angler take a half dozen trout during a trico hatch while I caught just one. That angler showed me his secret.

What are some of my favorite well-tested patterns that work when there's no hatch on the water? We'll discuss this and much much more about patterns and pattern selection in Chapter 2.

You'll find more about patterns in Chapter 3, especially those that match the hatches. The more you know about the hatches, when they appear, where they appear, and what patterns match them, the more trout you'll catch. Chapter 3 has plenty of charts to aid you in insect identification, times of emergence, and more. What are some of the most memorable fishing trips for me? Most of them occur around a hatch of stoneflies, caddisflies, or mayflies. Your probability of success increases geometrically if you fish the hatches—and if you're properly prepared for them. What about the time I hit one of the heaviest trico hatches I've ever encountered in my lifetime—in February? No other fly fisher knew about this hatch and for weeks I fished alone when these insects appeared.

Have you ever given much thought to at what level you place your fly when you're fishing? Do you fish on the surface, just under the surface, or near the bottom? Where you fish that pattern can again mean the difference between a successful or a barren fishing trip. We look at varying the depth of the fly in Chapter 4.

I'll always remember that trip to a Montana pond several years ago. I caught trout that first hour while my son and a friend caught none. We changed their tippets and they caught up to me within an hour with that new material. We'll discuss leaders and knots in Chapter 5.

Of all the things I've learned in the past 50 years of fly-fishing probably the most important ingredient to success is drag—or rather the lack of it. We'll examine what causes drag and how to prevent it in Chapter 6.

I'll never forget that trip to the Blue River near Dillon, Colorado, in 1976. I watched a spin fisher use a large clear bubble with a wet fly and I saw him literally clean up. We now have the same advantage with strike indicators, including the tandem. We'll look at all types of strike indicators and the advantages and disadvantages of each in Chapter 7

How can you increase your chances of success during the fishing season? Fish when weather conditions are at their worst. The best fly fishing days I've ever had have occurred when a hatch appeared on the surface and it couldn't take off because of cool weather, drizzle, or some other impediment. We'll also look at fishing heavily fished streams in Chapter 8. Chapter 8 also includes other suggestions to help you fish smarter not harder.

Chapter 9 includes just about every pattern recipe you'll ever need to tie, including a lot of relatively new ones. Have you ever heard of a bead head Glo Bug? Chapter 9 tells you how to tie this fish catcher.

At the beginning of each chapter you'll find a set of rules listed. These rules are a synthesis of the entire chapter. In most cases they're just common sense.

Where will these strategies we discuss in the book work? They work everywhere! If you use them you'll catch more trout on New Zealand's pristine waters like the Englinton River on the South Island. They work on heavily fished Western rivers like Henry's Fork in Idaho and on the San Juan in New Mexico. And they especially work on rivers like the AuSable in the Midwest on New York's Willowemoc and in the East.

Do you want to catch more trout? You will if you use what you've learned in this book on your next trip. Get ready for an educational and hopefully entertaining trip through the book.

– 2 –
SELECTING THE RIGHT PATTERN WHEN THERE'S NO HATCH

Rule 1. Be flexible. Change patterns if you're not catching trout.

Rule 2. What fly you use depends on the condition of the water you're fishing.

Rule 3. Try attractor patterns when no hatch appears.

Rule 4. Develop a short list of patterns that work for you when there is no hatch.

Donald DuBois wrote *The Fisherman's Handbook of Trout Flies* in 1960. I met him in 1975 on Penns Creek in central Pennsylvania and asked him to autograph my book. He said he wanted to fish with me first, then he would sign the book. I came back to his trailer several hours later to go fishing with him for the evening hatch and he declined because he wasn't feeling well. I never got that book signed. His book, however, remains a classic. In that book he listed almost 6000 different patterns. How many patterns have been devised since 1960? I'm certain the number has now grown geometrically—so have your choices.

So, one of the first important parts, and often the most challenging, of catching more trout is pattern selection. That first decision that you make on the stream—which fly will I use today—might mean the difference between a highly successful day and one full of frustration.

How many times have you seen somebody nearby catching a lot of trout while you're struggling to catch one or two? It's happened to me more times than I care to remember. How many times have you wished you had that same pattern that other angler was using? How many times have you finally broken down and approached that other fly fisher and asked him or her what pattern he or she was using? I've done it many times.

Selecting the right fly can make a day of fishing one of the most memorable trips of your life. I'll never ever forget that outstanding day on central Pennsylvania's Penns Creek. Here's how I described it in *Trout Streams and Hatches of Pennsylvania:*

Fourth of July on Penns Creek, the famous but sometimes frustrating limestone stream in central Pennsylvania. By 10:00 A.M. the temperature had barely reached 58 degrees, and a fine drizzle fell. At the lower end of the catch-and-release section on this holiday, no one was fly-fishing except me. Two other fair-weather anglers had returned their gear to their cars seemingly disgusted with the depressing weather. I was the only nut remaining on the entire stretch of that productive water. I headed up the abandoned railroad bed toward the R. B. Winter estate. Swallows cruised near the water's surface, crisscrossing upstream, downstream, and across stream. Just in front of me thousands of Blue-Winged Olive Duns floated, half-dazed, and swirling around in an eddy. Normally this species (*Drunella cornutella*) takes off rapidly from the surface when emerging, but the unusually cold weather today prevented the duns from escaping quickly from the water. Five, ten, fifteen trout rose in a small riffle in front of me.

I quickly tied on a size-16 Blue-Winged Olive Dun, nervously finishing the improved clinch knot. The leader slipped out of the second loop, and I had to retie the knot. More and more duns emerged and added to the incredible number already resting on the surface. When it seemed like every trout in that section had taken my Blue-Winged imitation, I moved upstream. Ahead of me lay some moderate water with a boulder-strewn area at its head. Here maybe 15 more trout lined up in a feeding lane and fed in frenzy on the duns. At least 10 of the trout in that stretch sucked in the dry fly. I continued upstream for about a half-mile, fishing every pool, riffle, and pocket that harbored rising trout. Remember, while this unbelievable fly-fishing over a hatch continued, not one other person took part in the excitement—not one other fly fisherman shared this memorable experience. Three hours, 65 trout, and seven imitations later, I quit.

Not long after I wrote about the preceding incident on Penns Creek I received a letter from Andrew Leitzinger of Collegeville, Pennsylvania. It seems Andrew had experienced that same memorable hatch on Penns that day, 10 years ago. Andrew fished the hatch two miles upstream from me. He wrote:

"On July 4, 1979, in the late morning after a cold rain, I fished the upper no-kill stretch of Penns Creek from the Broadwaters to the Upper Island. I found the surface covered with tiny Blue-Winged Olive mayflies. I fished this stretch with a size 20 midge Adams and hooked and released 30 trout between 10 and 17 inches long. I missed many, many more. The water surface was quite broken as far as you could see with feeding fish.

I fished that day in complete solitude (I thought). I was cold, happy, and alone. I can remember how my shoulders ached from so many hours, and my thumb had become tattered by the teeth of the many trout that I had released. I stopped fishing at about 5:00 P.M. because I had reached a state just short of exhaustion. I exalted the cold gray heavens above me and gave thanks for a wonderful and unique gift.

So when I read your book and came across the passage on your experience at Penns Creek, I wondered what the odds were that such conditions had occurred more than once on a fourth of July in the past 10 years: a cold rain, a great hatch of Blue-Winged Olives, and a nearly deserted stream. If our two days were separate in time, then a statistical phenomenon has occurred to be noted! But if, as I hope, those two days were one and the same, then I am glad to know that one other person was able to share the exhilaration I felt that day. Those days, when all things come together, are few and far between and should never be taken for granted."

I especially like Andy's ending. Selecting the right pattern can make those "things come together." Did I select the right pattern for the occasion? You bet I did!

How many times have you attempted to match a hatch but you had no appropriate pattern? It used to happen to me frequently. I'll never forget that first time I hit the brown drake hatch in Eastern United States. I tried using a March Brown, Black Quill, and a dozen other patterns and caught only a few trout while hundreds rose just a few feet in front of me. That's why it's important to know as much about the hatches as possible. We'll examine hatches and the patterns that match them in more detail in Chapter 3.

But, let's face it—you'll probably fish more often when no hatch appears than when one does. We'll examine what patterns seem to work on days when no hatch appears here.

Table 1. Which Pattern Will I Use Today?

Type of Day, Time of Year, or Condition of Stream	Suggested Dry Fly Patterns	Suggested Wet Fly Patterns	Reference to any Discussion in the Book	Fluoro-carbons (Chap. 5)	Suggested Leader Diameter (Chap. 5)	Type of Strike Indicator (Chap. 7)	Depth (Chap. 4)
Early Spring	Gray patterns like the Quill Gordon, Blue Quill, Hendrick-son and the Western March Brown	Gray wet flies Bead head patterns, Wooly Bugger, and Green Weenie	"See When Grays Appear" in Chapter 3	Yes	4X-5X	Tandem or poly	Top and bottom
Fall	Gray patterns like the Little Blue-winged Olive Dun and the Slate Drake	Gray wet flies and bead heads including the Glo Bug	See "When Grays Appear" in Chapter 3	Yes	4X-5X	Tandem, putty, or plastic bubble	Top and bottom
Summer— Evening	Light patterns like the Sulphur, Light Cahill, and Cream Cahill. Downwings like the Tan Caddis	Bead heads and emergers	See "Insect Identification Chart" and "When Grays Appear" in Chapter 3.	Yes	4X-6X	Tandem	Top and just underneath
Summer— Day	Olive and gray patterns like the Blue-winged Olive	Bead heads	See "Insect Identification Chart" and "When Grays Appear" in Chapter 3.	Yes	4X-6X	Tandem	Top and underneath

Table 1. Which Pattern Will I Use Today? *(continued)*

Type of Day, Time of Year, or Condition of Stream	Suggested Dry Fly Patterns	Suggested Wet Fly Patterns	Reference to any Discussion in the Book	Fluoro-carbons *(Chap. 5)*	Suggested Leader Diameter *(Chap. 5)*	Type of Strike Indicator *(Chap. 7)*	Depth *(Chap. 4)*
Winter	Midges, Little Blue-winged Olives	Bead heads, streamers, Glo Bugs, and Midge pupa	See Chapter 2 "My Top Five Patterns when the Water is High, Cold, or Off Color"	Yes	3X-5X	Tandem	Bottom
High Water		Streamers and Bead Heads	See Chapter 2 "My Top Five Patterns when the Water is High, Cold, or Off Color"	No	3X-5X	Poly	Deep
Low Water	Terrestrials, Midges, and imitations to match any hatch	Small bead heads		Yes	5X-7X	Tandem	Surface
Cold Water	Imitations to match any hatch	Streamers, Bead Heads	See Chapter 2 "My Top Five Patterns when the Water is High, Cold, or Off Color"	Yes	4X-6X	Poly or marker	Deep

Table 1. Which Pattern Will I Use Today? *(continued)*

Type of Day, Time of Year, or Condition of Stream	Suggested Dry Fly Patterns	Suggested Wet Fly Patterns	Reference to any Discussion in the Book	Fluoro-carbons *(Chap. 5)*	Suggested Leader Diameter *(Chap. 5)*	Type of Strike Indicator *(Chap. 7)*	Depth *(Chap. 4)*
Hatch in Progress	Match the hatch	Copy the emerger and the nymph	See Chapter 3 Tables 1-4 and 9 and 11 to help identify hatch and "Sinking Spinner and Dun Patterns" in Chapter 4. See Chapter 9 for tying details on nymphs and emergers.	Yes	4X-6X	You might want to try an emerger pattern behind an imitation matching the hatch— especially if trout are refusing your pattern	Use the tandem to fish two depths at once or try pulling your pattern "matching the hatch" underneath if a dry fly doesn't work.
Overcast, Drizzle Day	Little Blue-winged Olive, Blue-winged Olive, Pale Morning Dun, or Sulphur	Emerger patterns to copy the same hatches	See "Fish When Conditions are Terrible" in Chapter 8.	Yes	4X-7X	None	Surface
No Hatch	Patriot or other Attractor	Bead Heads like the Pheasant Tail, Olive Caddis, Tan Caddis, Glo Bug, or Green Weenie	See "My Wet Fly Choices When There's No Hatch" later in this chapter	Yes	4X-6X	Tandem	Surface and Underneath

Table 1. Which Pattern Will I Use Today? *(continued)*

Type of Day, Time of Year, or Condition of Stream	Suggested Dry Fly Patterns	Suggested Wet Fly Patterns	Reference to any Discussion in the Book	Fluoro-carbons *(Chap. 5)*	Suggested Leader Diameter *(Chap. 5)*	Type of Strike Indicator *(Chap. 7)*	Depth *(Chap. 4)*
Spinner Fall in Progress	Fish the spinner fall	Sink the spinner imitation	See Chapter 3 Tables 1-4, and 10 and 12 to help identify spinner fall and "Sinking Spinner and Dun Patterns" in Chapter 4	Yes	5X-8X	None	If surface pattern doesn't work try sinking the spinner. See Chapter 4
Night	Large dry flies	Streamers	See "Streamer Choices" later in This Chapter.	No	2X-4X	None	Surface and Underneath
Small Stream	Terrestrials and attractor dry flies	Small bead heads (Sizes 14 to 18)	See "My Top Dry Flies that Match No Hatch— Attractors" in Chapter 2	Yes	4X-7X	Tandem with a weighted terrestrial and a attractor dry fly	If ant and beetle patterns don't work on the surface try sinking them.
Heavily Fished Waters	Small dry fly patterns, and match the hatches	Small bead heads (sizes 16 to 22)	See "Special Tactics for Fishing Heavily Fished Waters" in Chapter 8	Yes	4X-7X	Tandem, none, or a marker on the fly line	Surface (Try all levels if surface patterns don't work)

Table 1. Which Pattern Will I Use Today? *(continued)*

Type of Day, Time of Year, or Condition of Stream	Suggested Dry Fly Patterns	Suggested Wet Fly Patterns	Reference to any Discussion in the Book	Fluoro-carbons *(Chap. 5)*	Suggested Leader Diameter *(Chap. 5)*	Type of Strike Indicator *(Chap. 7)*	Depth *(Chap. 4)*
Cloudy Water	None	Bright streamers like the Mickey Finn and Clouser Minnow	See "My Top Patterns When the Water is High, Cold, or Off Color" Later in this Chapter	No	3X-4X	Poly or plastic	Bottom
Lakes, Ponds and Still Water	Midges, Speckle-winged Dun	Midge pupa. Damselfly Nymph and Streamers like the Peacock Lady	See Chapter 3 on "Midges" and Table 12—Lake Hatch Chart	Yes	4X-7X	Tandem, none	Surface (Try all levels if surface patterns don't work)

Which Pattern Will I Use Today?

Which pattern will you use today? Table 1 should be helpful in making that decision. The table not only covers patterns, but also leaders (Chapter 5) and where you should fish that pattern (Chapter 4). There are many variables that go into making a decision of what pattern to use. We cover a few of the most important here. The patterns I suggest here might not work as well for you. Maybe over the years patterns like the Prince Nymph and Muskrat Nymph have been proven performers for you. *It's important that you develop a short list of patterns that work well for you when there is no hatch.*

I recently fished a nondescript stream in north central Pennsylvania—one I had never fly-fished before. As I waded upstream I saw no signs of trout, until I arrived at a deep, slow pool a few hundred years above my parked car. Here I saw another angler, Nicholas Somogi, making frantic casts and mumbling to himself. When he saw me he immediately pointed to several dozen trout directly in the water in front of him.

In a frustrated voice the other angler said: "I've tried just about every pattern in my fly box and nothing seems to work."

I opened my fly box and handed him two patterns—a Patriot dry fly and a size 16 bead head Pheasant Tail Nymph. I showed him how to tie the two patterns in tandem by tying a two-foot piece of 4X tippet material to the bend of the shank of the dry fly. I thought a tandem was a good choice there because the trout we saw were not on the bottom, but rather two feet below the surface.

On the very first cast with that duo of flies his Patriot dry fly sank, he set the hook, and released a 12-inch rainbow. Two casts later he caught a second trout on the bead head pattern. After an hour or so trout refused the pattern so we switched to a Green Weenie and continued to catch trout. For the next two hours the two of us caught more than 40 trout— most of them on the wet fly.

Every time a strong wind blew that afternoon I noted that a dozen or more trout began to feed in a shallow glide upstream from us. I tied on an ant pattern and picked up several trout.

Talk about a bad day tuned good—it certainly did for the two of us.

How many times has this same type of event happened to you? I can speak from experience and say it has happened to me hundreds of times. I know I'm fishing over plenty of trout, but I can't catch them. What pattern you select—and how you fish that pattern—can make all the difference in the world. Let's examine several questions you might ask before you select that pattern.

Which fly will you use today? It depends on a whole lot of variables like the stream you plan to fish and the time of year you're using that pattern. You should also consider other features like whether or not you'll see any insects on the water and which pattern or patterns you feel most confident with. Consider what your confidence level is for some patterns. If you like a pattern and it works well for you then stick with it You've also got to consider the size, shape, and color of the pattern, and the conditions of the stream. Above all if the pattern you've used with success like the bead head Pheasant Tail in our earlier story begins to fail you, *then switch*. By changing to another pattern in the earlier story we continued to catch trout. Ask yourself some of the following questions to find out what pattern you want to use.

What Stream Do I Plan To Fish?

Certain patterns seem to work better on certain streams. I would never go near Clarks Creek, just north of Harrisburg, Pennsylvania, without a good supply of Green Weenies. The same goes for Fishing Creek in Clinton County in the same state. I wouldn't fish Lee's Ferry on the Colorado River in Arizona without a good supply of chironomid patterns, both wet and dry. The Lee's Ferry area harbors more than 30 midge species and trout feed on them for several hours each day. If you ever plan to fish the Red River in northern New Mexico carry plenty of bead head Glo Bug patterns with you. Trout head up this river from the Rio Grande to breed in December and take a Glo Bug readily. If you plan to fish New Mexico's San Juan you've got to carry some Red Worms with you. Just about every stream that's worth fishing in the United States has one or two patterns that seem to work well on them. Before you fish a stream or river check with some local experts to see what patterns they recommend.

But, there are certain patterns that seem to work on any stream and river. I've listed my favorites later.

What are the Conditions?

Before you select a pattern determine what the conditions are? Is the stream high, or off color? If it is, select a bright colored wet fly pattern or a streamer. Is the stream low and extremely clear? Maybe you want to start off with a small wet fly like a size 18-bead head Pheasant Tail. *What fly you select should depend on the conditions of the water you're fishing.* Table 1 should help you select patterns for specific conditions.

I'll never forget that trip to the Little Colorado in the White Mountains of Arizona. Craig Josephson and I had arrived at the X-Diamond Ranch in mid May while the river was still swollen from snowmelt. We fished for more than an hour without any success. Finally, I tied on a bead head Wooly Bugger. That Wooly Bugger that day saved the trip. Craig and I landed more than 20 trout on that heavy pattern in that deep water.

Then there are those days when the water is low and extremely clear like the day Craig Shuman, Garry Sandstrom, and I hit Rocky Ford Creek near Moses Lake in eastern Washington. Only small midges and Blue-winged Olive patterns in sizes 22 to 24 would trick trout on these low, clear, and heavily fished, waters.

There's another condition that you've got to determine when you arrive at a river: Do you expect to see a hatch today? That brings back memories of the many trips to Western rivers to fish the Western green drake hatch. This huge species often appears on rivers of the West still high from snowmelt. It often brings trout to the surface for the first time in the season. If you expect to see a hatch—even in high water conditions—be prepared for it. Check Chapter 3 for most of the more common hatches you'll encounter.

What Time of Year am I Fishing the Stream?

Certain patterns work better certain times of the year. What is the predominant color of insects appearing in April and again in September and October? Where do these mayflies land to rest? They usually rest on branches of trees or bushes. What is the color of these branches or bushes in April? Gray, and that's the general coloration of just about every mayfly and stonefly that appears in the spring and fall. When leaves and flowers start appearing in May and June then you get your more colorful mayflies. That's when to use the light cahill. At that time of year you'll see hatches like the light cahill, sulphur, cream cahill, pink lady, especially in the evening. If major hatches occur during the day in the summer, these insects are usually darker in coloration than those emerging in the evening. For example, during May and June you'll see hatches like the blue-winged olive dun, chocolate dun, and blue quill appearing. All these dark-bodied mayflies emerge during the daylight hours. Table 1 should help you decide on the color of the pattern for certain times of the year.

So, as a general rule, you should use gray flies in April and again in September and October. On summer trips, if you plan to fly-fish during the day use a dark-colored mayfly, in the evening use a light-colored pattern. If I plan to fish a small heavily canopied stream in the summer I often resort to terrestrials. We'll look at this in more detail in Chapter 3.

Should I use a Downwing Pattern?

Don't overlook downwing patterns. I remember that summer trip to the Bighorn River in Montana with my son Bryan one mid July evening. Nothing we used caught trout—until we switched to a size 16 Black Caddis. We had arrived at the three-mile takeout area and Bryan wanted to continue to fish. Trout rose to black caddis for more than two hours that evening. The two of us had a similar experience on the Ruby River, in southwestern Montana. Here trout rose eagerly for a size 14 Tan Caddis pattern. We'll examine in more detail caddis and stonefly patterns in Chapter 3.

Recently I fished the Saucon Creek in southeastern Pennsylvania with Rich Heiserman. We hit the stream in early July during a trico spinner fall. Rich tried a Trico pattern for a half-hour without any success. He then switched to one of his favorite patterns, a size 16 Tan Elk Hair Caddis. Within an hour Rich picked up a half dozen trout on that pattern and missed as many more. He had all this success when there was no hatch on the water. Hatch or no hatch the Tan Caddis is one of the most productive patterns you can use during the summer.

What Hatches Do I Expect To See?

If you expect a hatch, pattern selection is rather simple—that is, if you're fairly familiar with most of the hatches. Tables 9-12 in Chapter 3 suggest specific patterns that match hatches and that might be best during certain times of the season. The chart should help you narrow the number of imitations you carry with you. I have three compartments in my chest fly box. One is marked "early," another "middle," and the third is labeled "late." I place the most common patterns to match the hatches for each season in these compartments. Chapter 3 will explain this aspect in detail.

You'll often encounter problems when you see more than one hatch or spinner fall occurring at the same time. I've already encountered three and four hatches appearing at the same time on Henry's Fork in Idaho. Schwiebert and others have called this water a virtual insect factory. I've seen blue-winged olives, Western green drakes, and pale morning duns on the surface at the same time. Read Chapter 3 for more details.

With Which Pattern Do I Feel Most Confident?

Often it's a case of which pattern you believe in—which one consistently works for you. Phil Baldacchino, an expert angler and fly shop owner, fishes Kettle Creek in north central Pennsylvania on a regular basis. The stream runs through his back yard. I'll never forget that day Phil and I fished the Adam's Hole during a hendrickson hatch. For every trout I caught on a Red Quill pattern Phil caught two on his pattern. What was he using during the hatch? Would you believe he used a Humpy pattern with a bright red body. While Phil sold hundreds of Hendrickson patterns in his shop during the hatch, he used the Humpy as his pattern of choice—and caught plenty of trout. Lots of times what will work for you will be the pattern in which you have the most confidence. For Phil that pattern is the Goofus or Humpy.

I've seen other anglers who swear by a Light Cahill and use that all summer. I like the bead head Pheasant Tail and I use it on just about every stream I fish. Rarely has this pattern failed me. I'm so confident with this bead head that if I don't get a strike within a half-hour with that pattern I often quit or move to another location. If that pattern doesn't work I'll switch to a bead head Green or Tan Caddis.

If you've been successful with a pattern on one stream it will probably work for you on another stream.

Should I Change Patterns?

I just mentioned that if I don't get a strike on the bead head Pheasant Tail in a half-hour of fishing I move. If I don't move I change patterns. Look at the example I noted earlier on the nondescript stream in northwestern Pennsylvania. After the two of us had caught quite a few trout on a bead head, the number of strikes began to decrease dramatically. Why? Were trout tired of seeing that particular pattern? Were most of the trout that were interested in the bead caught or hooked by us? It's probably a lot of the latter. Whatever it is, be prepared to switch patterns until you begin catching trout. I can often tell how frustrating a trip I'm having by how short my tippet is at the end of the day. A short tippet means I changed flies often. On some tough days I resort to all eight of my wet fly patterns. But, most often one, two, or three of them will produce.

What About Size, Color, Shape, and Type of Pattern?

I've suggested earlier that shape and color can make all the difference in the world. If trout are taking downwings like caddisflies, then it's important to copy the shape of that insect with its wings folded down over its body. If they're taking recently dead or dying mayfly spinners then maybe you should think of a using a spent-winged spinner pattern.

Size also can make a difference between a successful and a frustrating fishing trip. I've often had refusals with a size 12 or 14 Light Cahill, and switched to a size 18 or 20 and caught trout. Carry some of the more popular patterns in sizes 12 to 22 to cope with selective trout. Often trout surface feed on chironomids or midges. If you plan to fish over trout rising to these insects carry small patterns, sizes 20 to 26, to copy these. Above all, if you're fishing a spinner fall, be prepared to use a size or two smaller if the pattern you're presently using doesn't work. How many times have I heard other anglers say they had plenty of refusals using a size 22 or 24 Trico spinner? They then switched to a smaller spinner pattern and began catching trout. We'll discuss patterns that match the hatches in more detail in Chapter 3.

Shape also refers to what type of pattern you tie. Will it be a parachute, classic or Catskill, or a comparadun type? Over the years I've found that trout tend to take a fly more readily if the body of that pattern rests on the surface—not above. With a parachute style or a comparadun pattern the body rests on the surface. Not so with the classic style where the body tends to ride above the surface. I can still remember that day on the Arkansas River near Buena Vista, Colorado with Phil Camera. Phil's an expert fly fisher, fly tier, and inventor. He's developed many of the modern synthetics used for fly tying. He recently wrote a book on these materials. We had no luck that morning we fished when a pale morning dun appeared on the river—until we cut the hackle off the bottom of the high riding Catskill pattern so the fly rode flush with the surface. Trout took that lower profile dry fly with a vengeance.

Finally, which type of fly you use, sinking or floating, can mean the difference between success and failure. For more than 20 years I used dry flies almost exclusively. Rarely, if ever, did I ever resort to a wet fly. When I did, it was on those occasions when I hit high or cold water. The last 10 years I have switched to using the tandem, which consists of a wet and a dry fly. When I use two patterns in tandem I consistently catch 10 or 20 percent of the trout on the dry fly—but I catch about 80 to 90 percent on the wet fly. In high water I often use a poly strike indicator and just one wet fly. As soon as I began using wet flies I noticed a sharp increase in the number of trout caught. We'll look at varying the depth in Chapter 4.

My Top Wet Fly Choices When There's No Hatch

I just mentioned that for more than two decades fly-fishing to me meant using a dry fly and watching a trout take that fly on the surface. In fact, in *Meeting and Fishing the Hatches*, published in 1977, I indicated that the only true fly-fishing for trout was with a dry fly. In the Preface of that book I said, "enticing a trout to the surface is much more enjoyable, rewarding, and challenging than any other type of fishing." I have changed my beliefs completely in the past 20 years! Let me explain.

For years I realized that most good wet fly anglers would, on many occasions, out-fish someone using dry flies. Not until I began to use the tandem on streams and rivers across the United States did I actually realize how effective wet flies could be—on almost every occasion. I was first introduced to the two-fly system on Western rivers, but I quickly found out that that same technique works well on Eastern and Midwestern streams. I still remember the first time I used the tandem. I tied on a

My Top Wet Fly Choices When There's No Hatch (Table 2)

Wet Fly Choices	Attractor Dry Fly Choices*	Streamer Choices
Green Weenie	Patriot	Bead Head Wooly Bugger
Bead Head Pheasant Tail	Adams	Muddler Minnow
Bead Head Olive Caddis	Trout Fin	Lady Ghost
Flashback Nymph	Wulff Royal Coachman	Clouser Minnow
Bead Head Glo Bug		Peacock Lady
		Pink Ugly
		Mickey Finn
*Other pattern selections to match the hatches are found in Chapter 3.		

Use a large bright streamer like the Pink Ugly in cloudy waters.

large (size 12) dry fly, added a piece of 4X tippet at the bend of the hook, and tied on a wet fly. A 5X or 6X tippet will even produce more trout once you get accustomed to casting the pair (see Chapter 5). I pretended that there was no wet fly connected to the back of the dry fly. It took only a matter of days until I realized that the wet fly out-performed the dry fly by a wide margin. For every trout I caught on the dry fly I managed to land nine on the wet fly.

I then began to focus on some productive wet fly patterns. How many sinking patterns do you need? I mentioned earlier that Donald DuBois in his classic book, *The Fisherman's Handbook of Trout Flies,* list thousands of wet fly patterns. How can we reduce this number to a manageable few? In the past ten years, when no hatch appears, I've found that on almost every occasion I can rely on eight wet fly patterns to catch trout. These patterns—the bead head Glo Bug, Green Weenie, bead head Tan Caddis, Bead Head Olive Caddis Caddis, Flashback Nymph, bead head Pheasant Tail, bead head Hare's Ear, and the bead head Wooly Bugger have proved to be top producers for me. I've experienced so much success using them that I seldom use any other pattern—unless, of course, I encounter a hatch. These eight patterns will produce under almost every situation.

Bead heads arrived on the scene almost a decade ago. In those few years they have revolutionized how wet fly fishers fish. You can see from my selection how they've influenced me. Seven of the eight patterns I rely on contain bead heads. Yes, even the Glo Bug I use has a bead head! Why do bead heads work? Is it because the extra weight gets the wet fly deeper quicker? Does the shine from a copper or brass bead attract trout? Do the wet flies float differently with the bead head attached? Does the bead look like an insect ready to emerge? It might be one or a combination of the above—but bead heads really work. Let's examine each of the top eight patterns.

Bead Head Pheasant Tail

I'll never forget the first bead head Pheasant Tail nymph that Walt Young handed me. He said that the pattern had really produced for him on central Pennsylvania's lower Bald Eagle Creek in late August. I headed to the same stream a few days later, and fished a productive looking run for more than an hour with a caddis emerger pattern. In an hour of fishing I didn't have one strike. I decided to tie on that bead head Pheasant Tail that Walt had just given me and test it on the same stretch I just fished. In the next hour I caught six trout—in that same riffle that I had fished earlier with a caddis emerger. A total change had occurred in me in a half hour of fishing. Never—never again would I ever fly fish—on any stream without a good supply of size 12, 14, and 16 bead head Pheasant Tails. In the past five years I have used the Pheasant Tail on almost every trip and I haven't been disappointed. It has produced when other patterns have failed.

Why does the Pheasant Tail work so well? I believe one reason is that this pattern copies the sulphur nymph found in the East and Midwest and pale morning dun nymph found in the West. That trip to the Missouri River near Craig, Montana, proved forever the merits of the bead head Pheasant Tail to me. I hit a great hatch of pale morning duns but continued to use my tandem setup with a Patriot dry fly and a size 16 bead head Pheasant Tail Nymph. It was unbelievable: trout hit that wet fly on almost every cast. Five anglers below me fished the dry fly during the hatch. They caught very few trout. I could hear them mumbling from almost a hundred yards away because of my success with that bead head.

Don Baylor, an entomologist from Stroudsburg, Pennsylvania, studied the contents of several trout that had fed during a sulphur hatch. He found that the great majority of the insect phase that the trout took was the nymph or emerger. Don found only a couple sulphur duns in the sample. So, while we often fish to what we think are trout rising to sulphur or pale morning duns, we're really fishing to a lot of trout chasing the nymph and emerger near the surface. And, as I stated earlier, with its dark brown body the bead head Pheasant Tail copies the coloration of

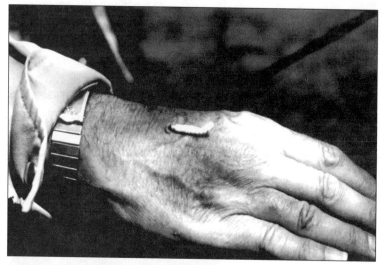

One reason the Green Weenie works is because it looks a lot like a green worm. The Green Weenie is a top producer when there's no hatch on the water.

both the sulphur and pale morning dun nymphs. That's why the bead head Pheasant Tail works so well in late May, June and July.

Green Weenie

I'll always recall that first time I saw the Green Weenie pattern used. That introduction to that effective pattern occurred on the Loyalhanna Creek in Ligonier in southwestern Pennsylvania. The late Russ Mowry, a famous fly tier and terrific person, fished with Tim Shaffer and Ken Igo. I sat on the bank of the stream that March afternoon and watched the trio catch 25 trout while six other anglers around them caught nothing. Since that day back in 1988 I have made certain I always carry a good supply of size 12 Green Weenies.

Mary Kuss of Media, Pennsylvania, recalls an instance where the Green Weenie worked well for her on Kettle Creek several years ago. On

The Green Weenie works extremely well on the McKenzie River in Oregon.

10 casts Mary caught a half dozen trout. Finally one of the anglers nearby came up to Mary and asked her what she was using. Mary showed the angler the Green Weenie and he walked away mumbling to himself.

The Green Weenie seems to work better on some trout streams than others. I use the pattern all winter on the Salt River near Phoenix, Arizona. Fred Brauburger, of nearby Scottsdale, and I caught 135 trout one day on the Salt River. The majority of those trout hit the Green Weenie.

Several years back I opened the New York trout season on Irondequoit Creek near Rochester, New York. We didn't arrive until some of the crowd had left. I tied on a Green Weenie and fished in a pool with five other anglers. While those five anglers watched I caught a half dozen trout. Several anglers came over to me to ask what I was using.

The Green Weenie works well on far Western rivers. I first used the pattern on a McKenzie River float trip with an expert guide, Ken Helfrich of Springfield, Oregon. The river ran at least a foot above its normal flow for early May and no pattern I used seemed to catch trout. Then, in a fit of frustration, I tied on a Green Weenie. In the next three hours I caught more than 20 trout on the Green Weenie and transformed the day into one

The Bead Head Tan Caddis produced this trout from Montana's Bighorn River. Ten wraps of .010 lead wire are a normal tying ingredient.

of those memorable trips. Was Ken impressed with the pattern? He asked me to give him a few for his customers he planned to guide the next day.

Bead Head Tan Caddis

Anyone can tie the bead head Tan Caddis in a minute or two, but it's one of the most productive patterns I've ever used. Recently a friend and expert guide, Dave McMullen, handed me a size 14 bead head pattern and said that pattern always worked well for him. The pattern—you guessed it—was a bead head Tan Caddis. That same caddis pattern, tied in sizes 12 to 16, has proved to be a top producer on just about every trout stream in the United States that I've fished.

The Tan Caddis saved the day for my son, Bryan, and me on the Ruby River near Alder, Montana. Bryan out-fished me by five to one for the first hour that day. Finally, I had enough and asked him what he was using. He showed me the Tan Caddis he tied. I finally had to beg him for one and he gave it to me reluctantly. I soon began catching more trout. That day and that pattern will remain a day of success forever.

I use tan Squirrel Brite or Krystal Dub to tie the pattern. This dubbing contains some bright synthetics that make the pattern sparkle. The bead head Tan Caddis is especially effective when you find a hatch of tan caddis emerging.

As with most the bead head patterns, I usually add about ten wraps of .010 lead to the body of the pattern. If you have the larger hole of the bead facing towards the rear of the hook you can push the lead wire forward and under the bead. Chapter 9 gives the recipe for tying this effective pattern.

Bead Head Olive Caddis

One of the top producing bead patterns at the present time is the Bead Head Olive Caddis. It's an important pattern because it copies so many caddis larvae. Let me explain.

Several years ago a long time fishing friend, Bob Budd, and I fished a section of the Little Juniata River in central Pennsylvania. We had experienced an extremely unproductive day and were about to quit. On one cast with a Pheasant Tail I got hung up on a pile of roots. When I retrieved my fly I noticed maybe a dozen or more dark olive caddis larva clinging to the root. That evening I went back to my fly tying bench and

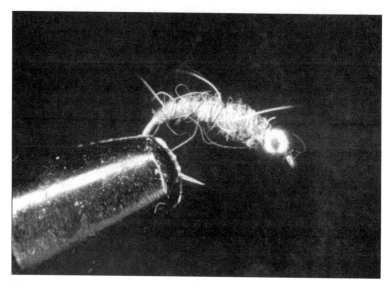

The Dark Olive Bead Head is a top producer because it copies so many different species of caddis larvae.

tied my first Bead Head Olive Caddis Caddis. I can still remember the first time Bob and I used that pattern a few days later. We caught literally dozens of trout on that pattern.

No pattern is ever really new. I remember watching Don Bastian catch several trout that same year that I first tied the Olive bead head Caddis. I asked what he caught them on and he showed me the same olive-colored fly.

Several weeks later I fished that same caddis wet fly on a spring creek. With a good green caddis hatch throughout the summer on this limestone stream trout see plenty of green caddis larva naturals. The pattern works well on all limestone streams. One of the best non-hatch days I ever had with the olive bead occurred on south-central Pennsylvania's Yellow Breeches Creek.

I tie the pattern in two shades of olive. On some I dub dark olive green angora and rib the pattern with a fine gold wire. On others I use a dark olive green Squirrel Brite or Krystal Dub. I tie the patterns in sizes 12 to 16. Use the scud type hooks for all your bead head patterns.

Flashback Nymph

The bead head nymph works so well because of the shiny bead. The Flashback Nymph also works for the same reason. I've tied the pattern for years but used it rarely. That is, until a recent fishing trip with Andy Leitzinger. Andy supplied the other anglers with Flashback Nymphs and they began to catch trout. We used a dark brown Flashback Nymph most of the day and caught trout.

Tie patterns with dark brown and gray bodies. Use a bright synthetic material for the flashback part and bring the material above and underneath the thorax. Tie off at the eye of the hook.

Bead Head Glo Bug

For years I scoffed at the Glo Bug. I contended that no good fly fisher would ever use a pattern that copied a salmon egg. Then one day Bryan Meck and I tried the Glo Bug on a small spring-fed pond in southwestern Montana. Bryan used the pattern as part of a tandem and kept the Glo Bug just a couple inches above the weed bed. That afternoon Bryan caught more than 40 trout in that pond on that pattern and I became an instant believer. There's one problem with the pattern: The Glo Bug doesn't sink quickly and you can't add weight to the body before you tie it. To overcome this problem I added a bead head.

I tried the first bead head Glo Bug on the Red River in New Mexico in mid December. Virgil Bradford, Manuel Monasterio, Ed Adams, and I hiked down the long trail to the river below. Before we headed down the gorge to the river Ed asked me what kind of shape I was in. He said that he didn't want to be known as the guide who killed Charlie Meck. We arrived at the river two hours after we began our trek. I immediately tied on a Bead Glo Bug because the cutbows in the stream had already paired up preparing for mating a couple months later. We had only two hours to fish before we had to head up the gorge, but in that short time the bead head Glo Bug showed its merits on Western rivers.

My Top Dry Fly Patterns that Match No Hatch—Attractors

The Patriot and the Royal Coachman dry fly, copy no insect, and are called attractor patterns. Attractor patterns often contain bright colors like red, yellow, or blue. These patterns often irritate into striking. With attractor patterns you'll often see trout swirling at and refusing the pattern. These patterns are often good for locating trout. On any day, but especially from June through September, when there's no hatch on, I often rely on an attractor pattern.

Why use attractor patterns? As I grow older I have more difficulty following that dry fly on the surface. When I fish small streams with a heavy canopy I often have difficulty following the float of an ant or beetle pattern. Try this experiment next time you fish one of these heavily shaded streams. First try a terrestrial like an ant, beetle, or cricket. Next try an attractor pattern like a size 12 Patriot, Trout Fin or Wulff Royal Coachman. Once you see how easy these attractor patterns are to follow—and how well they produce—you'll start using them. Attractor patterns also serve effectively as the lead fly on the tandem because they're easy to follow on the surface.

What dry flies will I often use when no hatch appears? I'm partial to the Adams—three varieties. I use a yellow-bellied one, the standard one with a gray body, and a gray bodied one ribbed with gold. But, there are other great patterns like the Patriot, Trout Fin, and the old standby, the Wulff Royal Coachman.

Patriot

I created this fly more than 20 years ago. At that time I read an article about a study two professors had conducted on rainbow trout. They colored salmon eggs all colors of the rainbow and then studied which color the trout preferred most. Under most light conditions (overcast and sunny) trout preferred a blue colored egg. But, you say there's nothing in nature that has that color. I don't know why this color works, but it does.

Several years back I carried two dozen Patriots with me to the South Island of New Zealand. I was anxious to see if these patterns worked as well there as they did in the United States. Twelve of the thirteen largest trout Mike Manfredo and I caught in that fantastic country were caught on the Patriot. By the end of our first week of fly-fishing we had completely

The Patriot is a great attractor dry fly pattern. Though most attractors are used during the warmer summer months, I've expanded their use for most of the season.

run out of Patriots. I'll never forget that one evening we spent fly tying in our room. We ran out of smolt blue krystal flash and we tore a back pack apart to get a similar colored thread to use for the body.

I often use the Patriot as the dry fly or strike indicator when I use the tandem. I usually tie a bead head behind the Patriot as the wet fly. The white calf body wings of the Patriot show up well even in a heavy canopy.

What time of the year do these patterns work best? I find that I have most of my strikes with attractors in June, July, and August—often in the middle of the day. But, attractors like the Patriot also work at other times of the year. Let me explain.

Paul Weamer runs a fly shop on the Delaware River. He recently shared one of his favorite streams with me. This stream does not receive trout on any regular basis but holds plenty of wild browns. The fly of the day on that stream was the Patriot. Several months later I reciprocated with Paul and showed him one of my favorite streams that held a good population of wild browns—again this stream has never been stocked. We selected a cold, blustery November day to fish. As I entered the stream I checked the water temperature. It was 45 degrees—in the middle of the afternoon. We certainly wouldn't catch any trout under these cold conditions. But, guess what? From the minute we entered the stream until we left three hours later we had almost constant action. Trout hit bead head Pheasant Tails and Green Weenies with a vengeance. We managed to land a couple trout almost 15 inches long. In that afternoon of cold weather fly-fishing, we even managed to catch two trout on the "strike indicator," the Patriot. Yes, two trout rose to the surface to take the dry fly that day. When should you use an attractor like the Patriot? Before that incident I would have suggested the summer months. Now, I have expanded that to include much of the fishing season.

The Patriot looks a lot like the Trout Fin and the Wulff Royal Coachman. The only difference with the three is the materials used for the body. For the Patriot I recommend brown hackle fibers for the tail, smolt blue Krystal Flash with a red midsection for the body, brown hackle, and white calf body wings.

The attractor type dry fly pattern to use when no hatch appears is the Patriot. Several years ago I conducted some experiments with 20 different dry fly patterns fishing them over water where no trout rose. The patterns included the Light Cahill, Adams, Quill Gordon, and the Wulff Royal Coachman. I cast each fly 1000 times over a period of several months. I carried a counter with me and kept a record of the number of strikes for each fly. The Patriot caught more trout than any other pattern. By the way, you can purchase the Patriot from the Orvis catalog.

I never cease to be amazed how wild trout take attractor patterns like the Patriot. I still remember that morning on the lower end of Virginia's Mossy Creek. I arrived with Bob Cramer just at the height of the Trico spinner fall on a late July morning. I still had the Patriot attached to the tippet from the day before and I made a couple casts to some risers with that bright blue dry fly. Two of three rising wild brown trout in front of me took that large odd colored fly before I switched to a smaller pattern that matched the Trico.

One of the toughest streams in Pennsylvania to catch trout can be the Tulpehocken Creek in southeast. Recently I fished this tailwater with two great local fly fishers Tony Gehman and Dave Eshenower. Just ask these two how difficult the trout in this stream can be. Tony and Dave said there are two noises you consistently hear on that great stream. One is the "Oh's" coming from anglers who just missed a trout. The other is the clicking of fly boxes from anglers constantly changing flies and looking for other patterns to use. Because these trout have seen a lot of patterns and a lot of anglers they've become highly selective. I missed the first ten trout that struck that morning because they let go of the pattern in a split second. I did manage to catch a few trout that morning—yes, two hit the attractor pattern, the Patriot. Maybe they hit that large blue-colored fly because they had not seen it before.

I hit Owego Creek in upstate New York on one of the worst days of the year. In late August this stream, filled with streambred brown trout, flowed with just a trickle of water. Thanks to the many stream improvements, trout still had places to hide. I hiked upstream from the lower end and began casting a size 18 Patriot. Because of the heavy canopy I couldn't see the ant pattern I used earlier so I switched. Four trout took that pattern in those low water conditions.

I never cease to be amazed how wild trout take attractor patterns like the Patriot. I still remember that morning on Colorado's South Platte River with Phil Camera. I arrived just at the height of the trico spinner fall on a late July morning. I still had a Patriot attached to the tippet from the day before and I made a couple casts to some risers with that bright blue dry fly. Two of three rising wild brown trout in front of me took that large odd colored fly before I switched to a smaller pattern that matched the Trico.

Wulff Royal Coachman

Lloyd Williams and John Weaver both of the Wilkes-Barre, Pennsylvania, area had many things in common. Both were excellent dry fly fishers almost totally ignoring wet flies for their favorite floating ones. They had much more in common when they fly-fished in the 1960's and 1970's. Just about every summer evening you'd find both anglers casting a dry fly on Bowman Creek. Both skilled fly fishers considered Bowman Creek as their favorite stream. Lloyd and John had one more point in common: both used attractor patterns almost exclusively. Lloyd preferred using the Wulff Royal Coachman while John would cast the Trout Fin. Look in the back of Lloyd's car any time of the fishing season and you'd see a Wulff Royal Coachman still attached to the tippet on his disassembled fly rod.

I had the opportunity to fly fish with Lloyd and John frequently when they fished twenty years ago. I saw Lloyd catch and release many trout over 15 inches long on the Coachman. On those rare trips when we'd hike up a small mountain stream or fish the upper end of Bowman Creek I'd commonly see Lloyd pick 20, 30, even 40 trout on his favorite attractor pattern.

Trout Fin

John Weaver fished his Trout Fins in the evening on Bowman Creek in northeastern Pennsylvania. He'd fish rings around me and caught two trout for every one I caught—on that darned attractor pattern. He tied his Trout Fin with a tail made from brown hackle fibers, a body of bright orange floss, brown hackle, and white quill wings. I've since substituted white calf body hair for the wings. John first introduced me to this pattern more than 30 years ago.   If you were fortunate enough to watch John Weaver fly fish in the 1960's you saw a skilled fly caster using not one but two attractor patterns.   John tied on two bright orange Trout Fins on the end of his leader and he'd cast the two of them as well as I cast one fly.

I have seen few other anglers use it with the skill John showed. That pattern worked then, and it still works now, especially on evenings in July and August. Why? It might suggest to trout a Light Cahill type mayfly that frequents many of the nation's streams that time of the year. I said earlier that the old pattern calls for white quill wings. Quill wings often split so I tie my Trout Fin patterns with wings of calf body hair. Also, quill wings tend to twist the tippet. The Trout Fin has a bright orange body. John Weaver made his body from floss or silk.   Bodies made with these tend to discolor easily so I prefer using bright orange poly.

Adams

The Adams is a top producer throughout the summer months. From June through August, if you prefer fishing on top, the Adams will catch trout. I know many fly fishers who use it, almost exclusively. Why does it work so well then?   It really shouldn't be classified as an attractor pattern because it copies so many mayfly naturals. Look at one of the best hatches, the slate drake, that you'll see on many trout streams throughout the East and Midwest at that time of year. Look at the rocks on the New York's Ausable or Black Rivers, and you'll see nymphal shucks of these drakes lining the rocks along the shore. Examine the banks and rocks along the shore on New Jersey's South Branch of the Raritan in the Ken Lockwood Gorge area, and you'll see evidence of slate drakes that appear throughout much of the summer.   Just about every evening from late May through July you can see this species emerging on many northeastern streams.   A second generation of the same species reappears again in September and early October on many trout streams. If you calculate the number of days that you'll find slate drakes appearing on any given stream it would be over 50 days of the fishing season. So, if trout see this hatch that many days, don't you think a dark gray-bodied fly, very similar to the body of the slate drake, would produce?

Does the Adams work in New Zealand? One morning on the Englinton River on the South Island, Mike Manfredo and I hit a spinner fall. As we arrived at the river we saw dozens of large fish sipping in spinners on the surface. I saw several dark gray spinners on the surface so I tied on the only Adams dry fly in my fly box. That Adams caught several trout over 20 inches long that morning before it fell apart and the spinner fall ended.

In addition to the gray-bodied pattern I often use a yellow-bodied one in midseason. This Yellow Adams seems especially effective during the sulphur and pale morning dun hatches.

Downwing and Spent-Winged Attractor Patterns

If the Patriot works with white upright wings why wouldn't downwing patterns copying the configuration of caddisflies and stoneflies work? And what about spent winged attractor patterns copying dying mayfly spinners. Will these catch trout? You bet they work!

Try a downwing attractor pattern on those streams that hold good caddisfly and stonefly hatches. I've found the downwing version of the Patriot especially effective on many of those August evenings just before dark.

My Top Patterns when the Water is High, Cold or Off Color

Let's face it—we often have a limited time to fly fish or we've committed ourselves to a week or day and we're confronted with less than ideal conditions. What do we do if we want to catch more trout? Try larger patterns that sink quickly or brightly colored patterns that trout can see in cloudy water. What about fishing early in the season?

What do fishing trips to Montana, Idaho and Oregon in early June have in common? How about trips to Arizona trout streams in April? And, those trips to Eastern and Midwestern waters in early April—what do they have in common with all the others? Most often you'll encounter high flow and cold water on these rivers and streams. What can you do at that time to catch more trout? Go deep early in the season. For the past 25 years I've begun each opening day on eastern streams in New York, New Jersey, and Pennsylvania. I've learned that trout on these cold days trout often stay near the bottom. Granted you'll occasionally see trout rising to a hatch on opening day, but this is the exception and not the rule. So if you've had little success the past few years you might want to change your method of fly-fishing. And the tactics and techniques that have

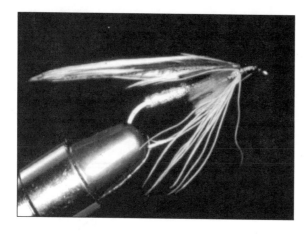

Carry streamers like the Lady Ghost with you. The brightly colored dressing is one that trout can see in cloudy water.

worked for me will work on any stream early in the season. Let me explain.

Why is it important to go deep in high water? You'll encounter two things early in the season that you don't see later. High water and cold temperatures often keep trout deep next to the bottom. In this type of setting, trout, if they do feed, do so near the bottom. Often anglers use patterns on opening day that sink but they don't sink far enough. Only when you get near the bottom will you begin experiencing success.

Patterns to Go Deep

Over the many years of opening days, I've had considerable success with several wet flies. My pick of patterns is below:

> **Bead Head Wooly Bugger**
> **Muddler Minnow**
> **Clouser Minnow**
> **Peacock Lady**
> **Lady Ghost***
> **Mickey Finn***
> **Pink Ugly***
>
> *Cloudy water patterns

I add weight to the body of all the wet flies when I'm tying them. Let's look at some of these and how much weight I add to each to sink them deep.

Always carry Bead Head Wooly Buggers with you for high water. They look like the very common fish fly larva.

Bead Head Wooly Bugger

It had rained for twelve straight days in early May. Now, even after five days of bright sunny weather just about every stream in the area still ran high and a bit off color. What pattern would work under these adverse conditions? Why, of course, the bead head Wooly Bugger. I'm convinced that one reason this pattern catches trout on streams and rivers across the United States is because it looks like the very common fish fly larva. Even in that high spring water I caught several trout on the Wooly Bugger.

But, the Wooly Bugger works well on Western rivers like the Little Colorado near Springerville, Arizona. Craig Josephson and I spent a week fly fishing streams of the southwest and we spent two days on the Little Colorado. Gerald Scott, the river keeper at the X-Diamond Ranch, apologized for the poor fishing we experienced that first morning at the ranch. He said fishing had been lousy the past week. With this 20-foot wide river running high and a bit off color I tied on a bead head Wooly Bugger to start off the afternoon. On the first cast I landed a 20-inch rainbow and the action didn't stop for two hours. Craig Josephson, fishing a hundred yards below me, had the same success with the same bead head pattern. We ended the day and tallied our number of releases. We hurried back to the ranch house and told Gerald how fishing that afternoon with the bead head Wooly Bugger turned into a splendid success.

I tie the Bugger with 10 to 20 wraps of .015 lead on the body to make it sink rapidly. If you plan to use the Wooly Bugger behind a dry fly you might not want to add the weight. I prefer using the bead head Wooly Bugger without the dry fly attached. If you're fishing heavy water with the pattern use a bright colored poly strike indicator.

Peacock Lady

If you ever plan to fly fish lakes in Arizona or New Mexico don't go without a good supply of Peacock Ladies. The first time I ever used the pattern was on Sunrise Lake in the White Mountains of Arizona. I fished with Bob David who suggested I start with the Peacock Lady pattern. I didn't—I thought I knew better and began fishing with a Green Weenie. For a half-hour Bob and Craig Josephson caught one trout after another on that Peacock Lady pattern while I caught nothing. After a half-hour I switched to the same pattern that they used and began catching trout.

Clouser Minnow

I consider Bob Clouser a friend. He's one of the finest fly tiers and fly fishers we have in the East. He's creative with his minnow patterns. However, I must admit that until a recent event I never tried the Clouser Minnow. Not until I planned to fish much of the day and a heavy storm hit at noon. By the time the storm had ended the stream became off color so I opted for a bright streamer pattern. A sparsely tied Clouser Minnow caught trout all afternoon long in that cloudy water.

There are other patterns you should keep with you for those days when the stream you plan to fish is high or off color. The Muddler Minnow and Lady Ghost seem to work on those trout waters. I often start off the season in New York, New Jersey, Maryland, or Pennsylvania with one of these two patterns. Also carry a few bright colored streamers like the Mickey Finn and the Pink Ugly. You ask what is a Pink Ugly. It's a huge pink colored streamer that catches trout in high, off color, water. Ron German first came up with the recipe and his wife, Flossie, ties the pattern by the hundreds for local anglers. I carried a couple with me but didn't use them for more than a year. Not until I hit high muddy water on Oatka Creek, near Rochester, New York, did I get a chance to use this pattern. In that high water in early April this pattern caught trout when other streamers failed me. Why is it called the Pink Ugly? Look at the photo and you'll immediately know that a streamer like that should never catch trout.

Do you want to catch more trout? Then try some of the patterns that have worked well for others and me throughout the years. Follow some of the other tactics I've suggested in this chapter. Above all if you have no success with the pattern you're using tie on another one. Selecting the right pattern when there's no hatch is only a part of the total strategy to catch more trout. Next, you must be prepared to match any hatch you'll see on the stream. Then you must remember how important leaders, drag and strike indicators are to your success.

– 3 –
KNOW THE MAJOR HATCHES AND WHAT MATCHES THEM

Rule 1. *Hatches appear most often in the afternoon during the late fall, winter, and spring.*

Rule 2. *You'll find midges emerging on many streams and rivers throughout the United States on almost every winter day.*

Rule 3. *Smaller hatches seem to appear for a longer time.*

Rule 4. *Some of the more famous hatches appear only a few days each year.*

Rule 5. *As a general rule, use gray patterns in March and April; and lighter colors on May, June, July, and August evenings.*

Rule 6. *Use darker patterns during the day in the summer.*

Rule 7. *Use darker patterns again in September and October.*

Rule 8. *Most hatches in April appear at the most comfortable time of day—the afternoon.*

Rule 9. *After mid-May many hatches appear in the evening.*

Rule 10. *In the southwest you'll find hatches like the blue-winged olive and trico in February and March.*

I 've enjoyed reading Charlie Brooks' books on fly-fishing for many years. The first time I met him in West Yellowstone, Montana, really set the tone for me and my three decades of fishing the West. Charlie helped me tremendously with my first book on fly-fishing, *Meeting and Fishing the Hatches*. I stayed in West Yellowstone for more than a month when I wrote the book. Almost daily I'd stop by Charlie's house to ask him where I should fish that day so I could see a hatch and fish over rising trout. Boy, did I see the hatches and rising trout! I spent more than a week fishing Henry's Fork and witnessing hatches like the Western green drake and pale morning dun. I spent hours on the Yellowstone River near Gardiner, Montana. On this latter river I truly experienced the ultimate hatch—the huge salmon fly. I saw two-foot cutthroats go crazy when one of these stoneflies landed on the surface. Even on the upper Gallatin River I saw hatches and matched them

I equate a good hatch of insects on the surface to a fish hatchery at feeding time. When feeding time comes at a hatchery trout go crazy, lose any timidity they have and feed voraciously. Talk about catching more trout—the time to do it effectively and efficiently is at feeding time—on a stream it occurs when a hatch appears.

Do you want to catch more trout? Then know as much as possible about the hatches. *You should know when and where they appear, and most important of all, what patterns match them. You should have enough information available to identify some of the more common hatches. Part of the overall knowledge should also include other aspects like how many times a year you expect to see a particular hatch, how long can you expect a hatch to continue to appear, and what colors of insects predominate at what time of year.*

We'll examine each one of these important aspects in this chapter. You'll find 12 tables to help you better understand the hatches and how to use them to your best advantage. In Tables 1 and 2 you'll see when and where the common hatches appear. Tables 3 through 6 suggest what time of day to use various patterns and what hatches these patterns match. Tables 7 and 8 will help you identify some of the more common hatches. Tables 9 and 10 show some of the hatches that appear for an extended period of time, and Tables 11 and 12 illustrate which hatches appear early in the season.

How to Fish the Hatches

I've fished mayfly, stonefly and caddisfly hatches for more than 40 years. On many occasions I've become frustrated, intimidated and downright confused over some of my matching-the-hatch episodes. As a result of many hours that were less than successful, I have developed a series of axioms that I follow when I fish the hatches.

1. Carry Several Sizes of the Same Pattern with You.

How many times have I seen trout refuse a size 22 or 24 Trico pattern and take a smaller size 26? In my lifetime I've seen that happen on many late summer trips. Always carry the size that most appropriately matches the hatch; but also carry a smaller pattern.

2. Carry Several Patterns that Match the Same Hatch.

How many times has my first selection of a pattern to match the hatch failed me? More times than I'd like to admit. On some of the more common hatches I carry three and four different patterns. I carry a standard high riding Sulphur, one tied parachute style and a comparadun type. If you only have a high riding dry fly and the trout refuse it, try cutting off the hackle on the underside so it rides more flush with the surface.

3. Sink the Pattern.

Maybe changing the size or the pattern won't work. What do you do then? In Chapter 4 read about sinking both dun and spinner patterns if nothing else works. Sunken patterns have been a godsend for me the past decade. Try them when you get frustrated with a hatch. Chapter 4 looks at this technique in more detail.

4. Move During the Hatch if you See No Risers.

Often when I hit hatches like the hendrickson in the East and Midwest or the Western green drake in the West and I see no action in front of me, I move up or downstream quickly and search for risers. I've done it so often during a hendrickson hatch that I now enjoy moving from one riffle to another constantly looking for rising trout. I've done the same thing on the Metolius River in Oregon during a little blue-winged olive hatch.

Even with the diminutive trico spinner fall I've followed the same procedure across the United States. On the McKenzie River near Eugene, Oregon, in late October, I hiked more than a mile before I saw trout rising to spent trico spinners. When I finally found risers, I found a pod of a

TheTrico Spinner

dozen trout rising to these spent spinners.

I've moved several times when a Western green drake has appeared on the surface. That first time occurred on the Bitterroot River near Victor, Montana. After I caught the four trout that rose in front of me I hurried downriver to cast over other risers. It happened a second time on the Fryingpan River near Basalt, Colorado, with Roy Palm. We moved three times that morning before we saw plenty of risers.

In Chapter 8 I discuss location. Location, or where you place yourself on a stream when a hatch appears, can mean the difference between a great or a lousy day of fishing.

5. Arrive at the Stream at the Right Time

I wrote an entire book about getting there at the right time. That's exactly what I proposed in *Meeting and Fishing the Hatches.* That philosophy has saved many fishing trips from being complete disasters. I still remember my first trip to a Western river more than 25 years ago. I arrived on the Bitterroot River near Missoula, Montana, and planned to fish for a week. I had no guide, no local contact—I was on my own. I realized that in early July, with the river still high from snowmelt from the nearby mountain that I had a good chance to see a Western green drake hatch. I arrived on the stream by 10:00 A.M. because this huge mayfly usually appears in late morning. I didn't have to wait very long. Soon hundreds of these large dark olive green mayflies appeared in the high water in front of me and trout fed freely on them. By knowing approximately what time this hatch appears on the water I was able to experience a successful day. Tables 1 and 2 should help you be on the stream at the proper time.

Ask John Gierach and A.K. Best about the time we fished the sulphur hatch in central Pennsylvania. John inquired early in the afternoon what time he could expect to see the sulphur dun appear that evening. I told him the sulphur would appear at 8:25 P.M. He laughed and laughed at the precise time that I had given him. Guess what? That hatch appeared that evening exactly at 8:25 P.M. (Read more about this subject in Chapter 8.)

6. Fish on Lousy Days

I devote an entire section in Chapter 8 to fishing on lousy days. Aquatic insects that appear on overcast dreary days tend to remain on the surface for a longer period than if they appear on a bright sunny day. Trout also tend to feed more readily on a cloudy, overcast day. You should take advantage of this. You can also get away with using a heavier tippet on those cloudy days. See Chapter 5 for a discussion of leaders.

7. Use the Tandem.

You find a lot of information on using the tandem in Chapter 4. If you're not certain what the trout are taking—the dun or the emerger—why not try both at the same time?

8. Extend the Time You Fish the Hatch

Some years I've fished green drake hatches for more than a month. How? I know the stream where this hatch comes off first. Then I move to a stream where I know the hatch will appear next, and so on until the hatch has ended for the year. I've begun with the green drake in Maryland in mid May and end with the same hatch on the Gennyganslett Creek in central New York in mid June.

9. Location

If you're familiar with a hatch then you probably know where it appears on a stream. Hatches like the sulphur and blue-winged olive appear on specific areas of a stream. In the section "Location, Location, Location" in Chapter 8 we explore this in more detail.

10. Take Time Out and See What's Hatching or Falling

It happened on a cold April afternoon. As several of us headed for the stream we saw another angler running to his car. As he raced past us he yelled that there was a hatch on the stream and he was going to the car to get his fly rod. As he hurried by us we asked him what hatch. He yelled back that he thought it might be a quill gordon. We stepped up our pace to the stream to see the hatch and look for rising trout. As we arrived at a high bank overlooking the stream, we saw at least a half dozen trout taking mayflies. I headed down to the stream and grabbed a stillborn and identified it as a hendrickson—not a quill gordon. *If you're in the midst of a hatch or spinner fall and you don't know what hatch or fall it is take time out and try to identify it. You don't have to know what the hatch is, all you have to know is what pattern you have with you matches it.* How many times I've been frustrated by a spinner fall at dusk and I didn't know how to match it?

Hatch Charts and Life Cycles

I was prepared to give a brief talk on mayflies, stoneflies, caddisflies and their life cycles at the University of Pittsburgh at Bradford. Before I even had a chance to get started an old time angler sitting in the back of the room said, "What good is all this information about the hatches? How will it help me be a better fly fisher? Don't I just have to match the general color of the insect with a pattern?" Several other attendees shouted out in agreement with the first angler.

I was prepared—I had gotten the same comments many times before. So I pulled a sheet out of my pocket and gave the group a pop quiz. Here are the questions I asked them:

1. If you're copying the natural and using a Quill Gordon Nymph in July why should you use a smaller size than you would in March?

2. Of a white fly, trico, or hendrickson which nymph would you use in early April?

3. Why is a Quill Gordon wet fly so effective?

4. Why should you add a shuck to the tail of some of your dun patterns?

5. Why do trout often prefer feeding on emergers?

6. If you had just one pattern for each month beginning with April, May, June, July, August, and September what would it be?

7. Why is it more important to copy a mayfly that sits on the surface to lay its eggs?

8. Why do I see two different sizes of green drake nymphs at the same time?

9. If you have a preference why should you fish a hatch on a less than ideal day?

I then spent a half-hour telling these fly fishers how more knowledge of the hatches would help them catch more trout. I told them they would learn the correct answers from my discussion.

I explained that many words may be foreign to the beginning fly-fisher like hatch, spinner, dun, spinner fall, nymph, natural, life cycle and so on. To understand why trout take wet flies, dry flies, and nymphs, it's essential to have a basic understanding of the biology of the aquatic insects on which they feed and so come to understand these terms. We then looked at a typical life cycle of a mayfly.

Mayflies lay their eggs in different ways. Some sit on the water to deposit the fertilized eggs, others drop the eggs while flying above the water and others sit on the water for a short period and deposit their eggs and then take flight again. Hendricksons, pale morning duns, and sulphurs (all *Ephemerella species*) carry their eggs in a ball or sac under the female's abdomen and drop them into the water. After depositing their eggs, female spinners, especially those that sit on the surface to lay their eggs (Answer to 7), die.

The eggs take several weeks to hatch into nymphs (the larval form of the mayfly). The eggs of those mayflies, like the trico and white fly that appear in fall, don't hatch into nymphs until the following May (Answer to 2.). Nymphs usually live in specific locations. Some closely related mayflies like the yellow drake, brown drake, and green drake (all *Ephemera* species) burrow in loose gravel. Others like the big slate drake (and all other *Hexagenia* species) burrow in mud or silt. Anglers refer to these mayfly nymphs as burrowers. Light cahills, quill gordons and many others (*Stenonema and Epeorus* species) cling to rocks. We often call these mayflies clingers. Still others like the blue-winged olives (some *Drunella* and *Ephemerella* species) live on or in aquatic weeds. These and other nymphs are called swimmers and move about freely on the bottom of the stream (*Isonychia*). Not only are scores of nymphs specific in their habitat, but also many are particular in the velocity of the water where they live. Slate drakes (*Isonychia*) usually inhabit fast-water sections of a stream. Hendricksons (*Ephemerella subvaria*) are found in all types of water, but yellow drakes (*Ephemera varia*) customarily occupy slower areas, usually pools of a stream. Other nymphs, like the speckle-winged dun (*Callibaetis*), regularly inhabit ponds and lakes. Look at the table in Chapter 8 for a complete list of species and where you'll find them.

Although there are numerous exceptions, most mayfly species live under water for about 340 days as nymphs. The green drake has a two-year life cycle and lives in a burrow for almost two years (Answer to 8). As the nymph feeds and grows, it regularly sheds its skin or exoskeleton and develops a new one. Some species, depending on size and length of time they live as nymphs, go through five or more of these transformations, called instars where they continue to grow (Answer to 1).

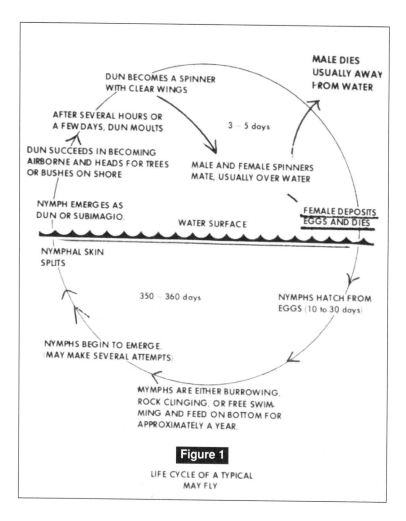

DUN BECOMES A SPINNER
WITH CLEAR WINGS

MALE DIES
USUALLY AWAY
FROM WATER

AFTER SEVERAL HOURS OR
A FEW DAYS, DUN MOULTS

3 — 5 days

DUN SUCCEEDS IN BECOMING
AIRBORNE AND HEADS FOR TREES
OR BUSHES ON SHORE

MALE AND FEMALE SPINNERS
MATE, USUALLY OVER WATER

NYMPH EMERGES AS
DUN OR SUBIMAGIO.

WATER SURFACE

FEMALE DEPOSITS
EGGS AND DIES

NYMPHAL SKIN
SPLITS

350 — 360 days

NYMPHS HATCH FROM
EGGS (10 to 30 days)

NYMPHS BEGIN TO EMERGE.
(MAY MAKE SEVERAL ATTEMPTS)

MYMPHS ARE EITHER BURROWING,
ROCK CLINGING, OR FREE SWIM-
MING AND FEED ON BOTTOM FOR
APPROXIMATELY A YEAR.

Figure 1

LIFE CYCLE OF A TYPICAL
MAY FLY

A year after the eggs were fertilized, the nymph begins to move toward the surface. At or near the water's surface the nymph splits its skin dorsally and appears on the surface as a mayfly *dun*, or *subimago*, an immature, non-mating adult. There are exceptions here, however, like *Epeorus*. This group emerges on the bottom (Answer to 3). The process of changing from an underwater insect to an air-breathing one often takes time. This stage, the transformation from a nymph to a dun, is the most vulnerable in the entire life cycle of the life mayfly. Trout sense that this is the most defenseless stage in the entire life cycle and readily feed on nymphs that are changing into duns (Answer to 5). The air-breathing mayfly dun rests on the water for a split second to several minutes, depending on the species

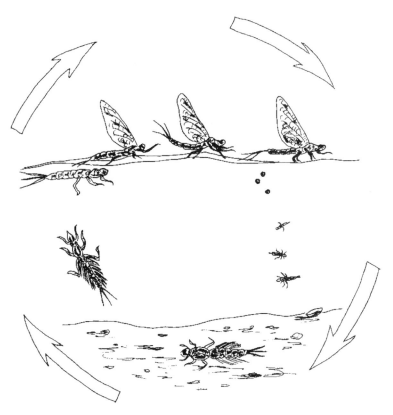

Figure 2. The average mayfly nymph lives underwater for about 340 days. It then moves towards the surface where it begins to shed its nympal shuck. The mayfly dun rests on the surface for a short time and then takes off to a nearby tree. A day or so later the mayfly dun changes to a mating spinner. Fertilized females move to the water and deposit eggs.

and the weather, before flying away. Abnormally cold weather, especially in the spring and fall, delays or prevents the dun from taking flight. Overcast, drizzly conditions will often slow duns from taking off even in midsummer. These conditions are of special importance to the dry fly-fisherman (Answer to 9) (See Chapter 8 for more information on this.).

If and when the dun escapes, it flies toward a branch to rest. On extremely cold, miserable days many duns struggle to reach rocks or debris on the shoreline and rest there. In a couple hours to a day or more the dun again goes through a change, loses its outer skin (pellicle), and becomes a spinner (also called an adult or imago) with glassy, clear wings. This spinner is a mating adult. Often, in the evening, male spinners form a

A female trico spinner.

A rusty spinner. Note the glassy, clear wings of the spinner.

swarm over or near the water, waiting for females to join them. When the females enter the swarm, the males impregnate them and the females then move toward the water's surface and deposit their fertilized eggs. Mayflies live out of the water as air-breathing duns and spinners usually less than five days. Thus the name for the order of insects that contains the mayflies is Ephemeroptera, which comes from the Greek for short-lived.

This is a very generalized description, and there are many exceptions. For example, some mayflies like the female white mayfly (*Ephoron*) never change into a spinner but mate as a dun. A few species remain as nymphs for two years (some *Ephemera* species) and many life cycles last only a few months (some *Baetis, Isonychia, Tricorythodes, and Callibaetis*). This latter type, with multiple broods, may appear as many as three times a year.

When the term *hatch* is used in this book, it usually refers to duns

A Sulphur nymph. The most vulnerable time in the entire life cycle of the mayfly is when the nymph begins changing into a dun.

The Bitterroot River in western Montana holds some great hatches.

emerging on the surface. When the nymph splits its pellicle or skin near the surface and changes into a dun, it is referred to as an *emerger*. *Spinner fall* is that time when females (and in some instances males) return to the water to deposit eggs and fall onto the surface spent, or with wings

A "mat" of dead trico and pale morning spinners on Montana's Missouri River.

Colorado's North Fork of the Cache La Poudre holds some great hatches.

outstretched. *Natural* refers to the nymph, dun, or spinner of a species.

Caddisflies (Order Trichoptera) and stoneflies (Order Plecoptera) are similar to the mayfly in their development. Anglers often call these insects downwings because of the configuration of their wings when at rest. Stoneflies and mayflies, however, lack one stage of the complete insect life cycle and are, therefore, considered to have incomplete metamorphosis. Caddisflies pass through this phase called the pupa or resting phase (diapause). This period usually lasts several weeks. Caddisfly larvae, like mayfly nymphs,

The Missouri River holds one of the heaviest hatches of tricos in the nation.

Henry's Fork has a hatch just about every day of the fishing season.

New Zealand's Oreti River on the South Island holds great mayfly spinner falls.

are specific in their habitat. Unlike stonefly and mayfly nymphs, however, caddis larvae lack the tough outer shell called the exoskeleton. Therefore, some caddis (but not all) construct a protective shelter or case. Caddisflies can be grouped according to the type of case they build. Some, like the green caddis (*Rhyacophila*), are free swimmers on the bottom and construct no shelter. Other important caddis, like grannoms (*Brachycentrus*), builds a case of twigs. Still others build a cover in the form of a net (the little black caddis), and the dark-blue sedge (*Psilotreta*) makes a case of coarse stone fragments. The nymph turns into a pupa inside its case. You can often predict what species you'll encounter in a stream by what's available for the larvae to use for cases.

Stonefly nymphs take one to three years to develop, depending on the species. You'll see different sizes of salmon fly nymphs on Western waters because they take three years to complete their life cycle. When they do emerge, mating usually takes place while they are resting on some surface rather than while they are in flight.

You can see by the brief description of the life cycles of mayflies, stoneflies, and caddis flies that the nymph or larva of a species is available to trout almost every day of the year, whereas the adult is available for only about a few days. Nymph fishing by a skilled angler will usually outperform fly-fishing using dry flies—*when there is no hatch.*

Emergers

Just what is an emerger? It's a nymph changing into a dun near the surface. When the nymph moves to the surface to change into a dun it goes through some dramatic changes.

The nymph breaks its outer skin (exoskeleton) and becomes an air-breathing dun. Why is the emerger important to copy? As I stated earlier, in this phase of its development the mayfly is very vulnerable. As a nymph it can swim and hide to get away from trout. As a dun it can fly away. But, for a short time—while it's changing from a nymph to an air-breathing dun—the mayfly is helpless and can't escape. Trout seem to sense this and seek out emergers eagerly.

Not all emergers should be tied in the same manner. The emerger is a transition from the nymph to the dun. As such, fly tiers should make some patterns with a crystal flash or other bright synthetic material to imitate an air bubble as the nymph pushes out its wing pad. On other patterns add a piece of poly to imitate the wing coming out of the nymph's wing pad. In a third type of emerger you might tie the front half of the body to copy the dun and the back half tied to copy the nymph. In yet another phase, the fourth one, attach a piece of Z-lon to the tail of the dun pattern (Answer to 4). Match the color of the nymph with the Z-lon. For instance, with the sulphur and pale morning dun, add a piece of dark brown Z-lon. In Chapter 9 the recipes give many of the colors for the shucks.

Are emergers an important part of a trout's diet? Look at a study that

In early September you'll find a great Little Blue-winged Olive hatch on the Cache La Poudre just outside Fort Collins, Colorado.

A later stage Sulphur emerger. Note the trailing nymphal shuck.

A Sulphur emerger. Note the imitation looks like the wings are just appearing.

A Sulphur emerger. Note the front half looks like the dun and the rear half like the nymph.

A Hendrickson dun with a shuck.

Don Baylor, an entomologist of note, conducted during a sulphur hatch. Don extracted the stomach contents of several trout. He found that 36 of 38 insects eaten were emergers. Are emergers important? You bet they are!

What about caddis hatches—does the emerger work when these downwings appear? As with mayflies the emerging phase of the caddisfly, the pupa, is extremely vulnerable. How many times have I heard anglers complain that they had little success during a caddis hatch? Many, many times! One of the greatest caddisfly hatches in the West is the Mother's Day emergence found on many trout waters, including the Bitterroot River in Montana and the Yakima River in eastern Washington. Try using an emerging caddis pattern for that hatch after you've become frustrated with a downwing dry fly.

Notes about the
Emergence Charts

In Tables 3 and 4 you'll see some of the more common mayflies, stoneflies and caddisflies and when they appear. These emergence dates are only approximate and vary considerably from location to location—especially in the West. Look at the salmon fly as an example. This huge stonefly usually begins appearing on Western waters like the Deschutes River in central Oregon around May 25. You can fish the same hatch on the Yellowstone River just outside the park in early July. That's a difference of more than a month. I've seen the pale morning dun emerge on the Metolius River in central Oregon as early as late May. The same pale morning dun emerges on the Kootenai River in northwestern Montana in late June and early July. If you plan to fish this same hatch on the Bighorn River in Montana don't expect to see the hatch until late July or August.

Fishing the trico hatch and spinner fall is even more interesting in the West. I've hit great trico spinner falls on southwestern Montana's Ruby River in early August. On the McKenzie River in western Oregon, I've seen hatches in late October and early November. But, the most unusual situation of all for the trico spinner fall occurs in the Southwest. I've seen tricos in the air in December, January, February, and March in this sector. I've experienced heavy spinner falls on the upper Verde River at Cottonwood, Arizona, in mid-February and saw pods of 30 and 40 trout feeding on the spinners.

Yes, emergence dates do vary tremendously—especially in the West. If you're aware of these variations you can readily take advantage of them. Look at the brown drake as an example. On many Eastern rivers this hatch appears in late May and early June. In Michigan and Wisconsin you'll find the hatch appearing in early to mid June. This same hatch appears on Henry's Fork and Silver Creek in Idaho in late June.

Table 3. HATCH CHART for Western Streams and Rivers					
Dun	Spinner	Species	Date	Hook Size	Time of Day
Little Black Stonefly (s)		*Eucapnopsis brevicauda*	February to April	16	Afternoon
Early Blue or Little Blue-winged Olive Dun	Rusty Spinner (Early evening)	*Baetis tricaudatus*	January** to December	16-20	Afternoon
Little Blue-winged Olive Dun	Rusty Spinner (Early evening)	*Beatis tricaudatus*	January** to December	20-22	Afternoon
Early Blue or Little Blue-winged Olive Dun	Rusty Spinner	*Acentrella turbida*	January to December	22-24	Afternoon
Western March Brown	Western March Brown	*Rhithrogena morrisoni*	February to May	14	Afternoon
Little Golden Stonefly (s)		*Skawala parallela*	April 1	18	Afternoon
Blue Quill	Rusty Spinner	*Paraleptophlebia memorialis*	March to July	18	Morning
Quill Gordon	Quill Gordon Spinner	*Epeorus longimanus*	March to May	16	Afternoon
Trico Dun	Trico Spinner (mid-to-late morning)	*Tricorythodes minutus*	February** to December	24	Morning
Trico Dun	Trico Spinner (mid-to-late morning)	*Tricorythodes fictus*	February** to December	20-24	Morning
Speckle-winged Dun	Speckle-winged Spinner	*Callibaetis americanus*	April to November	16	Morning
Little Brown Stonefly (c)		*Amphinemura* species	April 1	16	Afternoon
Grannom (c)		*Brachycentrus occidentalis*	May 1	16	Afternoon
Western Green Drake	Dark Olive Spinner (afternoon)	*Drunella Grandis*	May to July	12	Morning

Table 3. HATCH CHART *(continued)* for Western Streams and Rivers

Dun	Spinner	Species	Date	Hook Size	Time of Day
Dark Brown Dun	Dark Brown Spinner	*Cinygmula par*	May 15	16	Noon
Salmon Fly (s)		*Pteronarcys californica*	May 20	6	Morning
Blue-winged Olive Dun	Dark Olive Spinner	*Drunella spinifera*	June 1	16	Noon
Pale Morning Dun	Pale Morning Spinner	*Ephemerella inermis*	May 20	16	Morning
Little Blue-winged Olive Dun	Rusty Spinner	*Baetis bicaudatus*	May 20	20	Afternoon
Black Quill	Black Quill Spinner	*Leptophlebia* species	May 20	16	Afternoon
Little Yellow Stonefly (s)		*Sweltsa coloradensis*	May 20	16	Evening
Pale Morning Dun	Pale Morning Spinner	*Ephemerella infrequens*	May 20	18	Morning
Blue-winged Olive	Dark Olive Spinner	*Drunella flavilinea*	June 15	14	Morning & Evening
Pale Evening Dun	Pale Evening Spinner	*Heptagenia elegantula*	June 15	16	Evening
Green Caddis (c)		*Rhyacophila vagrita*	June 15	12-14	Evening
Yellow Caddis (c)		*Oecetis* species	June 15	14-16	Evening
Dark Brown Dun	Dark Brown Spinner	*Ameletus velox*	June 15	14	Late Morning
Brown Caddis (c)		*Oecetis* species	June 15	14-16	Evening
Golden Stonefly (s)		*Hesperoperla pacifica*	June 15	4	Evening
Blue Quill	Dark Brown Spinner	*Paraleptophlebia heteronea*	June 15	18	Morning

Table 3. HATCH CHART (continued) for Western Streams and Rivers

Dun	Spinner	Species	Date	Hook Size	Time of Day
Blue Quill	Dark Brown Spinner	Paraleptophlebia memorialis	July 1	18	Morning
Pink Lady	Salmon Spinner	Epeorus albertae	July 1	12	Evening
Brown Drake	Dark Brown Spinner	Ephemera simulans	July 1	10	Evening
Cream Dun	Cream Spinner	Leptohyphes species	July 1	22-24	Evening
Little White Mayfly	Little Cream Spinner	Caenis species	July 1	24-26	Evening
Gray Drake	Gray Drake Spinner	Siphlonurus occidentalis	July 1	10	Afternoon

* More than one generation each year.
** Early dates refer to hatches in the Southwest.
(s) Stonefly
(c) Caddisfly

Montana's Kootenai River holds a great mid-season Pale Morning Dun.

Table 4. HATCH CHART
for Eastern & Midwestern Streams and Rivers

Dun	Spinner	Species	Date	Hook Size	Time of Day
Little Black Stonefly (s)		*Capnia vernalis*	February 1	14-18	Afternoon
Little Blue-winged Olive Dun	Rusty Spinner	*Baetis tricaudatus**	April 1	18	Afternoon
Early Brown Stonefly (s)		*Strophopteryx faciata*	April 10	14	Afternoon
Blue Quill	Dark Brown Spinner	*Paraleptophlebia adoptiva*	April 15	18	Afternoon
Quill Gordon	Red Quill Spinner	*Epeorus pleruralis*	April 15	14	Afternoon
Dark Quill Gordon	Quill Gordon Spinner	*Ameletus ludens*	April 18	14	Afternoon
Little Black Caddis (c)		*Chimarra atterima*	April 20	16	Afternoon
Male dun: Red Quill *Female dun:* Hendrickson	Red Quill	*Ephemerella subvaria*	April 20	14	Afternoon
Black Quill	Early Brown Spinner	*Leptophlebia cupida*	April 22	14	Afternoon
Grannom (c)		*Brachycentrus fulliginosis*	April 22	12-16	Afternoon
Grannom (c)		*Brachycentrus numerosis*	April 22	10-14	Afternoon
Light Stonefly (s)		*Isoperla signata*	May 8	14	Afternoon
Sulphur	Sulphur Spinner	*Ephemerella rotunda*	May 8	16	Evening
Blue Dun	Dark Rusty Spinner	*Baetis cinctutus**	May 8	22	Afternoon
Green Caddis (c)		*Rhyacophilia lobifera*	May 8	14-16	Afternoon

Above: A grayling
caught on
Handkerchief Lake
in northern
Montana during a
Speckle-winged Dun
hatch.

Right: Michigan's
Au Sable holds great
hatches throughout
the season.

Table 4. HATCH CHART (continued) for Eastern & Midwestern Streams and Rivers

Dun	Spinner	Species	Date	Hook Size	Time of Day
Little Blue-winged Olive Dun	Rusty Spinner	*Baetis brunneicolor*	May 10	20	Afternoon
Gray Fox	Ginger Quill	*Stenonema fuscum***	May 15	14	Afternoon & Evening
Pale Evening Dun	Pale Evening Spinner	*Ephemerella septentrionalis*	May 18	16	Evening
American March Brown	Great Red Spinner	*Stenonema vicarium*	May 20	12	Afternoon *Spinner:* Evening
Pale Evening Dun	Pale Evening Spinner	*Leucrota aphrodite*	May 20	16	Evening
Sulphur	Sulphur Spinner	*Ephemerella invaria*	May 20	16	Evening
Chocolate Dun	Chocolate Spinner	*Eurylophella bicolor*	May 22	16	*Dun:* Afternoon *Spinner:* Evening
Spotted Sedge (c)		*Hydropsyche slossanae*	May 23	14	Afternoon
Light Cahill	Light Cahill Spinner	*Stenonema ithaca*	May 25	14	Evening
Slate Drake	White-gloved Howdy	*Isonychia bicolor**	May 25	12	Evening
Female: Pink Lady *Male:* Light Cahill	Salmon Spinner	*Epeorus vitreus**	May 25	14	Evening
Light Cahill	Light Cahill Spinner	*Stenacron interpunctatum*	May 25	14	Evening
Dark Green Drake	Brown Drake	*Litobrancha recurvata*	May 25	8	*Dun:* Afternoon *Spinner:* Evening
Brown Drake	Brown Drake Spinner	*Ephemera simulans*	May 25	10	Evening

Table 4. HATCH CHART (continued) for Eastern & Midwestern Streams and Rivers

Dun	Spinner	Species	Date	Hook Size	Time of Day
Green Drake	Coffin Fly	*Ephemera guttulata*	May 25	8	Evening
Gray Drake	Gray Drake Spinner	*Siphlonurus quebecensis*	May 25	10	*Dun:* Day *Spinner:* Evening
Blue-winged Olive Dun	Dark Olive Spinner	*Drunella cornuta*	May 25		*Dun:* Morning *Spinner:* Evening
Blue Quill	*Female:* Dark Brown Spinner *Male:* Jenny Spinner	*Paraleptophlebia mollis*	May 26	18	Morning & Afternoon
Chocolate Dun— male Olive Sulphur— female	Chocolate Spinner —male Dark Olive Spinner—female	*Ephemerella needhami*	May 30	16	*Dun:* Morning *Spinner:* Evening
Pale Evening Dun	Pale Evening Spinner	*Ephemerella dorothea*	May 31	18	Evening
Dark Blue Sedge		*Psilotreta frontalis*	June 1	14	Evening
Blue-winged Olive Dun	Dark Olive Spinner	*Drunella cornutella*	June 10	16	*Dun:* Morning *Spinner:* Evening
Blue-winged Olive Dun	Dark Olive Spinner	*Danella simplex*	June 15	20	*Dun:* Morning *Spinner:* Evening
Light Cahill	Olive Cahill Spinner	*Heptagenia marginalis*	June 15	14	Evening
Cream Cahill	Cream Cahill Spinner	*Stenonema pulchellum*	June 15	14	Evening
Yellow Drake	Yellow Drake Spinner	*Ephemera varia*	June 15	12	Evening

Table 4. HATCH CHART (continued)
for Eastern & Midwestern Streams and Rivers

Dun	Spinner	Species	Date	Hook Size	Time of Day
Pale Evening Dun	Pale Evening Spinner	*Leucrocuta hebe*	June 22	16	Evening
Blue Quill	*Female:* Dark Brown Spinner *Male:* Jenny Spinner	*Paraleptophlebia guttata*	June 25	18	Morning & Afternoon
Golden Drake	Golden Drake Spinner	*Anthopotaman-thus distinctus*	June 25	12	Evening
Trico Dun	Trico Spinner	*Tricorythodes allectus (attratus)**	July 15	24	Morning
Cream Cahill	Cream Spinner	*Stenonema modestum*	August 1	16	Evening
White Fly	White Fly	*Ephoron leukon*	August 12	14	Evening
Big Slate Drake	Dark Rusty Spinner	*Hexagenia atrocaudata*	August 15	6	Evening
Little Blue-winged	Rusty Spinner	*Baetis tricaudatus**	September 1	20	*Dun:* Afternoon *Spinner:* Afternoon & Evening
Slate Drake	White-gloved Howdy	*Isonychia bicolor**	September 1	14	Afternoon & Evening
Autumn Sedge (c)		*Neophylax* species	September 15	10-14	Afternoon

* *More than one generation each year.*
•• *Now grouped with S. vicarium*
(s) *Stonefly*
(c) *Caddisfly*

The Slate Drake appears much of the season.

A Little Blue-winged Olive *(Baetis tricaudatus)* found across the United States.

A Great Red Spinner.

A March Brown.

Patterns to Match the Hatches

Tables 3 and 4 list most of the major hatches found on United States trout streams. These tables also suggest common patterns and sizes. Tables 5, 6, 7 and 8 suggest what patterns you should carry with you at certain times of the year and specific times of the day. I try to carry copies of just about every hatch I expect to encounter. The result: I carry thousands and thousands of patterns with me on every trip. In this section I'll try to limit the number of patterns you'll need to take with you on your fishing trips. We'll look at patterns that copy mayfly duns and spinners, imitations for some of the common stoneflies and caddisflies; and patterns to copy midges and terrestrials. Chapter 9 gives tying descriptions for most of the common hatches you'll find.

Time of Day Hatches Appear

It's interesting to look at Tables 5 through 8. Look at the early season and you'll see that most of the hatches appear at the most comfortable time of day. Early in the season that occurs in the afternoon. Look at the Western March brown as an example. This unusual mayfly begins emerging on near coastal and coastal rivers of Oregon, California and Washington in late February and continues daily until early May. It usually appears shortly after noon and goes on for an hour or two. The hendrickson, in the East and Midwest, usually begins its annual appearance in mid April in Pennsylvania and New Jersey and late April and early May in New York and Michigan. It, too, appears early in the afternoon.

A dramatic change takes place in the East and Midwest with the onset of the sulphur hatch in mid May. Hatches shift to the evening in May and continue to appear in the evening until early September.

The East Koy in New York holds great hatches.

You'll find Little Blue-wings appearing in September and October in New York's Willowemoc.

The Delaware River near Hancock, New York, holds great hatches from March through October.

Table 5. Time of Day Selected Mayfly, Stonefly and Caddisfly Hatches Appear and Patterns that Match Them — East and Midwest

MONTH	MORNING	AFTERNOON	EVENING
MARCH		Little Blue-winged Olive Dun - #20 Little Black Stonefly (s) - #14	
APRIL	Little Blue-winged Olive Dun - #20 Blue Quill - #18	Little Blue-winged Olive Dun - #20 Early Brown Stonefly (s) - #12 Blue Quill - #18 Quill Gordon - #14 Hendrickson - #14 Black Quill - #14 Dark Quill Gordon - #14 Great Speckled Olive Dun - #12 Grannom (c) - #12-16	
MAY	Blue-winged Olive Dun - #14 Blue Quill - #18	Light Stonefly (s) - #14 Hendrickson - #14 Black Quill - #14 March Brown - #12 Sulphur - #16 Blue-winged Olive Dun - #16-22 Chocolate Dun - #16 Gray Drake - #12	Sulphur - #16 Light Cahill - #14 Slate Drake - #12-14 Green Drake - #8-10 Brown Drake - #10-12 Cream Cahill - #14
JUNE	Blue-winged Olive Dun - #14		Dark Blue Sedge - #14

Table 5. Time of Day Selected Mayfly, Stonefly and Caddisfly Hatches Appear and Patterns that Match Them — East and Midwest (continued)

MONTH	MORNING	AFTERNOON	EVENING
	Blue Quill Blue-winged Olive Dun - #16	Gray Drake - #12 Chocolate Dun - #16	Green Drake - #8-10 Brown Drake - #10-12 Sulphur - #16 Pale Evening Dun - #18 Olive Sulphur - #16 Hex *(H. limbata)* - #6 Yellow Drake - #12 Giant Yellow *(H. rigida)* - #8 Golden Drake - #12
JULY	Blue-winged Olive Dun - #16 Blue Quill - #18		Giant Yellow *(H. rigida)* - #8 Golden Drake - #12 Pale Evening Dun - #18 Yellow Drake - #12
AUGUST	Trico - #24 Blue Quill - #18	Little Blue-winged Olive Dun - #20	Slate Drake - #14 White Fly - #14 Cream Cahill - #14-16 Hex *(H. atrocaudata)* - #8
SEPT	Trico - #24 Blue Quill - #18	Little Blue-winged Olive Dun - #18	Slate Drake - #14 White Fly - #14 Cream Cahill - #14-16
OCTOBER	Trico - #24 Blue Quill - #18	Trico - #24	

Table 6. Time of Day Mayfly Spinners Appear and Patterns that Match Them — East and Midwest

MONTH	MORNING	AFTERNOON	EVENING
MARCH		Rusty Spinner - *#20* *(Baetis tricaudatus)*	
APRIL		Red Quill Spinner - #14 *(Ephemerella subvaria)* Dark Brown Spinner - #18 *(Paraleptophlebia adoptiva)* Rusty Spinner - #20 *(Baetis tricaudatus)* Early Brown Spinner - #14 *(Leptophlebia cupida)* Dark Quill Gordon Spinner - #14 *(Ameletus ludens)*	Red Quill Spinner - #14 *(Ephemerella subvaria)* Rusty Spinner - #20 *(Baetis tricaudatus)*
MAY		Red Quill Spinner - #14 *(Ephemerella subvaria)*	Red Quill Spinner - #14 *(Ephemerella subvaria)* Sulphur Spinner - #16 *(Ephemerella rotunda)* March Brown Spinner - #12 *(Stenonema vicarium)* White-gloved Howdy - #12 *(Isonychia bicolor)* Light Cahill Spinner - #14 *(Stenacron interpunctatum)* Coffin Fly - #8 *(Ephemera guttulata)* Brown Drake Spinner - #10 *(Ephemera simulans)* Dark Olive Spinner - #14 *(Drunella cornuta)* Chocolate Spinner - #16 *(Eurylophella bicolor)* Cream Cahill Spinner - #14 *(Stenonema modestum)*

MONTH	MORNING	AFTERNOON	EVENING
			Salmon Spinner - #14 *(Epeorus vitreus)*
JUNE	Dark Brown Spinner - #18 *(Paraleptophlebia mollis)*		Chocolate Spinner - #16 *(Eurylophella bicolor)*
	Blue Quill Spinner - #20 *(Serratella deficiens)*		White-gloved Howdy - #12 *(Isonychia bicolor)*
			Sulphur Spinner - #16 *(Ephemerella rotunda* and *invaria)*
			Coffin Fly - #8 *(Ephemera guttulata)*
			Brown Drake Spinner - #10 *(Ephemera simulans)*
			Gray Drake Spinner - #12 *(S. quebecensis* and *fictus)*
			Olive Sulphur Spinner - #16 *(E. needhami)*
			Yellow Drake Spinner - #12
			Dark Olive Spinner - #14 *(Drunella cornuta)*
			Dark Olive Spinner - #16 *(Drunella cornutella)*
			Pale Evening Spinner - #18 *(Ephemerella dorothea)*
			Cream Cahill Spinner - #14 *(Stenonema modestum)*
			Hex *(Hexagenia limbata)*
			Hex *(Hexagenia rigida)*
JULY	Trico Spinner - #24 *(Tricorythodes allectus)*		White-gloved Howdy - #12 *(Isonychia bicolor)*

Table 6. Time of Day Mayfly Spinners Appear and Patterns that Match Them — East and Midwest (continued)

MONTH	MORNING	AFTERNOON	EVENING
	Dark Brown Spinner - #18 (Paraleptophlebia guttata)		Dark Olive Spinner (Drunella cornutella) Hex (Hexagenia rigida)
AUGUST	Dark Brown Spinner - #18 (Paraleptophlebia guttata) Trico Spinner - #24 (Tricorythodes allectus)		White Fly - #14 (Ephoron leukon) Hex (Hexagenia atrodaudata)
SEPT	Trico Spinner - #24 (Tricorythodes allectus) Dark Brown Spinner - #18 (Paraleptophlebia guttata)	Rusty Spinner - #20 (Baetis tricaudatus)	White-gloved Howdy - #14 (Isonychia bicolor) Rusty Spinner - #20 (Baetis tricaudatus)

Above left: A Little Blue-winged Olive found in the Southwest *(Baetis intercalaris).*

Above right: A Trico species found in the Southwest *(Tricorythodes fictus).*

Right: Great Trico hatches appear on Arizona's Upper Verde River in late winter.

Table 7. Time of Day Selected Mayfly, Stonefly and Caddisfly Hatches Appear and Patterns that Match Them — West

MONTH	MORNING	AFTERNOON	EVENING
FEBRUARY	Little Blue-winged Olive Dun - #20 *(Baetis tricaudatus)* Trico - #24* *(Tricorythodes minutus* and *fictus)*	Little Blue-Winged Olive Dun - #20 *(Baetis tricaudatus* and *intercalaris)* Western March Brown - #14 *(Rhithrogena morrisoni)***	
MARCH	Little Blue-winged Olive Dun - #20 *(Baetis tricaudatus* and *intercalaris)* Trico - #20-24* *(Tricorythodes minutus* and *fictus)*	Little Blue-winged Olive Dun - #20 *(Baetis tricaudatus* and *intercalaris)* Trico - #20-24 Western March Brown - #14 *(Rhithrogena morrisoni)*	
APRIL	Little Blue-winged Olive Dun - #20 *(Baetis tricaudatus* and *intercalaris)* Trico - #24* *(Tricorythodes minutus* and *fictus)*	Western March Brown - #14 *(Rhithrogena morrisoni)*	
MAY	Trico - #24* *(Tricorythodes minutus* and *fictus)* Blue-winged Olive Dun - #14 *(Drunella flavilinea)* Blue Quill - #18 *(Paraleptophlebia heteronea)* Western Green Drake - #12 *(Ephemerella heteronea)* Salmon Fly (s) - #8 *(Pteronarcys californica)*	Western March Brown - #14 *(Rhithrogena morrisoni)*	

Table 7. Time of Day Selected Mayfly, Stonefly and Caddisfly Hatches Appear and Patterns that Match Them — West *(continued)*

MONTH	MORNING	AFTERNOON	EVENING
	Grannom #16 *(brachycentrus occidentalis)*		
	Pale Morning Dun - #16 *(Ephemerella inermis)*		Pale Morning Dun - #16 *(Ephemerella inermis)*
	Pale Morning Dun - #18 *(Ephemerella infrequens)*		
	Speckle-winged Dun - #16 *(Callibaetis americanus)*		
	Blue-winged Olive Dun - #14 *(Drunella flavilinea)*		Blue-winged Olive Dun - #14 *(Drunella flavilinea)*
JUNE			Brown Drake - #10 *(Ephemera simulans)*
	Pale Morning Dun - #16 *(Ephemerella inermis)*		Pale Morning Dun - #16 *(Ephemerella inermis)*
	Western Green Drake - #12 *(Ephemerella grandis)*	Dark Brown Dun - #20 *(Diphetor hagani)*	Pale Evening Dun - #16 *(Heptagenia elegantula)*
	Salmon Fly (s)- #8 *(Pteronarcys californica)*		
	Pale Morning Dun - #18 *(Ephemerella infrequens)*		
	Blue-winged Olive Dun - #14 *(Drunella flavilinea)*		Blue-winged Olive Dun - #14 *(Drunella flavilinea)*
	Blue Quill - #18 *(Paraleptophlebia heteronea)*		
	Speckle-winged Dun - #16 *(Callibaetis americanus)*		
JULY	Western Green Drake - #12 *(Ephemerella grandis)*	Dark Brown Dun - #20 *(Diphetor hagani)*	Gray Fox - #14 *Heptagenia solitaria*

Table 7. Time of Day Selected Mayfly, Stonefly and Caddisfly Hatches Appear and Patterns that Match Them — West *(continued)*

MONTH	MORNING	AFTERNOON	EVENING
	Quill Gordon - #12 *(Rhithrogena futilis)*	Quill Gordon - #12 *(Rhithrogena futilis)*	Light Cahill - #12 *(Cinygmula dimicki)*
	Pale Brown Dun - #14 *(Cinygmula reticulata)*	Pale Brown Dun - #14 *(Cinygmula reticulata)*	
	Trico - #24* *(Tricorythodes minutus and fictus)*		
	Blue Quill - #18 *(Paraleptophlebia memorialis)*		
	Pale Brown Dun - #14 *(Rhithrogena hagani)*	Pale Brown Dun - #14 *(Rhithrogena hagani)*	
	Dark Brown Dun - #14 *(Ameletus cooki)*	Dark Brown Dun - #14 *(Ameletus cooki)*	
AUGUST	Trico - #24* *(Tricorythodes minutus and fictus)*	Gray Drake - #12 *(Siphlonurus occidentalis)*	Gray Fox - #14 *(Heptagenia solitaria)*
	Blue Quill - #18 *(Paraleptophlebia memorialis)*		White Fly - #14 *(Ephoron album)*
SEPT	Blue Quill - #18 *(Paraleptophlebia memorialis)*		
	Trico - #24* *(Tricorythodes minutus and fictus)*	Little Blue-winged Olive Dun - #20 *(Baetis tricaudatus and intercalaris)*	Gray Fox - #14 *(Heptagenia solitaria)*

  * *Southwestern rivers like the Salt and Verde Rivers in Arizona*
 ** *Willamette and McKenzie Rivers in Oregon*

Table 8. Time of Day Mayfly Spinners Appear and Patterns that Match Them—West

MONTH	MORNING	AFTERNOON	EVENING
JANUARY		Rusty Spinner - #20 *(Baetis tricaudatus* and *intercalaris)*	Rusty Spinner - #20 *(Baetis tricaudatus* and *intercalaris)**
FEBRUARY		Rusty Spinner - #20 *(Baetis tricaudatus* and *intercalaris)*	Rusty Spinner - #20 *(Baetis tricaudatus* and *intercalaris)*
		Western March Brown Spinner *(Rhithrogena morrisoni)*	Western March Brown Spinner *(Rhithrogena morrisoni)*
	Trico - #24 *(Tricorythodes fictus)* Southwestern rivers	Trico - #24 *(Tricorythodes fictus)* Southwestern rivers	
MARCH	Trico - #24 *(Tricorythodes fictus)* Southwestern rivers		
APRIL	Trico - #24 *(Tricorythodes fictus)* Southwestern rivers		
MAY	Pale Morning Spinner - #16-18 *(Ephemerella inermis)*	Pale Morning Spinner - #16-18 *(Ephemerella inermis)*	
JUNE	Pale Morning Spinner - #16-18 *(Ephemerella inermis)*	Pale Morning Spinner - #16-18 *(Ephemerella inermis)*	Brown Drake Spinner - #10 *(Ephemera simulans)*
JULY			Brown Drake Spinner - #10 *(Ephemera simulans)*
	Pale Morning Spinner - #16-18 *(Ephemerella inermis)* Trico - #24 *(Tricorythodes minutus)*		
AUGUST	Pale Morning Spinner - #16-18 *(Ephemerella inermis)* Trico - #24 *(Tricorythodes minutus)*		
SEPT	Trico - #24 *(Tricorythodes minutus)*		Rusty Spinner - #20 *(Baetis tricaudatus)*
OCTOBER	Trico - #24 *(Tricorythodes minutus)*		Rusty Spinner - #20 *(Baetis tricaudatus)*

* *Mainly on southwestern rivers and streams*

Patterns that Copy Emerging Mayflies

How do you limit the number of patterns that copy mayflies to a manageable few? Look at Tables 9, 10, 13 and 14 for hints on color selection. Tables 9 and 10 suggest methods to identify some of the more common hatches and Tables 13 and 14 suggest what hatches you'll see early in the season. A good rule of thumb to remember: *If you're fishing in the early season (April and early May) you'll see mostly gray flies, so use a pattern that color. If you're fishing in mid summer at dusk remember that most light colored mayflies appear at that time. If you fish during the day in the summer gray or dark olive might be a good color. Finally, if you plan to fish in the fall gray mayflies again predominate.* (Answer to 6.) (See "When Grays Appear" on page 108.)

The patterns can be tied as wet flies or dry flies depending on your preference. With those thoughts in mind here are some suggestions for a short list of patterns that match the hatches in all parts of the country.

Spring
Little Blue-winged Olive Dun—sizes 16 to 22
Quill Gordon—sizes 12 to 16
Blue Quill—sizes 16 to 20
Hendrickson—sizes 14 to 16

Midseason
Light Cahill—sizes 10 to 20
Sulphur or Pale Morning Dun—sizes 14 to 20
Slate Drake—sizes 12 to 16
Blue-winged Olive Dun—sizes 12 to 16

Fall
Little Blue-winged Olive Dun—sizes 16 to 22
Slate Drake—sizes 12 to 16
Cream Cahill—sizes 12 to 18

Patterns that Copy Spinners

How many times have I been frustrated by a spinner fall? I can't begin to count the number of times I've seen spinners on the surface, and I didn't have a good pattern to match the fall. One of the most frustrating events occurred when I first met the brown spinner. Thousands of brown drake spinners dotted the surface and more than a hundred trout rose within casting distance of me. That evening I tried just about every dark pattern I had in my box without much success. After that troublesome evening I vowed never to be without a good supply of spinner patterns ever again. How would I accomplish that? I used 2 Wheatley fly boxes and placed in the individual compartments different colors in sizes 10 through 24. Figure 3 shows the different spinner patterns in these boxes.

SIZE	COLOR of BODY	COLOR of BODY	COLOR of BODY	COLOR of BODY	COLOR of BODY	COLOR of BODY	COLOR of BODY
10	Cream	Pale Yellow	Tan	Brown	Dark Olive	Dark Brown	Black
12	Cream	Pale Yellow	Tan	Brown	Dark Olive	Dark Brown	Black
14	Cream	Pale Yellow	Tan	Brown	Dark Olive	Dark Brown	Black
16	Cream	Pale Yellow	Tan	Brown	Dark Olive	Dark Brown	Black
18	Cream	Pale Yellow	Tan	Brown	Dark Olive	Dark Brown	Black
20	Cream	Pale Yellow	Tan	Brown	Dark Olive	Dark Brown	Black
22	Cream	Pale Yellow	Tan	Brown	Dark Olive	Dark Brown	Black
24	Cream	Pale Yellow	Tan	Brown	Dark Olive	Dark Brown	Black

Figure 3. Two Wheatley boxes with different body colors to match most spinner falls.

You can see from Figure 3 that the most popular spinner colors are all included. You might want to throw in a few dark gray body patterns to cover yourself. This system has worked well for me over the years. If you don't have the luxury of a large selection here are a few basic spinners that you should include in your selection whether you're fishing the East, Midwest or West.

Spring
Red Quill Spinner – sizes 14 and 16
Dark Brown Spinner – sizes 16 and 18
Rusty Spinner – sizes 18 to 22

Midseason
Sulphur and Pale Morning Spinner – sizes 16 to 18
Dark Brown Spinner – sizes 12 to 18
Brown Drake Spinner – sizes 10 to 14
White-gloved Howdy – sizes 12 and 14
Quill Gordon Spinner – sizes 12 and 14
Dark Olive Spinner – sizes 14 and 16
Trico Spinner – sizes 22 to 26
White Fly – sizes 14 and 16

Fall
Rusty Spinner – sizes 18 to 22
White-gloved Howdy – sizes 12 and 14

Patterns that Copy Caddisflies and Stoneflies

It's important to carry plenty of downwing patterns with you. On almost every day I fish during spring, summer and fall I will see some hatches of caddisflies and stoneflies. You'll find these patterns important to match hatches across the United States. Following are some of the more important patterns.

Black Caddis and Grannom

Craig Shuman and Jack Mitchell have guided on Washington's Yakima River for several years. Ask both of them what time of year they enjoy most on the river and without doubt both would say the last two weeks in May. Why? The Yakima, along with the Bitterroot in Montana and the Yellowstone in the Montana, harbor great hatches of black caddis. Locals call it the "Mothers Day caddis" since they appear around that Sunday in May.

I hit the Black Caddis on the Yakima recently. Craig and Jack

You'll find downwings like the grannom caddis early in the season nationwide.

contacted Al Novotny of Casper, Wyoming, about doing a video on the Yakima's great fly-fishing. Al Novotny has produced many award winning outdoor films. He has produced videos on Greece, Hawaii, Miami, South Carolina, and the Grand Canyon. Al, his wife Carol, and his son Jarod came to the Yakima River to complete a production on the Kittitas and Yakima Valleys. As a major part of this video Al wanted to include a float trip fishing the Yakima River. Craig and Jack invited Dave Engerbrettson and me to fly fish on the river. It took us a week to complete the video, and each day we hit grannom hatches.

Travel thousands of miles to the East and you'll find caddisfly hatches with the same general appearance. In fact, the patterns I used to copy the Eastern and Midwestern grannom hatches work well with on the Western ones. Penns Creek boasts a black-bodied downwing that appears near the end of April. Anglers also call this black caddis a grannom. This hatch, better copied with a size 12 pattern, often promotes early season matching-the-hatch opportunities.

I said earlier that I carry a couple Wheatley boxes for my spinner patterns. I also carry one for my downwings. I have a row in the box assigned to each size 12 through 20 (Figure 4). Each row has six slots where I place downwing patterns from light to dark. I'll place cream, tan, green, brown, gray, and black patterns for each size. With this setup I can match just any caddis hatch I see.

If your floating downwing doesn't produce, sink it. Add shucks to some of your patterns to imitate the caddisfly emerging. You'll read more about this tactic in Chapter 4. Here's a list of downwings that you should carry with you.

Above: **Michigan's Muskegon River holds great caddis hatches in the fall.**

Right: **A Black Caddis.**

Spring
Grannom - sizes 12 to 16
Green Caddis - size 12 to 16
Tan Caddis - sizes 12 to 16
Cream Caddis – sizes 14 to 16

Midseason
Dark Blue Sedge - sizes 12 to 16
Tan Caddis - sizes 12 to 16

Fall
Amber Caddis - sizes 10 to 16
October Caddis - sizes 10 to 14

SIZE	COLOR of BODY	COLOR of BODY	COLOR of BODY	COLOR of BODY	COLOR of BODY	COLOR of BODY
12	Cream	Tan	Brown	Green	Gray	Black
14	Cream	Tan	Brown	Green	Gray	Black
16	Cream	Tan	Brown	Green	Gray	Black
18	Cream	Tan	Brown	Green	Gray	Black
20	Cream	Tan	Brown	Green	Gray	Black

Figure 4. Configuration for a Wheatley box to match most caddisfly hatches.

Patterns that Copy Land Borne Insects

If you want to catch more trout in midsummer then you've got to carry a good selection of terrestrial patterns with you. Ants, beetles, grasshoppers, and crickets in several sizes are a must especially if you

Terrestrial patterns work well throughout the summer.

A winged ant pattern.

Terrestrials
Ant - sizes 14 to 22
Beetle - sizes 14 to 20
Grasshopper - sizes 10 to 16
Caterpillar – sizes 10 to 14
Cricket – sizes 12 to 16

plan to fish small or well-canopied streams. In 1992 I wrote *Fishing Small Streams with a Fly Rod.* In preparation for the manuscript I fished small streams across the country. I spent more than a week fishing some of the tributaries of the McKenzie River near Eugene, Oregon. Ken Helfrich, a great guide on the McKenzie, accompanied me on these trips to some of his favorite small streams. On each of these August fishing trips we resorted to ants and beetles to save the day.

Talk about saving the day—that Chernobyl Cricket did it on those dredging ponds near Alder, Montana. You can read more about that event in Chapter 5. I will always remember another trip saved by the LeTort Hopper. After two hours of fishing the Arkansas River in Browns Canyon, Colorado, I had no trout to show for my intense fishing. My luck immediately changed when I switched to a hopper pattern that I skittered across the surface. Talk about saving the day—the hopper and cricket did it on those two occasions.

Don't forget about sinking your terrestrial pattern. When all else fails on those midsummer afternoons, I sink the ant or beetle pattern. I place the terrestrial behind a Patriot dry fly on a tandem. See Chapter 4 for more details.

Patterns that Copy True Flies like Midges

I fished exclusively in the East and Midwest for the first 20 years. Not until 1976 did I begin fly fishing Western waters. Those trips to the Cache la Poudre and Fryingpan in Colorado; to the San Juan in New Mexico; the Green River in Utah; and to Rocky Ford Creek and Nunnally Lake in eastern Washington had one thing in common—I witnessed plenty of midge hatches. Even that weekend I spent on Cave Lake near Ely, Nevada, brings back memories of tremendous midge hatches. No pattern—and I mean no pattern—caught any trout except size 24 midge patterns. To catch more trout—especially from November through May—and especially in the West—you must carry plenty of midge patterns with you.

More recently I fished the Colorado River at Lee's Ferry in Arizona. That river holds more than 30 chironomid species that appear just about every day of the year. On that trip I witnessed trout feeding on chironomids for more than eight hours. Why do they feed here for eight hours? I speculate that they have to feed that long because the chironomids are so small. To catch more trout on that river you've got to carry a good supply of midge patterns—both dries and wets—with you. Without plenty of gray and black midge pupa and floating patterns I would have done miserably on those waters.

But, a second trip to Lee's Ferry proved the merits of an important new midge pattern, the Zebra Midge. Frank Nofer, a Philadelphia attorney, looks forward to the opening of trout season in Pennsylvania. Recently he wanted to begin the season a bit earlier so the two of us traveled to Arizona's Lee's Ferry for a mid-March fishing trip. The Lee's Ferry section of the Colorado boasts two sections—a 1-mile walk in area and a 9-mile area upriver reached only by motorized boats. I wanted Frank to see the spectacular natural beauty of this part of the river so we took a boat up to the Glen Canyon Dam.

On the ride up to the dam our guide, Chad Bayles, stopped and suggested the three of us fish a productive riffle. Chad recommended that we use a tandem with a large dry fly and a wet fly placed about two feet behind it. I started with a size 20-bead head Pheasant Tail. For the first hour I didn't land one trout. Then the three of us started to catch trout and plenty of them. It all began with a pattern, the Zebra Midge, that had been developed specifically for the Ferry several years ago. For almost two hours Frank, Chad or I had a 14-18-inch rainbow on almost

Above: A typical midge pattern.

Right: Dead chironomids on Colorado's upper Cache La Poudre River.

continuously. On several occasions we had two trout on at the same time. These Lee's Ferry rainbows sometimes took two and three runs before we netted them. The Zebra Midge saved the day! No, it saved the entire trip and immediately became one of my favorite patterns.

Gary Hitterman of Casa Grande, Arizona, is one of the finest innovative fly tiers I know. He first turned me on to this important sinking midge imitation. He extolled the virtues of the Zebra Midge at least a year before I tied the pattern.

Some local anglers say the Zebra Midge was originally called Ted's Silver Bullet and that it was first developed by a local fly tier, Edward (Ted) Welling. Tie the pattern with brown and black bodies. Rib the black pattern with fine silver and the brown pattern with a fine copper wire. This pattern should work well on all those great rivers and lakes that host terrific midge hatches.

You'll also need midge patterns on Eastern and Midwestern water also—especially in fall, winter, and spring. If trout are rising to midges try a size 24 dark, gray pattern—especially shortly after noon.

Midges
Griffith's Gnat - sizes 20 to 24
Black Midge - sizes 20 to 26*
Gray Midge - sizes 20 to 24*
Cream Midge - size 20 to 24*
Zebra Midge - sizes 16 to 20

Tie as dry flies or midge pupa

Stream Side Identification

How many times have you seen a hatch in progress and wondered what that hatch was? Why do you need to know what hatch is appearing? As I've said many times before the more you know about the hatch the better fly fisher you'll be. The better fly fisher you'll be the more trout you'll catch. The Mayfly Identification Chart should help you identify many of the more common hatches. All you have to know is several obvious answers. You need to know the number of tails—two or three; and whether the insect is large (size 14 hook and larger) or small (size 16 and smaller). If it's near the cutoff (size 14 or 16) the mayfly is included in both the large and small category. Other categories that will help you identify the mayfly are the season it appears, the time of day, and whether the mayfly dun is light or dark in coloration.

The chart should help you identify what hatch you've seen. Here are some of the features of the hatch identification chart.

A Little Blue-winged Olive Dun.

Table 9. Mayfly Identification Chart Eastern and Midwestern

<u>Size:</u> S = Small - #16 and smaller; L = Large - #14 and larger
Insect in **BOLD** type = emerge at evening or dark

EARLY SEASON — March 1 - May 10

TWO TAILS

Dark Body

(S) Little Blue-winged Olive Dun–*Baetis tricaudatus* (Note Other *Baetis* species appear in the early season. Dun and spinner move abdomen from side to side

(L) Quill Gordon—*Epeorus pleuralis*—Can appear as late as late June

(L) Dark Quill Gordon—*Ameletus luden*—Usually find duns on rocks next to stream

(L) Speckle-winged Dun—*Callibaetis skokianus*-slow water or lake species

(L) Great Olive Dun—*Siphloplecton basale*—Rare in Pennsylvania

THREE TAILS

Dark Body

(L) Hendrickson—*Ephemerella subvaria*

(L) Black Quill—*Leptophlebia cupida*—Middle tail is somewhat shorter than outer two

(S) Blue Quill—*Paraleptophlebia adoptiva*

A Sulphur
(Ephemerella
rotunda).

Table 9. Mayfly Identification Chart
Eastern and Midwestern *(continued)*

Size: S = Small - #16 and smaller; L = Large - #14 and larger
Insect in **BOLD** type = emerge at evening or dark

MIDDLE SEASON — May 11 - June 30

TWO TAILS

Light Body

(L) Light Cahill—*Stenacron interpunctatum canadense*—Often appears heaviest around 7 P.M.

(L) Light Cahill—*Epeorus vitreus*-male—Male is yellow and female has a pink body

(L) Light Cahill—*Stenonema ithaca*

(L) Pink Lady—*Epeorus vitreus*-female

(L) Cream Cahill—*Stenonema modestum*—Spinner is chalky white

(L) March Brown (Gray Fox)—*Stenonema vicarium*

Dark Body

(L) Quill Gordon—*Epeorus pleuralis* (I've seen this mayfly appear in fishable numbers into June

(L) Dark Green Drake—*Litobrancha recurvata*—Usually appears around 2 P.M. Has a middle vestigal (just a trace) tail

(L) Gray Drake—*Siphlonurus quebecensis and mirus*—Male spinner *(S. mirus)* has black rear wing. Very common in early June in Northwestern Pennsylvania

THREE TAILS

Light Body

(L) Golden Drake—*Antopotomantus distinctus*—Weak veins in wing

(L) Sulphur—*Ephemerella rotunda* (and *invaria*)

(L) Sulphur—*Ephemerella invaria*

Table 9. Mayfly Identification Chart
Eastern and Midwestern *(continued)*

Size: S = Small - #16 and smaller; L = Large - #14 and larger

Insect in **BOLD** type = emerge at evening or dark

(L) Pale Evening Dun—*Ephemerella septentrionalis*

(S) Pale Evening Dun—*Ephemerella dorothea*

Dark Body   (S) Blue Quill—*Paraleptophlebia mollis and guttata*

(L) Green Drake—*Ephemera guttulata* (dark on top and cream on bottom)

(L) Brown Drake—*Ephemera simulans*

(L) Blue-winged Olive Dun—*Drunella cornuta*

(L&S) Blue-winged Olive Dun—*Drunella cornutella* (a size smaller than cornuta) appears in early to mid June

(L&S) Blue-winged Olive Dun—*Drunella lata* (appears three weeks later than *cornutella*)

(L) Slate Drake—*Isonychia bicolor* Front legs are dark brown; rear two pair are cream

(S) Dark Blue Quill—*Seratella deficiens*

(S) Little Blue-winged Olive Dun—*Danella simplex*

(L) Chocolate Dun—*Eurylophella bicolor* (Legs are cream)

(S) Olive Sulphur—*Ephemerella needhami* (legs, tail, and wings are cream. Body of female dun is medium olive; body of male dun is dark brown)

LATE SEASON — July 1 - October 30

TWO TAILS

Light Body   (L&S) **Cream Cahill—*Stenonema modestum***

Table 9. Mayfly Identification Chart
Eastern and Midwestern *(continued)*

<u>Size:</u> S = Small - #16 and smaller; L = Large - #14 and larger
<u>Insect in **BOLD** type</u> = emerge at evening or dark

(L) **White Fly—*Ephoron leukon*-male**

Dark Body

(L) **Dark Slate Drake—Hexagenia atrocaudata—**Male spinners undulate about 30 feet in the air around 7 P.M.

(S) Little Blue-winged Olive Dun—*Baetis tricaudatus*

THREE TAILS

Light Body

(L) **White Fly—*Ephoron leukon*-female**

(L) **Yellow Drake—*Ehpemera varia***

(S) Trico—*Tricorythodes allectus*—female

(S) **Little White Mayfly—*Caenis* species**

Dark Body

(S) Trico—*Tricorythodes allectus*-male

(L) **Slate Drake—*Isonychia bicolor***

(L) Blue Quill—*Paraleptophlebia guttata*

Table 10. Mayfly Identification Chart
Western

Size: S = Small - #16 and smaller; L = Large - #14 and larger
Insect in **BOLD** type = emerge at evening or dark

EARLY SEASON — March 1 - May 10

TWO TAILS

Dark Body   (S) Little Blue-winged Olive Dun –*Baetis tricaudatus*
                         (Note: Other *Baetis* species appear in the early
                         season.

                     (S) Little Blue-winged Olive Dun—*Baetis intercalaris*

                     (L) Western March Brown—*Rhithrogena morrisoni—*
                         appears fro more than three months on some
                         western rivers

THREE TAILS

Dark Body   (S) Blue Quill—*Paraleptophlebia memorialis*

MIDDLE SEASON — May 11 - June 30

THREE TAILS

Light Body   (S) Pale Morning Dun—*Ephemerella infrequens*

                     (S) Pale Morning Dun—*Ephemerella inermis*—Body color
                         of this mayfly varies considerably from stream to
                         stream.

Dark Body   **(L)   Brown Drake—*Ephemera simulans***

                     (L)   Western Green Drake—Ephemerella grandis

LATE SEASON — July 1 - September 30

THREE TAILS

Light Body   (S)   Trico—Tricorythodes minutus and fictus

Notes about the Hatch Identification Charts

Season

I've divided hatches into early, middle, and late season. Some— like the blue quill (*Paraleptophlebia guttata)* and the yellow drake (*Ephemera varia*) emerge in two of the time frames. Just about every common hatch you'll ever encounter is listed in this hatch chart.

A Brown Drake *(Ephemera simulans).*

The Western Green Drake *(Drunella grandis).*

Tails

A simple way of helping you determine which mayfly you're matching is to count the number of tails. This works with most species—except the white fly. When the white fly emerges, the male changes from a dun to a spinner—usually in a few minutes. The female however, never molts and remains and breeds as a dun. The male spinner has two tails and the female dun three. All mayflies have either two or three tails.

Light and Dark

"Light and Dark" refers to the coloration of the back of the body. For example, look at the green drake. If you examine the belly or abdomen of this mayfly you'll see cream. But, look at the back and you see a darker mayfly.

From the chart you can gather several bits of information when looking at "light" and "dark." First, take note of the coloration of mayflies in the "early season." Note that there are no mayflies appearing early in the season that have light backs. Why? When mayfly duns emerge from the water they most often rest for a day or more before they come back to the stream to mate and lay eggs. Where do they rest for that day or two? You'll most often find them on rocks near the stream or on branches of a nearby bush or tree. Normally mayflies rest on the underside of leaves. But, leaves have not yet appeared for the season. What predominant color will you find the rocks near the shore and the branches of nearby trees? The only color is dark gray. Over the eons mayflies that did emerge with lighter colored backs were easy prey for predators like birds. Those mayflies with darker backs were less easy to see and they prevailed. See "When Grays Appear" later in this chapter.

How does this information affect your choice of patterns in the early season? After knowing this would you select a light cahill or a dark cahill to match most of the April hatches? Of course you'd select the darker pattern.

Second, look also at the hatches for midseason. All hatches that appear during the day are dark in color. This is nature's way of protecting them. This doesn't mean that all dark mayflies appear during the day, but those that do are usually dark.

Variation in Color

Dave McMullen owns and operates the Six Springs Fly Shop in Spruce Creek, Pennsylvania. He's one of the finest fly casters I've ever seen. Show him a narrow opening between two trees and he'll land that dry fly delicately on the surface and not get hung up on a single branch. Dave also operates a trout hatchery in Spruce Creek and has made some keen observations there. Recently he showed me one of his findings. Dave netted three trout from a hatchery pool and placed them in a white bucket. Within minutes these trout became much lighter in color. He then returned the three back to the hatchery and for almost five minutes we could tell which three they were because they were much lighter than the other trout.

So what does this prove? Many life forms are probably capable of changing color to some extent. Call it protective coloration or whatever you want, it happens. What about the coloration of nymphs? Have you heard someone say that nymphs in one area or on one stream are lighter or darker than on another area or stream? Do you think many aquatic insects have the same capability?

When I prepared the manuscript for *Meeting and Fishing the Hatches* back in 1977 I sent Wills Flowers, a skilled entomologist, male spinners from Rocky Mountain streams for him to identify. I remember sending him a reddish brown mayfly, an olive one, and a cream one—all colors refer to the dun stage. The identification for all three came back as the same species—the pale morning dun (*Ephemerella inermis*). Wills told me that this species, possibly more than any other, varies in color from stream to stream—it varies in color even on the same stream. Another, closely related species, *Ephemerella needhami,* also varies in color tremendously. I recently experienced a hatch of the latter mayfly and the female dun had a distinct olive body with cream legs, tail, and wings. The male of this same species had a dark brown body in the dun stage.

Night or Day Emergers

Those mayflies listed in bold usually emerge at night and those in regular type usually appear during the day. Of course times vary with temperature and weather. I've seen hendrickson hatches appear as early as 9:00 A.M. on hot April days and as late as 6:00 P.M. on others. The sulphur is another story. Often the first couple days that the sulphur appears it often does so in the afternoon. After a few days the hatch usually changes to an evening one that appears just before dusk. Pale morning duns in the West hatch in the morning, afternoon and evening. I fished with Dave Blackburn on the Kootenai River and we hit one of the heaviest pale morning dun hatches that I've ever seen—in the afternoon and evening.

Add a drizzly, overcast day and all kinds of things can happen. I've seen sulphurs and pale morning duns emerge all day long on inclement days. Green drakes, too, will often appear earlier on overcast days and on streams with a heavy canopy.

Large and Small

You'll see an S or an L in front of each mayfly in the chart. Hatches that can be matched with a size 14 or larger hook (14-6) have an L in front of them. Those matches with a size 16 or smaller hook (16-26) have an S. Size varies tremendously.

Other Features

To further help you identify some of the mayflies we've added comments that might set one mayfly off from another. If male and female duns have different colors we mention them in this column. Many of the features in this column refer to coloration of the mayfly.

More Hatch Information that will Help You Catch More Trout

Emergence charts and pattern selection will help you tremendously when you're fishing a hatch or spinner fall. Here's some additional information that should help. Did you know that you could predict to some extent what color mayfly would appear at what time of the year and the time of day? Did you know that some mayflies appear for only a few days a year while other species may appear for several months. We'll examine these two features so you know more about the hatches.

Number of Days the Hatch Appears

Why should you know how long a hatch appears? How will this help you catch more trout? Compare a hatch to the daily feeding of trout at a hatchery. In a hatchery trout feed voraciously on trout pellets. In the wild, trout do the same thing. I've seen difficult trout lose their timidity completely and immediately when a hatch appears on the surface. So, the more days a hatch occurs in the year the more important it is to be there when that hatch appears, and with an appropriate pattern. What hatch appears for probably the most days of the year in the East and Midwest? Is it the trico, the little blue-winged olive dun, or the slate drake? Which hatches appear for a long time in the West? Is it the trico or the speckle-winged dun?

In the Southwest you'll find tricos appearing almost every day of the year. I've seen hatches on the Salt River near Phoenix, Arizona, on Christmas and New Year's morning. But, the little blue-winged olive dun also appears for many days on most Western waters. Fish the San Juan in New Mexico almost any day of the year and you're likely to see some little blue-winged olives appearing.

New Mexico's Red River north of Taos holds a good number of cutbows that move upriver in late fall and early spring from the Rio Grande River. Manuel Monasterio, Ed Adams, Virgil Bradford, and I hiked into the Red River in mid December a few years ago. Manuel owns the Reel Life fly shops in Albuquerque and Santa Fe. It's extremely difficult getting into the lower end of the Red River. You have to descend a steep, rocky, narrow trail to reach the river below. Once we reached this 30-foot wide water we had other obstacles. Nature placed huge boulders in our path as

Length of Hatches

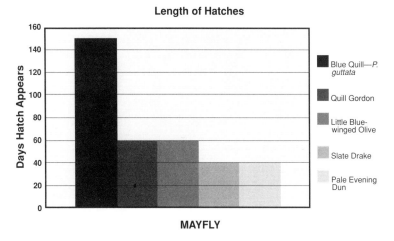

The number of days during a year that a mayfly hatch is in evidence varies widely from species to species.

we hiked upriver. Boulders in the stream and along the bank protected each pool. Almost every cast was an effort to complete. About noon hundreds of little blue-winged olives appeared and a few trout fed on them. These mayflies appeared on a cold mid-December afternoon. Hatches of this species appear in good numbers on the Red River in March, April, September, and October.

But, many of the hatches and spinner falls that appear for 30 or more days also have a downside. Trout seem to become extremely selective on some of these after feeding on the hatch for a week or two. Let me explain. Fish the sulphur on Spring Creek in central Pennsylvania in mid May, if you can find a spot to fish, and you'll probably do well matching the hatch. But, come back a few weeks later and you might well find a different story. In the many weeks that tricos, pale morning duns, or sulphurs appear, trout see a lot of anglers and patterns on some of the more heavily fished streams. These trout become highly selective in the process.

Why do some hatches appear for an extended period of time? Some hatches like the blue quill just have a long period of emergence, while others like the little blue-winged olive and trico have more than one generation each year. We'll examine a few of the major hatches that appear for an extended period.

Winter Tricos

What a fabulous way to spend a midwinter day! Phoenix and the Valley of the Sun in Arizona experience mild winter days in January and February. Craig Josephson and I headed 90 miles north of the valley to the Cottonwood area to fish the upper Verde River for a morning in mid-February. Craig had landed at Skyport Airport from Syracuse, New York, and wanted to experience some midwinter fishing. He had a few days to spend in the valley of the sun before he had to return to snowy Syracuse, New York. I planned to take him 90 miles north of Phoenix to fly fish on the upper Verde River near Cottonwood, Arizona.

Weather forecasters predicted a great day for the Valley of the Sun. Temperatures on that mid-February Saturday were expected to rise into the mid seventies. Even at Cottonwood they expected temperatures to peak out near 70 degrees. It took two hours to travel up I-17 to the Dead Horse State Park where we planned to fly fish. When we arrived at the river we were amazed at the number of anglers out on this Saturday morning. The upper Verde gets plenty of angling pressure—especially on the weekends. But, guess what? Each one of the anglers had a spinning rod in hand. Not during the entire morning did Craig or I see another fly fisher.

Shortly after we arrived on the Verde we saw several small mayflies emerge. I felt confident it was one of the little blue-winged olives appearing and tied on an a size 20 imitation to copy that hatch. By 10:00 AM hundreds of these duns emerged in the pool in front of Craig and me. I quickly grabbed one of the duns and blurted out in amazement to Craig that these were trico duns emerging. Trico duns in mid February? A winter trico hatch? I had seen a few tricos appear on the Salt River near Phoenix in December and January. But, they didn't appear in numbers to bring trout to the surface. By 10:30, however, trico spinners began to fall onto the surface and a half dozen trout rose in front of me for this early-season food. Craig and I hurriedly tied on Trico Spinner imitations and we began casting to surfacing trout. I missed the first trout that rose to the pattern—but hooked the second one. I wanted so desperately to land that trout taken on a Trico pattern in mid-February. It was a first—a trout caught on a Trico pattern in midwinter.

We headed upriver to the next pool and found two pods of 20 to 30 rising trout in each feeding on spent spinners. Trico spinners continued to fall onto the surface for two more hours that late February morning. Craig and I continued to match the spinner fall and landed more than a dozen trout rising to the spent spinners. What a midwinter hatch! What a midwinter day of fly-fishing! That's one that will go down in my memory

Table 11. Eastern and Midwestern Hatches and the Number of Days They Appear

IMITATION AND SIZE	SPECIES	NUMBER OF DAYS THE HATCH APPEARS EACH YEAR ON THE SAME STREAM*	TIME OF YEAR THE HATCH APPEARS
Blue Quill—18	*Paraleptophlebia guttata* and *strigula*	120	June, July, August and September
Trico**—24	*Tricorythodes allectus*	75	July, August and September
Quill Gordon—14	*Epeorus pleuralis*	60	April, May and June
Little Blue-winged Olive Dun**—20	*Baetis tricaudatus*	60	March, April, September and October
Slate Drake**—12 and 14	*Isonychia bicolor*	40	June and September
Pale Evening Dun —20	*Ephemerella dorothea*	40	June and July
Sulphur—16	*Ephemerella rotunda*	40	May and June
Blue-winged Olive Dun—14	*Drunella cornuta*	30	May and June
Blue-winged Olive Dun—16	*Drunella cornutella*	30	June and July
Light Cahill—14	*Stenacron interpunctatum*	30	May and June
Yellow Drake—12	*Ephemera varia*	30	June and July
March Brown—12	*Stenonema vicarium*	20	May and June
Blue Quill—18	*Paraleptophlebia adoptiva*	20	April
Olive Sulphur—16	*Ephemerella needhami*	20	June
Black Quill—14	*Leptophlebia cupida*	20	April and May
White Fly—14	*Ephoron leukon*	15	August and September
Hendrickson—14	*Ephemerella subvaria*	10	April
Green Drake—10	*Ephemera guttulata*	8	May and June
Brown Drake—12	*Ephemera simulans*	5	May and June

* *Number of days varies from stream to stream*
** *More than one generation per year*

bank and remain there forever. The upper Verde River produced a great day!

Was that trico hatch in February an aberration? I came back to the upper Verde two weeks later in early March. Would I see the same intensity with the trico hatch in March? I didn't have to wait long to get my answer. By 10:00 A.M. a fairly heavy swarm of trico spinners formed a sphere ten feet above a riffle in front of me. Trout seemed like they knew the spinner fall would appear and they began feeding almost as soon as the first spinner hit the surface. The spinner fall again lasted for more than two hours and dozens of trout broke the surface to feed on these tiny egg layers. The trico indeed did present some great matching-the-hatch opportunities—even in late winter.

How many days does the trico appear on some New Mexico and Arizona streams and rivers? It appears almost continuously throughout the year.

Blue Quill

In Tables 11 and 12 you can see which hatches appear the most days of the fishing season. In the East and Midwest the distinction goes to the blue quill, followed by the trico, little blue-winged olive, the slate drake, and the sulphur. The quill gordon also appears much longer than I or other anglers had thought—especially on cold mountain streams of the East.

This early Blue Quill (Paraleptophlebia adoptiva) appears on many waters in the East and Midwest.

Table 12. Western Hatches and the Number of Days They Appear

IMITATION AND SIZE	SPECIES	NUMBER OF DAYS THE HATCH APPEARS EACH YEAR ON THE SAME STREAM*	TIME OF YEAR THE HATCH APPEARS
Little Blue-winged Olive Dun*	*Baetis tricaudatus*	120	Much of the Year
Little Blue-winged Olive Dun*	*Baetis intercalaris*	120	Much of the Year
Trico	*Tricorythodes fictus*	120 (even longer on many south-western streams	July through Septmber
Trico	*Tricorythodes minutus*	100 (even longer on many south-western streams	July through September
Speckle-winged Dun*	*Callabaetis*	100	April through August
Blue Quill	*Paraleptophlebia memorialis*	30	May through July
Pale Morning Dun	*Ephemerella inermis*	30	May to September
Pale Morning Dun	*Ephemerella infrequens*	30	May to September
Blue Quill	*Paraleptophlebia heteronea*	50	June to August
Rhithrogena	*Rhithrigena futilis*	25	June and July
Blue-winged Olive	*Drunella flavilinea*		Late May to July
Pale Evening Dun	*Heptagenia elegantula*		May to July
Gray Fox	*Heptagenia solitaria*	30	July to September
Gray Drake	*Siphlonurus occidentalis*	30	August to September
Western Green Drake	*Drunella grandis*	20	Late May to August
Pink Lady	*Epeorus albertae*	20	June to July
Brown Drake	*Ephemera simulans*	10	June to July

* *Number of days varies from stream to stream*

In the West you'll find little blue-winged olive duns on rivers just about any time of the year. In New Mexico on the San Juan River just below the Navajo Dam I fished over a hatch of little blue-winged olives in February. If you fish the Salt River just outside Phoenix, Arizona, you can fish over trout rising to little blue-winged olives in January and February. The same goes for Oak Creek just north of Sedona, Arizona. Fish this spectacular stream from late February through much of the year and you'll see what the locals call the early blue. I've even seen little blue-winged olives on the lower end of the Ruby River in Montana in November.

Few, if any, anglers ever look for and fish the summer blue quill. Big Fishing Creek in north central Pennsylvania holds a good hatch of this summer blue quill species. The same tactics go wherever you see this hatch. Arrive early and your chances of fishing a dry fly to rising trout with this hatch are enhanced if weather conditions are less than good. You'll find closely related blue quill hatch on Henry's Fork in Idaho in late June. Here the blue quills seem to take more time escaping from the surface.

One way to take advantage of this summer blue quill, or any of the hatches that appear for a long time, is to fish it when the weather is less than perfect. Look for the hatch on cool, overcast, drizzly mornings in June and July. But, there are other ways you can fish these hatches in good weather conditions—fish the nymph or emerger

Wherever you find the summer blue quill hatch remember that these mayflies often escape rapidly from the surface so you might want to use a dark brownish black nymph pattern or an emerger. Trout most often take that phase of the mayfly, caddisfly, or stonefly that's easiest for them to capture. When a mayfly like the blue quill escapes rapidly from the surface trout tend to take the nymph that is changing into a dun. We mentioned earlier that anglers call this stage the emerger. For that fleeting time when the mayfly transforms from an aquatic insect to an air breathing one it is extremely defenseless. Trout sense this and often take an emerger and neglect the dun. Fish the nymph or emerger on a tandem rig behind a Blue Quill dry fly. If you fish it in this manner you'll find out quickly which phase of the insect trout are taking.

I've used the tandem on several occasions on Wiscoy Creek near Lamont in Western New York when the summer blue quills emerged. On one early morning trip in July I tied a small Blue Quill emerger a foot behind the Blue Quill dry fly. If you have difficulty following that small size 18 Blue Quill dry fly on the surface try tying the dry fly with a white poly wing or tie it on a size 16 hook. I've indicated dozens of times before that I connect the wet fly to the bend of the hook of the dry fly and secure

Blue Quill Hatches

Date	Time	Species
April 10 - May 10	10:00 a.m. - 5:00 p.m.	*Paraleptophlebia adoptiva* - East and Midwest *Paraleptophlebia memorialis* -West
May 20 - June 20	10:00 a.m. - 6:00 p.m.	*Paraleptophlebia mollis* - East and Midwest *Paraleptophlebia memorialis*-West
June 15 - Oct. 30	5:00 a.m. - Noon	*Paraleptophlebia guttata and strigula* - East and Midwest *Paraleptophlebia heteronea* - West

Figure 5. Common Blue Quill Hatches

it with an improved clinch knot. Look for the dry fly to go under the surface and you have a strike on the emerger.

You'll see this summer, morning hatch on plenty of streams throughout the United States. I've seen blue quills on Wyoming rivers like the North Platte near Saratoga in late August. I mentioned earlier the hatch Henry's Fork holds in Idaho.

If you're not certain whether or not your favorite late season trout streams hold this hatch spend some mornings looking for the male spinners undulating or moving up and down in their mating flight. Once you find the hatch you can reappear on the stream around dawn and hit the duns emerging. Many streams hold both the Trico and blue quill hatches so learn to differentiate between the two.

When will blue quills appear? I indicated earlier that you'd see great hatches early in the season. But, very similar hatches occur near the end of May and again in late June. The late June hatches of blue quills continue well into October. I've even seen sizable hatches in early November. So there are very few days during the fishing season that you won't see blue quills emerging (See Table 11 and Figure 5).

I mentioned before that the midsummer blue quill emerges about the same time as the trico. I also stated that many streams hold both hatches so it's important to learn to differentiate between the two. Some anglers confuse the two hatches. Both appear in the morning and the spinners of both form mating swarms 10 to 20 feet above the surface of the stream. The trico is the smaller of the two, often copied with a size 24 pattern; whereas the blue quill is most often copied with a size 18 pattern. Both mating swarms move. The male spinners of the blue quill, called jenny spinners by anglers, undulate or move up and down, vertically, whereas tricos normally move in a more horizontal plane. The female spinner of the blue quill is often called the dark brown spinner. Male trico spinners are dark blackish brown and the female has a cream abdomen with a dark brown thorax. There are other differences with the two spinners. Trico spinners often fall in numbers on the surface and encourage trout to feed on them. Few of the male jenny spinners fall onto the surface.

On occasion you need a pattern to copy the male or female spinner of the blue quill. Seldom, however, does either the female or male spinner fall onto the surface in any concentrated numbers. One mid-May afternoon, however, I did encounter a good spinner fall on Washington's Yakima River. If you see spinners in the air and trout are rising try a Dark Brown Spinner. Like most mayflies, the male spinners seldom land on the surface. If, however, you encounter a windy day some of the male spinners will be blown there.

Sulphur and Pale Morning Dun

I have seen pale morning dun hatches in the West from late May on the Deschutes and Metolius Rivers in Oregon; to June and July on Henry's Fork in Idaho; to August on the Bighorn River in Montana. Since there are multiple species that extend over much of the season in the East, Midwest, and West be prepared with imitations that copy the hatches.

Hatches with More than One Generation Per Year

What does one generation per year mean? Let's look at the sulphur as an example. The sulphur of the East and Midwest, and the pale morning dun of the West appear from late May into late July. A day or two after the dun emerges, it reappears over the stream as a mating adult or spinner. Male and female spinners meet and mate and the females drop their eggs onto the surface and die spent. These fertilized eggs usually develop into nymphs in about 20 days. For the next 340 days the nymph grows by shedding its pellicle. One generation per year means that the mayfly appears only one time a year.

Some mayflies, however, have more than one generation per year.

Arizona's Sunrise Lake holds a great Speckle-winged Dun hatch early in the season.

Hatches like the slate drake, little blue-winged olive dun, and trico have at least two generations each year. Speckle-winged duns and tricos in some areas of the nation have more than two generations each year. Of course, the more generations a mayfly has each year the more days of the year the hatch will appear.

I indicated that slate drakes (*Isonychia bicolor*) have two generations or broods each year. The first brood appears in late May and June and the second one emerges in September and October. The slate drake appearing in May is a size larger than the one appearing in the fall (size 12 versus 14). Often you'll find one brood larger than another. Why? The spring emerger has approximately eight months to develop whereas the fall one does so in three months.

Many little blue-winged olive duns also have more than one generation each year. But this has a different sequence. Following are some of the more common mayflies that have more than one generation per year:

Little Blue-winged Olive Dun (*Baetis tricaudatus* and other *Baetis* species*)*
Slate Drake *(Isonychia bicolor*)
Speckle-winged Dun (*Callibaetis* species)
Trico (*Tricorythodes* species)

A Little Blue-winged Olive Dun.

When Grays Appear

L ook at the list of mayflies that appear in March and April across the United States. In all sections of the country one of the first hatches to appear is the little blue-winged olive dun (*Baetis tricaudatus* and *Baetis intercalaris*). On some waters these species continue to appear throughout the winter. You can find little blue-winged olives on many of the trout streams and rivers across the United States. One species (*Baetis tricaudatus*) can be found from California to Maine. This very same species appears on Arizona rivers and streams as early as late February. Local anglers in the southwest call the hatch the early blue. On the San Juan in New Mexico not a day goes by in the winter that you don't at least see a few of these small dark mayflies.

What other hatches appear in April? In the East and Midwest you find great Hendrickson hatches appearing every afternoon for a couple weeks in late April or early May. Also in the East and Midwest you'll also find blue quills (*Paraleptophlebia adoptiva*), black quills (*Leptophlebia cupida*), and dark quill gordons (*Ameletus ludens*). Throughout the East, quill gordons (*Epeorus pleuralis*) appear much of the month—and continue into May.

What can you expect to see on Western rivers in the spring? In the West, in addition to the little blue-winged olive dun, you'll encounter hatches of the Western March brown (*Rhithrogena morrisoni*) and *blue quills (Paraleptophlebia* species*)*. The Western March brown begins appearing as early as late February on trout streams near the Oregon coast. The hatch appears in early afternoon and continues for a couple months

You'll find great early season hatches on New Jersey's South Branch of the Raritan River.

on rivers like the McKenzie and Willamette near Eugene, Oregon.

I remember the first time I hit the Western March brown hatch with Mike Manfredo on the McKenzie in mid-April. Ken Helfrich, agreed to be our guide for the day. We floated through a heavy mist most of the morning and caught a few trout on heavy wet flies, but the best was yet to come. Shortly after noon, a couple miles upriver from where the McKenzie empties into the Willamette, mayflies began to emerge and trout fed. At one point so many trout fed that we left our drift boat and fished to a pod of rising rainbows from the shore. The Western March brown continues to appear into May on the McKenzie and many of the other Oregon and Washington trout waters.

You'll also find several other hatches common on Western waters appearing in March, April, and May. Plenty of blue quills emerge in late April and May on southwestern rivers like the Little Colorado River near Springerville, Arizona. I still remember that afternoon at the X-Diamond Ranch when Virgil Bradford and I hit a blue quill hatch. It happened in late April and trout went crazy chasing laggards on the surface all afternoon long. A size 18 Blue Quill imitation took plenty of trout during the hatch. What do all these early Western hatches have in common?

In talks across the United States I show slides of hatches found in April and that appear in the East, Midwest, and West. All of these have one thing in common—they all have dark gray backs. The abdomen may vary, but the back of all of these March-and-April-appearing mayflies is dark gray. Why? Where do these mayflies rest after they've emerged? They usually land on a rock or stone near the stream or on a tree near the water. What color predominates at that time of year? Gray! Every place you look you see gray. Whether it's the bark of the tree or the color of the rock, the prevailing color is gray. It's nature's way of protecting these early season emergers while they're resting.

Then, in mid-to-late-May a transformation takes place in all parts of the country. Almost overnight many of the mayflies appearing have yellow or tan backs. Look in the East and Midwest in mid-May. One of the first emergers at this time of year is the Sulphur. Look to the West and in late May and you'll begin to see pale morning duns appearing. Look also at the vegetation near a stream or river and you'll see that too has changed. Now, yellow flowers, green leaves, and other colors dominate the surroundings. Color at this time is not as dangerous to mayflies as it is earlier in the season.

That doesn't mean that you won't see dark colored mayflies appearing in late spring and summer. *A good rule of thumb is dark mayflies appear in the day and early evening at this time and light colored mayflies appearing near dusk.* There are some notable exceptions to this premise like the pale morning dun in the West. But, the pale morning dun doesn't appear in the morning on all streams and rivers in the West. Look at the hatch on the Kootenai River in northwestern Montana.

Look at the blue quill, blue-winged olive dun, or the Western green drake. All three are dark mayflies and all three appear mainly in the morning during the summer.

What happens in the fall when trees lose their leaves and flowers die? What hatches will you see at that time? Blue quills, slate drakes, and little blue-winged olives still appear in late September, October, and part of November. And all three have dark gray backs. You'll also see tricos still emerging. These latter tiny mayflies have an olive to dark olive back.

And what about the winter—will you see any hatches at that time? I've hit dark gray midge hatches from the Cache la Poudre in Colorado to Spring Creek in Pennsylvania. Little blue-winged olives often appear during the winter on many of our streams and rivers across the United States.

What does all of this mean for the angler? Whether you fish in the East, Midwest, or West in the early spring and late fall and you fish over a hatch, that hatch will probably be dark gray—at least the back will be. If you fish trout streams and rivers in late spring and summer you can expect to see more colorful mayflies appearing. Many of these appear at

Table 13. Early Mayflies of the East and Midwest

Common Name	Mayfly Species	Hook Size	Time of Year the Hatch Appears	Color of the Back of the Mayfly	Time of Day the Hatch Appears
Little Blue-winged Olive Dun	*Baetis tricaudatus*	20	March, April, September, October	Dark olive gray	Afternoon
Blue Quill	*Paraleptophleiba adoptiva*	18	April	Dark brownish gray	Afternoon
Quill Gordon	*Epeorus pleuralis*	14	April	Dark gray	Afternoon
Hendrickson	*Ephemerella subvaria*	14	April and early May	Dark brownish gray	Afternoon
Dark Quill Gordon	*Ameletus ludens*	14	April	Dark gray	Afternoon
Speckle-winged	*Callabaetis*	16	April, May, June	Dark gray	Morning and afternoon
Black Quill	*Leptophlebia cupida*	14	April and early May	Dark brownish gray	Afternoon
Sulphur	*Ephemerella rotunda*	16	May and June	Yellow with some brown ribbing	Evening
March Brown	*Stenonema vicarium*	12	May and June	Medium to dark brown	Afternoon
Green Drake	*Ephemera guttulata*	8	May and June	Dark gray some lighter ribbing	Evening
Brown Drake	*Ephemera simulans*	10	May and June	Dark brown	Evening

or near dusk. If you see dark mayflies appearing like the blue-winged olive, little blue-winged olive or the blue quill, you'll often see these darker hatches appearing during daylight hours. And again in the fall, if you see hatches appearing they'll probably be dark. What can you gain from this information to help you catch more trout? *Use gray patterns in*

Common Name	Mayfly Species	Hook Size	Time of Year the Hatch Appears	Color of the Back of the Mayfly	Time of Day the Hatch Appears
Little Blue-winged Olive Dun	*Baetis tricaudatus*	20	All year		Afternoon
Little Blue-winged Olive Dun	*Baetis intercalaris*	20	All year		Afternoon
Western March Brown	*Rhithrogena morrisoni*	14	February to May	Dark brown	Afternoon
Speckle-winged Dun	*Callabaetis americanus*	14-16	April to August	Dark gray	Morning
Trico	*Tricorythodes minutus*	24	February to December	Olive	Morning
Trico	*Tricorythodes fictus*	20-24	All year in the Southwest	Olive	Morning
Pale Morning Dun	*Ephemerella inermis*	16	May to September		Variable
Western Green Darke	*Drunella grandis*		May to August	Dark brownish black	Morning
Blue-winged Olive Dun	*Drunella flavilinea*		May to August	Dark brownish olive	Morning

the spring and late fall and during the day in the summer. Use lighter patterns on late spring and summer evenings.

There's a lot of information on the hatches in this chapter. I've said it a dozen times that the more you know about the hatches the more trout you'll catch. By knowing that many of the dark colored mayflies appear in the spring and fall and that most of the lighter colored mayflies tend to appear in the evening should help you on your quest. Knowledge of the hatches and when and where they appear should help you select a good pattern. But, selecting the pattern is only part of the total strategy to catch more trout. Once you've selected that pattern you now must remember several other important aspects. You must use the correct leader, and decide at what depth and how you'll fish the pattern. All of these will help you catch more trout. These important features are covered in Chapters 4 through 10.

– 4 –

VARY THE DEPTH OF THAT PATTERN

Rule 1. If you're fishing wet flies without much success, vary the depth of the pattern.

Rule 2. Use a tandem to fish two locations at the same time.

Rule 3. If there's a hatch or a spinner fall occurring and you're not catching trout, sink the pattern.

I often experiment when I fly fish. Wednesday is my day to test new products, new ideas, and new techniques. Not too long ago on a Wednesday I fished a weighted bead head Pheasant Tail in a two-hundred-foot-long heavy glide. I fished that heavy wet fly two and one half feet behind a Patriot dry fly. In addition to the bead, the body of the Pheasant Tail held 8 wraps of .010 lead. The combined weight of the bead head and the lead on the body kept the pattern fairly deep. I caught four trout in that section that afternoon. I then added another foot and a half of leader between the wet and the dry fly so that now the bead head was four feet behind the dry fly. I fished the same glide with the same size 16-bead head, albeit this time deeper, and I picked up four more trout.

What about some of the great Western rivers—does depth really mean the difference between a successful trip and a barren one? Let me tell you about a trip to the Colorado River at Lee's Ferry in northern Arizona. I fished upriver for more than a 100 yards in a heavy glide on this spectacular river. In an hour of fishing I landed four heavy trout. I then moved the wet fly from 2+ feet from the dry fly to 4 feet. I fished the same productive riffle that I had fished before with the same pattern—but now 1¹/₂ feet farther from the dry fly. I picked up five more trout with that deeper wet fly.

What do these events prove? Experiment. If you don't have any action near the bottom, then try fishing the wet fly nearer the surface and visa versa. *If you feel confident that you have a good pattern and that you're fishing a productive stretch, then maybe you want to drift that pattern at a different level. What does this mean? Vary the depth of the pattern. That goes for dry flies—if their not producing sink them— especially during a hatch or spinner fall!*

Sinking Spinner and Dun Patterns

*O*n most occasions when a hatch occurs and trout are rising you want to float the pattern you're using. If you hit a trico spinner fall or a sulphur hatch normally you want to use a floating fly to fish to risers. But, if you feel you're using the right leader, the correct pattern, and drifting it drag free, maybe you want to change the depth of the pattern— yes, sink it. Let me explain.

For years the trico hatch and spinner fall have frustrated me. I found that trout rise readily to an imitation for a week or two—when the hatch first begins—then they become highly selective and take spent winged spinner imitations only occasionally after that. That was, until I met an aged fly fisher on Falling Springs Run in south central Pennsylvania. One morning, more than 20 years ago, I fished a trico spinner fall on that small fertile limestone stream. Across from me and downstream a few feet another angler cast his pattern in the direction of rising trout. I saw that aged angler pull out ten trout while I had but one to show for more than an hour of intense fishing. He made me look silly—like a beginner. I had to ask him how he did it. Was it the pattern he used? Was it his technique? Was it a finer tippet? Or, was he just a more experienced trico fisher?

Finally, I had enough and blurted out, "What the devil are you doing to catch all of those trout?" He didn't say anything for almost a minute, and then he looked at me and said in a half-whisper. "I'm sinking the pattern." He walked away a few minutes later and never said another word. I never saw that angler after that encounter.

For more than ten years ago I totally put that frustrating embarrassing day completely out of my mind—until another event where I again fished over trico spinners—and once more became frustrated. Then I remembered what that old angler muttered, "sink the pattern." My first

A weighted Trico spinner pattern.

opportunity to sink a Trico spinner pattern occurred on the Ruby River about twenty miles upriver from Alder, Montana. I conducted a fly fishing workshop for the Upper Canyon Outfitters and Jake and Donna McDonald, and I had a day to fish before the workshop began. Jake and Donna suggested I fish right behind their ranch house that morning. When I arrived at the river's edge at 9:00 A.M. tricos already had formed huge swarms. An occasional gust blew the swarm a hundred feet away, but they returned over the fast stretch in a few seconds. The spinners formed a huge cluster and the slightest breeze blew them in my mouth, ears, and eyes.

Soon dozens of 12 to 15-inch rainbows began feeding on the spent trico spinners. I had no success at all with a size 24 female spinner that I cast over the risers. I tried several other dry fly patterns with no luck. Several of the conferees for the workshop arrived early and watched me fly fish, and they too could see the frustration on my face. I had to produce now—my future students were watching.

Then I remembered the advice that old man gave me many years ago and 2000 miles away—sink the pattern. I tied on a weighted Trico spinner-—one I had tied years before. It contained several wraps of .050 lead on its body and had a dubbed angora body and wings made from Krystal Flash. How would I detect a subtle strike with this small sunken pattern? I got a two-foot piece of Orvis Mirage 6X tippet, made an improved clinch knot, and tied it to the bend of the hook of a size 16 Patriot dry fly. To the end of the new piece of tippet I tied on the weighted Trico spinner. The dry fly acted as a strike indicator for me. I didn't have to wait long to see if this darned thing worked. On maybe the second cast the dry fly sank, I set the hook, and I landed a 14-inch rainbow. Soon the students watching the action began applauding as I caught trout. At least 10 trout took that sunken Trico that morning before the spinner fall ended. Talk about a terrible, frustrating event that turned around quickly—that one certainly did!

I have difficulty often following a size 24 Trico spinner on the surface. Some of the takes are extremely subtle. By using a Patriot dry fly as a strike indicator I have no trouble knowing when trout take the sunken spinner.

Why does this technique using a sunken spinner work? Think of some of the streams and rivers where you've seen trico hatches. What happens to those spent tricos that have floated downstream through three or four pools and sets of rapids? They sink. Why should trout come to the surface when they can stay underneath and feed on the same insect—with much less effort? And plenty of trout do stay underneath and feed off of these sunken naturals.

Sunken spinners work especially well with hatches that last a long time (See Chapter 8). The trico is only one of those. Think of situations where you've seen heavy concentrations of spinners. Sulphur spinners (*Ephemerella rotunda* and *invaria*) pale morning spinners (*Ephemerella inermis* and *infrequens*), rusty spinners (*Baetis* species), coffin flies (*Ephemera guttulata*), red quill spinners (*Ephemerella subvaria*) and brown drakes (*Ephemera simulans*) are only a few of the spinner falls where you should try fishing sunken spinners.

If you never have fished when a green drake hatch emerges make it a point to do so. On some streams this hatch appears in unbelievable numbers—at dusk and after dark—for several days. Spinners, called coffin flies by anglers, reappear over the stream a day or two later. I've often fished when spent winged coffin flies literally covered the surface of a stream—and I've quit fishing because I knew I had little chance of tricking trout into taking my spinner pattern. But, wait, your sunken pattern has a much better chance of getting a trout's attention. Next time you encounter this situation try fishing a submerged Coffin Fly pattern.

Let me explain what happened the first time that I tried a sunken Coffin Fly. Green drakes had appeared on Penns Creek in central Pennsylvania for the past three evenings. As darkness progressed that evening thousands of female coffin fly spinners reappeared over the water in front of me. I tied on a large, weighted spent Coffin Fly spinner and began casting. When I tied the pattern I added about 10 wraps of .010 lead wire to the shank, then dubbed a body of white angora. I placed the spinner behind a size 10 Green Drake dry fly. The latter acted as a strike indicator. By the time I had secured the Coffin Fly thousands upon thousands of coffin mated female spinners moved upstream 10 feet above the surface in a seemingly unending flow. Soon these females laid their eggs, and fell onto the surface spent. Trout went crazy taking as many as two and three spent spinners with each sip. I cast my weighted Coffin Fly spinner into the midst of a dozen rising trout. It didn't take long to see if this new method would work. Within seconds in that half light I saw the dry fly sink, I set the hook and landed a 12-inch brown trout.

That evening I released six trout on that pattern. On some frustrating evenings with a floating Coffin Fly I'd be lucky to land a trout or two. Does sinking a spinner pattern really work? You bet it does! Try it!

Look at the brown drake hatch and spinner fall. This species appears from the East Coast to the Far West. On most streams and rivers where it appears it does so for just a few days. Often most duns emerge in one evening and the spinner fall might last for two or three evenings. The mating process seems to last a few more days on Michigan, Wisconsin, and Idaho waters, and on lakes like Skinneatales Lake near Syracuse, New York.

When the brown drake spinner fall occurs, usually just at dusk, the surface is literally covered with spent spinners. Henry's Fork in Idaho has a spectacular hatch of brown drakes. Al Gretz and I first fished the brown drake spinner fall on that unbelievably fertile river more than 20 years ago. But, it wasn't until a few years ago—on Honey Creek in south central Pennsylvania—that I had an opportunity to test my sunken spinner pattern. That sunken Brown Drake caught five trout that early June evening.

I'm not the only angler to recognize the importance of sunken spinners. Eugene Gordon fishes the Casselman River in western Maryland. The state stocks plenty of large trout in this marginal stream and the river boasts some great early season hatches. Eugene fished the river in mid April recently when a red quill spinner fall occurred. That evening spinners fell for more than an hour. For the first 15 minutes Eugene had no strikes on his spinner pattern—until it accidentally sank on one cast. He immediately caught a trout on that errant cast. Now he purposely sank the fly and began catching trout on almost every cast.

We've seen how sinking the fly works with spinner patterns. What about dry fly patterns that copy emerging mayfly duns? Until a decade ago few anglers had heard little about using emergers. Now this phase has become an important part of many fly fishers arsenal (Chapter 3 discusses emergers in detail).

Years ago I used an emerger pattern and I never realized it. On two occasions I've had some of the best fishing I've ever experienced with the Green Drake. Both of those occurred while I used a pattern copying the dun. The first occurred on Penns Creek more than 30 years ago. I became frustrated with my inability to even catch one trout on my Green Drake pattern, so I yanked it under the surface and fished it as a wet fly. On the second cast a trout struck violently. I landed the 19-inch brown trout and cast that 'wet fly' pattern again. I ended the day catching a number of heavy trout on that emerger pattern fished just under the surface.

It happened a second time on Sinnemahoning Creek in north central Pennsylvania. I fished with Craig Hudson while a green drake hatch appeared. Craig purposely sank his Green Drake dry fly and began catching trout. I followed suit and also had success. I don't think I would have caught a trout that evening if I hadn't sunk that dry fly.

So remember on those frustrating hatches and spinner falls to sink your fly if trout aren't taking the pattern on the surface. Vary the depth of that dry that copies a dun or spinner

Fishing the Emerger

During a hatch I often have trouble deciding whether trout are rising to natural on the surface or taking emergers just under the surface. By using a dry fly and an emerger pattern just behind it you've got yourself covered.

Andy Leitzinger is one of the top young fly fishers I know. On good fishing days it's not uncommon for him to catch 50 or 60 trout. I normally use a grading system for fly fishers with whom I fish. I rate them from a 1 (beginner) to 10 (a professional expert). I've only seen one or two 10's in my lifetime (I'm not one of them). Andy, still in his 30's, is a true 9. Andy uses the tandem when he's fishing the sulphur and the pale morning dun hatches. He uses a Sulphur Dun and ties a Sulphur Emerger a foot behind the dry fly. Using the two patterns with this configuration, the emerger sinks just beneath the surface. He adds a bit of weight to the body of the emerger to make it sink just beneath the surface. One evening I fished with him he caught more than 20 trout on that combination.

Does this same method work with other hatches? Bryan Meck and I fished the white fly hatch several years back on Yellow Breeches Creek in south central Pennsylvania. Talk about heavy angler pressure—the crowd that appears at the stream to fish this hatch has to be the heaviest I've ever encountered. Because of this pressure trout quickly become highly selective. By the end of the first week of the hatch it's often extremely difficult to catch even one trout. Bryan and I used a tandem made of a White Fly dry fly and a White Fly emerger. That evening we caught almost 20 trout on the tandem. We caught four trout on the emerger for every trout we caught on the dry fly. So, while other anglers fished only the dry fly, the two of us used the tandem—with a lot of success. The advantage of the tandem is that you're fishing two levels—the surface and underneath—at the same time.

Next time you become frustrated with one of your favorite hatches try something different. If your dry fly doesn't work yank it under the surface. If you're competing with too many spinners on the surface, use a sunken spinner. If you have difficulty following your wet fly or nymph, use a tandem or poly strike indicator.

How to Fish Terrestrials

It first happened on the Arkansas River in central Colorado just below Buena Vista. I had little success catching any of the heavy brown trout in the river. I had caught a couple browns on a LeTort Hopper pattern that I let dance across the surface. But after an hour of using the hopper I switched to a weighted Beetle pattern. That Beetle, attached to a Patriot dry fly, sank a couple feet beneath the surface. In an hour of fishing with that Beetle I landed six heavy brown trout.

Weighted ant patterns also work well. I remember well the day on Michigan's Little Manistee where a sunken ant saved the day. Often I use a bead to represent one of the humps on the ant. I use a marker to make it black. The weight of the bead sinks the terrestrial quickly. Both ant and beetle patterns are difficult to follow on the surface. If you use the terrestrial pattern behind a dry fly or a regular strike indicator it's easy to detect any strike. The Patriot dry fly with its white calf body wings shows up well in even in the half-light often encountered in small heavily shaded trout streams.

How To Vary the Depth

If varying the depth is so important how do you best accomplish it? The easiest way to vary the depth of your wet fly or nymph is to fish the pattern with some weight so it sinks near the bottom. Anglers usually cast the pattern across stream or three-quarters downstream and let it make a swing or arc. How many times have you had a strike on that swing? That's where you get many of them (strikes) because that's where the pattern moves from the bottom and rises towards the top. Here's an example where you fish several levels underneath with one cast. What

I'm suggesting in this chapter is that you fish a certain depth, and if that proves unproductive then switch to another depth—shallower or deeper.

Getting the Wet Fly Deeper

There are lots of ways of getting your wet fly deeper. First, and I think the easiest way, is to add weight to the body of the pattern when you're tying it. You can vary the weight as I do when I tie Green Weenie patterns. I use .015 lead wire and on some of the patterns I add 10 wraps, on others 15, and on others 20. Or you can add the same number of wraps but use heavier wire on some. After you've tied a pattern how do you know which patterns are lighter and which are heavier? On the Green Weenie I use red thread on those tied with 10 wraps, olive thread for those with 15 wraps and black for those tied with 20 wraps. I put a note in each fly box indicating what color represents what number of wraps.

A second way, and one I described earlier, is to add a longer piece of leader between the dry fly and the wet fly if you're using the tandem. Shorten the distance between the two if you want the wet fly nearer the

With the tandem rig, you can catch trout on the strike indicator—the dry fly.

surface and lengthen the leader if you want the wet fly to go deeper.

A third way to get the wet fly deeper if you're using another type of strike indicator is to move the indicator away from the wet fly. If you're using one of the floating plastic type indicators lengthen the distance to the wet fly and the pattern will go deeper.

A fourth way, and one most anglers use, is to add a lead shot or two just above the wet fly. Don't try this if you're using the tandem. I've learned the hard way that it will tangle the tandem on many of your casts.

A fifth way is to add a bead to the wet fly pattern. If you want even more weight try using one of the tungsten beads. But, don't try to use the tandem if you plan to use these tungsten beads. They'll sink the dry fly quickly.

Using the Tandem to Vary the Depth

You've selected a pattern you feel will work on the water you're fishing. But, that's only part of a successful fishing trip. A second ingredient of fly-fishing I feel is extremely important is where you plan to fish that pattern. Will you use a dry fly, wet fly, or an emerger? Do you plan to fish on the surface, just under the surface, or near the bottom? Where did I place my patterns for my first 40 years of fly-fishing? I first talked about it in *Meeting and Fishing the Hatches* published in 1977. I said I had a strong personal bias for using dry flies and "enticing trout to the surface with a lifelike dry fly is much more enjoyable, rewarding, and challenging than any other type of fishing."

But, wait, something changed about 10 years ago for me. I talked about it in *Patterns, Hatches, Tactics, and Trout.* I was introduced to an old western method of fly-fishing with a dry fly and wet fly. Some anglers call this method of fly-fishing using a tandem. I connect a piece of tippet material to the bend of the hook of the lead fly. Let's say for example I'm using a dry fly like the Patriot (an attractor type pattern) as my lead fly (fly closest to the fly rod). I might attach a two-feet piece of 4X tippet to the bend of the hook of the lead fly, secure it with an improved clinch knot and tie on a bead head pheasant tail as the dropper. I'm now using two flies at one time. I'm using a fairly large dry fly that floats, and a weighted bead head behind it that sinks beneath the surface. I add 6 to 10 wraps of lead to the body of the bead head pattern to make the pattern sink more quickly. The weight of the bead plus the weight added to the body of the fly assures that the pattern sinks rapidly. I've seen anglers use two dry flies, two wet flies, or a dry fly and a wet fly in the tandem setup. I vary the length between the two, if I'm using a wet and a dry fly,

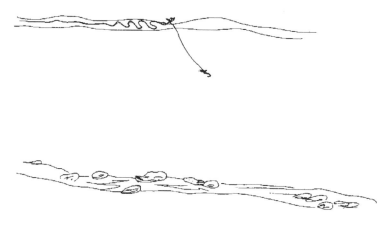

Figures 6 & 7. If you're using the tandem rig, one way you can vary the depth of a wet fly is by increasing the distance between the dry fly and the wet fly.

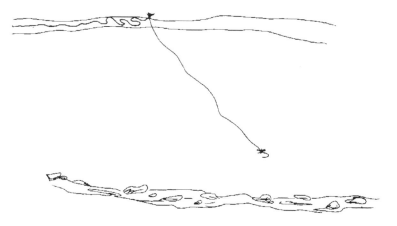

according to the type of water I'm fishing. If I'm fishing while a sulphur or pale morning dun hatch appears I often attach an emerger pattern just a foot behind the sulphur dry fly. In deep, fast, or cool water I often want to get the wet fly near the bottom so I increase the distance between the wet and dry flies to three or four feet.

How can you fish two depths at the same time? That's easy: use the tandem. The dry fly of course floats on the surface and the wet fly, often weighted, sinks beneath the surface. This is an extremely deadly method of fly fishing that you've got to master if you want to catch more trout.

I said earlier that I first wrote about the tandem in *Patterns, Hatches, Tactics, and Trout*. I'll never forget one review of that book. The reviewer

A heavy brown trout taken in early March on a wet fly on Oak Creek in Arizona.

said that anglers have used the tandem for many years in the West and that it wasn't anything new. He forgot the whole gist of the book: The tandem works equally well in *all parts of the country—no, all over the world.* Prior to that book few anglers used this highly productive technique in the East and Midwest. The tandem works much better than an ordinary strike indicator and even better than one made of poly. Let me explain.

Most strike indicators allow you to vary the depth of your wet fly. Strike indicators come in a variety of shapes, sizes, and materials. Some anglers use just a brightly colored dot or mark on their leader or line. Others use a bobberlike contraption or poly, while others use a dry fly that floats. (See Chapter 7 for a full description of strike indicators.) On extremely fast, deep water like the Colorado at Lee's Ferry in Arizona I prefer using a poly indicator—on most others I use the tandem with a wet and dry fly. The dry fly floats while the wet fly behind it sinks under the surface. If a trout strikes the wet fly, the dry fly, floating on the surface, sinks. Anglers can attach the wet fly to the dry fly "strike indicator" by using a clinch knot and attaching the leader from the wet fly to the dry fly at the bend of the hook of the dry fly.

Why use the tandem? First and foremost if you use the tandem—a wet fly and a dry fly—you can catch trout on either. I call the dry fly on the tandem a strike indicator with an attitude. On several occasions I've landed two trout at the same time—one on the dry fly and one on the wet fly. What a mess! On many trips I've averaged thirty per cent of the trout caught on the dry fly—especially during the summer. Second, the dry fly will show you even the subtlest of strikes. If trout are striking quickly or short the tandem should be the indicator of choice. Third, the dry fly will float all day under most conditions. As I indicated earlier, however, under extremely fast water conditions like those on many Western waters the dry fly often sinks and the better choice would be a poly or plastic strike indicator.

I've mentioned many times before the four important tactics necessary to become a better fly fisher. The four are pattern selection, where you fish that pattern, what leader you use to connect that pattern, and how naturally you drift that pattern. Probably the most important of the four is how you drift the pattern. I always tell fly fishers to follow a nearby bubble or other object on the surface and have their pattern float in synchrony with that. By using the tandem not only can you have the dry float drag free, but also you can have the sunken fly drifting freely underneath. But, the tandem and other strike indicators allow you to vary the depth.

The tandem or two level system works whether you're using chironomid, caddis, or mayfly patterns. Fishing two levels is almost always more productive than just one.

I'll never forget that first time I fished on the upper Cache la Poudre outside of Fort Collins, Colorado. Mike Manfredo and Don Rodriguez accompanied me on the trip. We arrived on the river in late morning in mid-April. By the time we arrived at the stream dozens of trout had already begun feeding on diminutive chironomids. The feeding frenzy continued for more than two hours. I get frustrated when I go to someone's home stream and they don't tell me what to use. Believe me, I was frustrated with this hatch. For more than an hour I caught nothing—I had one trout look at my dry fly pattern in that 60-minute period. Then I switched. I added a black midge pupa and fished it a foot behind a size 18 Patriot. My luck certainly changed immediately with the new pattern. Within the next hour I had released a half dozen trout. What does this show? When fishing over trout that have fed on the same hatches for many days and have had a lot of pressure, try something different. If a floating pattern doesn't work, then try something just under the surface. If that doesn't work try something deeper. Be ready to change patterns. After fishing over many risers for a half an hour and not getting one strike I should have changed.

The most common mayfly hatch on New Mexico's San Juan River has got to be the little blue-winged olive dun. This same river, in its

Fishing two separate depths—this section of the Colorado River at Lee's Ferry produces trout.

upper reaches holds one of the heaviest and most frustrating midge hatches just about every morning of the year. Fish within sight the breast of the Navajo Dam and you'll see hundreds of heavy trout feeding on midges most of the morning. There's one other thing you'll see—constant fly fishing pressure over these trout.   Travel downriver just a few hundred yards and you'll see the little blue-winged olive appear just about every month of the year—and in great numbers. Trout see imitations of these mayflies almost every day of the year.

I hit a great hatch of little blue-winged olives one early March afternoon just below the Navajo Dam. By 2:00 P.M. thousands of duns rested on the surface and dozens of trout rose in the water in front of me. A very light drizzle slowed up the duns even further. I tied on a Little Blue-winged emerger pattern a foot behind a Little Blue-winged dry fly.

Depth can be critical in lake fishing.

I tied the dry fly with white wings so I could easily follow it. For every trout I caught on that dry fly I caught four on the emerger just under the surface.

That float trip down the Green River in Utah really showed me the value of using two flies at one time. I drifted the river just below the Flaming Gorge. For the first half mile I fished very little. I found myself scanning the bottom for trout. The river in this section is extremely clear and reminded me of my experience on the rivers of New Zealand's South Island. An emerging pupa fished behind a Patriot dry fly caught trout throughout the entire drift on the Green.

What do you do if the water is just too fast and too deep to use a dry fly and a wet fly? I often then resort to a piece of poly as a strike indicator. (See Chapter 7 for a list of good strike indicators.) Make a loop in the leader and attach the poly indicator about three to six feet up from the fly, depending on the type of water you're fishing. These poly indicators now come with a braided loop in them so they're easy to tie onto your leader. Recently, I've used large poly strike indicators that will float even if you use a heavy Wooly Bugger.

Has using the tandem and a wet fly increased the number of trout I catch? It really has, especially on trips when no hatch appears. Look at these situations as proof. Recently I fly fished with several well-known writers during a sulphur hatch. We fished an entire day waiting for the hatch to appear—it normally emerges just at dusk. Few trout rose during the daylight hours so Bob Budd and I used the tandem during the day. Four of the other fly fishers who accompanied us used only dry flies during the same period prior to the hatch. In two riffled sections Bob and I caught more than 20 trout on the sunken bead head pheasant tail. The others, using only dry flies, caught only a few trout that entire afternoon.

I've fished with others who only fish over rising trout. I've seen these anglers make only a half dozen casts on some evenings. While I fished the entire evening, my dry fly friends made only a couple casts.

So, fishing the pattern under the surface works when no hatch appears—it also works early in the spring or in high water conditions. How many times early in the season have I found myself using the tandem to get the wet fly deep and that tactic has saved the day? More often than I care to remember.

Here's a rule of thumb where to fish a wet fly pattern and how much distance between the wet and dry flies on a tandem rig:

A nice trout caught on a wet fly.

1. Deep, fast water—2+ to 5 feet
2. Cold water—2+ to 5 feet
3. Fishing the tandem during a hatch—1 to 2 feet
4. Late fall, winter and early spring—2+ to 5 feet
5. Summer in normal and low water—1-3 feet
6. Lakes and ponds—1-6 feet

Note in the chart of distances between the wet and dry flies the large variation I recommend for lakes and ponds. I often make the distance between the two even less than one foot. If I see trout rising or cruising near the surface I'll often tie a wet fly just a few inches behind the dry fly. Does this work? Look at the experiment I did on Saguaro Lake just outside Phoenix, Arizona. Arizona Game and Fish had just planted trout in this impoundment and within minutes these trout began looking for food on the surface. I tied a tandem made up of a Patriot dry fly and a bead head Pheasant Tail nymph placed three feet behind. In an hour of casting to the school of cruising trout I caught two. I then shortened the length between the two to one foot. In the next hour I landed more than a dozen trout. Does depth matter in lakes and ponds? You bet it does! For days these trout swam around in a loose school.

I normally use 4X Mirage tippet (fluorocarbon) to connect the wet fly to the dry fly. I've found that the 4X leader doesn't tangle as quickly as some of the finer tippets. (We'll talk about tippets in Chapter 5.) Once you get accustomed to casting the tandem you shouldn't have difficulty using a 5X or even a 6X tippet. You'll see in Chapter 5 that these smaller diameter tippets often catch more trout.

The tandem setup can be extremely effective on ponds and lakes. Several years ago my son, Bryan Meck, and I fished at the Upper Canyon Outfitters near Alder, Montana. The ranch holds a spring fed pond filled with 2 to 3 pound rainbow trout. Weeds fill much of the bottom of the impoundment making it difficult to fish any wet fly. Bryan used a bead head Glo Bug and tied it on two feet behind the Patriot dry fly. At this depth the bead head barely drifted above the weeds. That afternoon Bryan landed more than 30 trout on that tandem. By the end of the day five other anglers fishing the same pond used the same technique that Bryan had.

Once you've selected a pattern you've got to decide where you're going to fish it. So, another important ingredient of a productive fly fishing trip is where you fish that pattern. *Vary the depth from the bottom to the surface.* Remember, if that pattern copying a dun or spinner doesn't work during a hatch sink it.

Pattern selection and where you fish that fly are only part of the equation that equals more trout. Leaders, drag, and strike indicators help round out the equation.

– 5 –

CONNECT THAT PATTERN WITH THE CORRECT LEADER

Rule 1. A leader can be as important as the pattern you use.

Rule 2. Use fluorocarbon tippets as often as possible

Rule 3. Tippet diameter is critical.

Rule 4. In heavily fished waters, and under low water conditions, a longer, finer tippet has an important impact on your success.

Rule 5. If the water you're fishing is low and extremely clear start off with 5X-fluorocarbon tippet on cloudy days and a 6X-fluorocarbon tippet on bright, sunny days.

Fluorocarbons

Fluorocarbons have come on the scene just a few years ago. Fluorocarbon is a non-nylon synthetic material used originally in commercial fishing nets. When this new leader material first came out many anglers thought it was just another expensive gimmick, and that it wouldn't be any better than any other leader material on the market.. Consequently, many fly fishers rebelled against buying it. But, fluorocarbons can make the difference between a terrible and a spectacular day of fishing. They can definitely help you catch more trout. Let me explain.

Chernobyl Cricket.

It first happened on a small but difficult pond in southwestern Montana. Ken Rictor, Lynn Rotz, my son Bryan, and I fished for a day on a series of ponds formed by gold dredging operations conducted decades ago. These four small ponds had a constant release of cool spring water and became the home for a good number of heavy brown trout. I stayed at the first pond—the one closest to the car, while Bryan, Ken, and Lynn wandered off in different directions to the other ponds. Almost immediately I began catching trout. In an hour I released seven heavy brown trout measuring up to 20 inches long. After fishing the other ponds for a couple hours Bryan and Ken had not caught one trout and headed back to fish with me. We sat down on the bank overlooking the pond and tried to figure out why these two skilled fly fishers had nothing to show for a couple hours of fishing. They were both excellent fly casters and both reached the brushy bank on the far side of the pond with the same degree of accuracy that I did. They used the same pattern that I used—a Chernobyl Cricket. After a minute or two Bryan and Ken looked at my tippet material and both blurted out almost in unison: "What's that tippet material?" Both anglers used regular 5X-tippet material. During that successful hour I had, however, used a 5X-fluorocarbon tippet from Orvis called Mirage. That tippet material seemed to be the only difference in our approach to fly fishing that morning.

I tore off a 2¹/₂-foot piece of 5X-fluorocarbon tippet and gave one to Ken and another to Bryan. They both tied on the new tippet material and began casting with the same cricket pattern they had used before. Within an hour Ken and Bryan each caught seven huge brown trout on that new rig. I never would have believed what an effect a leader can have if I hadn't experienced that incident that day. Does fluorocarbon really work? You bet it does—especially on or in slow, clear water. After we finished fishing we hurried to Tom Harmon's Orvis Shop in nearby Sheridan, Montana, and bought every spool of 4X and 5X Mirage he had in the shop. I became such a believer in fluorocarbons that after I arrived back from my trip to Montana I sent Orvis a letter praising Mirage. Orvis felt the letter deserved special merit and placed my testimonial in their catalog—for two years in a row!

Do an experiment to prove to yourself that fluorocarbons are less visible than regular leaders. Place two, three, or four different 4X leaders in a jar and attach a weight like a small bolt or nut to each one. Make certain one of

A long, fine fluorocarbon leader works well on the Ruby River.

these is a fluorocarbon and the others are not. Put holes through the lid of the jar and add water. Now look how well you can see the leaders. Tom Finkbiner first showed me this experiment. I conducted the experiment before a group one day and some anglers in the audience complained that one of the leaders in the jar was a smaller diameter because they couldn't see it as well. The one they couldn't see as well was the fluorocarbon leader material.

So the first rule to follow is to get some fluorocarbon and use it when you're confronted with any of the following problems. First, use it if you plan to fish clear, slow water. Second, try it if you want to use a heavier leader, but yet want it to be less visible. I often use a 5X fluorocarbon for trico fishing and I catch plenty of trout with that size tippet. Third, use fluorocarbons on heavily fished waters. On waters where you see plenty of anglers you need every advantage you can get. A fluorocarbon leader will definitely give you the edge.

Tippet Diameter	X	Type of leader	Number of Casts	Number of Strikes on the Wet Fly	Number of Strikes on the Dry Fly	Total Number of Strikes
.005	6X	Fluorocarbon	100	12	4	16
.005	6X	Regular Leader Tippet	100	4	0	4

Figure 8. Tests comparing fluorocarbon and regular 6X-tippet material on a bright sunny day on a low clear stream.

A fluorocarbon leader does have two distinct disadvantages. First, it doesn't have quite the strength that regular leaders have (Figure 5). Second it seems to have more memory and once twisted it will remain twisted.

Can my experiences with fluorocarbons be substantiated? Over the past couple years I have conducted many experiments with leaders, tippets, leader formulas, and the effectiveness of fluorocarbons. In all the tests I used the tandem rig—a size 12 Patriot as the dry fly and a size 16 bead head Glo Bug (egg color) as the point or wet fly. I used a 32-inch tippet to connect the dry fly and the same length tippet between the dry fly and the wet fly. In one of these experiments (Figure 1) I compared the effectiveness of a 6X regular with a 6X-fluorocarbon tippet. I conducted this test under extreme conditions—low, clear water and a bright sunny day. I made 100 casts with each tippet in the same general area on a private stream. I did not cast over any rising trout and I used two fly rods. Both fly rods had the same patterns and leader length—one had the regular leader and the other had fluorocarbon. First I cast the fly rod with the 6X regular tippet for 25 casts, then I cast the fly rod that held the 6X fluorocarbon for 25 casts. I switched from one fly rod to the other for 25 casts until I had made 100 casts with each tippet.

I noticed one important thing when I ran the tests. I saw many trout follow the wet fly and dry fly attached to the 6X regular tippet, then turn away at the last moment. These same trout often took the patterns attached to the 6X-fluorocarbon tippet. **I'm convinced, more than ever, that often trout turn away from a pattern because they see the leader, not because they're refusing the imitation.**

Look at the results in Figure 8. In that test the fluorocarbon tippet caught four times as many trout as the regular leader. Any scientist would say that 100 casts are not enough to prove anything—and they're correct. But combine this test with the others you'll see later and you'll definitely agree that leaders and diameter are extremely important.

Tippet Diameter

I've mentioned "4X, 5X and 6X " in a previous paragraphs. What do these mean and how can you use these numbers to help you determine what you're using? I always remember the number 11 when I'm referring to diameter and what X it is. Diameter refers to the size of the leader. Added together, the diameter and the X always equal 11. (Diameters, however are not always consistent and sometimes vary from manufacturer to manufacturer—even from one spool to another of the same material. The only precise way to determine the diameter is to carry an expensive micrometer with you.). In other words, a 5X leader has a diameter of .006. Usually the thicker the leader (the higher the number and the lower the X) the easier the leader is to see. That's where fluorocarbons come into play. Fluorocarbons are not normally as easy to see as regular leader materials. Look at the chart below and remember that the number 11 is important in determining the X or the diameter.

$$1X = .010$$
$$2X = .009$$
$$3X = .008$$
$$4X = .007$$
$$5X = .006$$
$$6X = .005$$
$$7X = .004$$
$$8X = .003$$
$$9X = .002$$
$$10X = .001$$

Back in the 1960's I got on a kick about using extremely fine leaders. I often used a 9X (yes, 9X) leader when I fished for selective trout in the Northeast. I can remember how I compared that leader to a fine gossamer strand floating in the early morning breeze. We often hooked trout on that fine leader, but we landed very few of them

Is leader diameter critical? You bet it is! But, as you use finer tippets you lose tippet strength. Leader strength and leader diameter—it's a trade off between the two. What you want is the finest, least visible leader with the strength you need to successfully land trout. I can remember recently I invited a friend to a private fishing stream loaded with a lot of trout over 20 inches long. He'd been fly fishing for only a couple years and was not accustomed to landing trout like this. He used a three-pound test leader tippet and broke off the first six trout he had hooked. I changed his tippet to a six-pound test one and he began landing trout. In Chapter 1 I mentioned

Tippet Diameter (All Fluorocarbons)	X	Number of Casts	Total Strikes	Number of Trout Caught on the Dry Fly	Number of Fish that Broke Off
.007	4X	25	1	0	0
.006	5X	25	4	0	0
.005	6X	25	10	2	2

Figure 9. Experiment with several diameter fluorocarbon tippets on a low clear stream on a bright, sunny day.

an incident that happened recently during a trico spinner fall. Ron Dorula tied on a 1½-pound test 8X-fluorocarbon. Ron fished over some heavy trout that broke him off almost immediately. I try to get away with as strong a leader as possible—especially when I'm fishing over heavy trout. Why use a light leader and break off almost every trout you hook?

Here are some times you should use as light a leader as possible:

1. Use as light a leader as possible on heavily fished streams (See Chapter 8).
2. Use a light leader during small hatches and spinner falls.
3. Use a light leader on hatches that appear for a long time. (See Chapter 3)
4. Use as light a leader as possible on low, clear streams and bright sunny days. (See Figures 8 and 9).

For years I've told anglers to use a 4X tippet for most situations. *I no longer say that. Tippet diameter is critical if you want to catch more trout.* You don't believe that tippet makes a difference? Look at a second test I conducted with different fluorocarbon tippet diameters.

I recently conducted another experiment with several leader sizes on a bright, sunny day on a low clear stream. In all three tests I used the same tandem made up of a Patriot dry fly and a bead head Glo Bug and the same length of tippet between the two. I conducted the experiments on a private stretch of water on a long deep pool with a lot of large fish, but also with plenty of fishing pressure. I first made 25 casts with the 4 X-fluorocarbon tippet and recorded the number of casts, strikes, and fish that broke off in Figure 9. I then switched to a 5X-fluorocarbon tippet, same length as the previous tippet, and made another 25 casts—this time over the same water where I had made the 25 casts with the 4X tippet. Finally, I used a 6X-fluorocarbon tippet and made another 25 casts—again over the same water. In each case I used a 32-inch piece of 4X, 5X,

Tippet Diameter	X	Type of Fly	Number of Casts	Number of Trout Caught on the Dry Fly	Number of Trout Caught on the Wet Fly	Total of Trout Caught on the Tandem	Number of Fish that Broke Off
.007	4	Dry fly Only	25	0	N/A	N/A	0
.007	4	Tandem	25	1	3	4	0
.006	5	Dry fly Only	25	4	N/A	N/A	0
.006	5	Tandem	25	2	5	7	1

Figure 10. Results of fluorocarbons on a cloudy day on a low, clear stream.

or 6X between the dry fly and the wet fly, and for the tippet connecting the dry fly. You'll see the amazing results in Figure 9. Of course anyone can say that 25 casts is not enough to prove anything, and they're correct— but results give one food for thought. These results combined with the other experiments should show to you the value of finer fluorocarbon tippets.

Tandem, Leaders and Weather Conditions

Figure 9 shows another important feature. I used the tandem setup— a dry fly as my strike indicator with a wet fly behind it. Only with the 6X leader did I get strikes on the dry fly. But, that test was conducted on a bright sunny day. What about a cloudy day—what leader should I start off with under those conditions?

In Figure 10 you see results obtained on a cloudy day when the water was low and clear. In this experiment I made some casts with just a dry fly and others with the tandem. Even under these conditions a 5X tippet seemed to be the finest leader required to catch more trout. So, the next time somebody says to you that leader diameter doesn't make any difference you can mention these experiments. *When you encounter low water conditions on cloudy days start off with a 5X-fluorocarbon leader.*

I conducted a fourth test (Figure 11) with different leader diameters on a cloudy day when the water was a bit off color. Even under those conditions leader diameter seemed to effect the number of strikes. Even then a finer leader caught more trout—by a wide margin. As with the

Tippet Diameter	X	Number of Casts	Number of Trout Caught on Wet Fly	Number of Trout Caught on Dry Fly	Total Trout
.006 (Fluorocarbon)	5X	25	10	3	13
.007 (Fluorocarbon)	4X	25	5	0	5
.008 (Regular)	3X	25	3	0	3

Figure 11. Experiment results using several different diameters of fluorocarbon and regular tippet material on a cloudy day with the water slightly off color.

other tests the results shown in Figure 11 show a wide divergence in number of trout caught with different tippet diameters.

What do all of these experiments tend to prove? *Leader diameter and fluorocarbons do matter—the finer the leader the more trout you'll catch.* But, as I said before, like every good thing a finer tippet has its downside: You'll break off more trout. There's a second distinct disadvantage to a finer leader: The older you get the difficult it is to put that finer leader through the eye of the hook.

Length of Leader

What else can you do to increase the number of trout you catch? You can increase the length of your tippet. If you're using a 30-inch piece of 6X fluorocarbon and not having any success try a 36-inch piece of the same leader. If that doesn't work you might want to go to a 7X tippet. But, normally a 6X fluorocarbon should work.

Length of tippet should also help you with drag. The longer and finer the tippet the longer the drag free float.

A Review of the Experiments

Earlier in this chapter I talked about the value of fluorocarbons. I am convinced that they catch more trout especially under low, clear water conditions. Toss in slow water or lake or pond fishing and you'll find that they might make the difference between a so-so day and a highly eventful one. I said earlier how well fluorocarbons worked on the slow water I

Table 15. Suggested Leader Tippets for Varied Stream and Weather Conditions

Water Conditions	Weather	First Choice in Diameter of and Type of Tippet*
Low, clear	Sunny	6X Fluorocarbon
Low, clear	Cloudy	5X Fluorocarbon
Low, slightly off color	Sunny	5X Fluorocarbon
Low, slightly off color	Cloudy	4X Fluorocarbon
High, off color	Sunny	3X or 4X
High	Sunny	4X

* *Start with this tippet. You might have to go lighter.*

encountered in Montana. In the preceding series of tests we saw that fluorocarbons work just as well on eastern waters. Tom Large of Hollidaysburg and Dale Johnson of Greensburg, Pennsylvania, watched me test the regular and fluorocarbon types of tippet material. As soon as the tests were finished both men headed to the nearest fly shop to purchase some fluorocarbon leader.

There's another important item revealed as a result of two of the four experiments: *the value of the tandem.* Using the tandem rather than just a dry fly when there's no hatch is more effective than just using a dry fly.

As a result of the four experiments I've suggested tippet materials and diameters with which you should that you should begin in Table 15. For example, if you encounter a cloudy day but the stream is low and extremely clear, start with a 5X fluorocarbon. If you feel you should be catching more trout then switch to a smaller diameter leader like a 6X fluorocarbon. Start with a 27 to 32 inch piece of tippet material and lengthen that if you feel you should be catching more trout. Length of the tippet can also help you get a better drift.

Leader Strength

With the advent of much better leaders anglers can use a fairly light tippet and not sacrifice strength. Here are a few of the more popular leaders and their strength in pounds:

4X	Regular	Fluorocarbon
Orvis	6.0	4.75
Rio	6.4	5.0
Dai-Riki (Velvet)	5.3	4.0
Climax	6.0	5.5
5X	**Regular**	**Fluorocarbon**
Climax	5.2	4.5
Orvis	4.75	4.0
Dai-Riki (Velvet)	4.4	3.5

Figure 12. Strength of some of the more common tippet materials in regular and fluorocarbon.

The diameter or the X tells you nothing about the strength of the leader. Leaders have become stronger in the past decade. Just a few years ago a 4X tippet had an average pound test of 3 or 4. More recently that average among leader materials (like Orvis's Super Strong) is 6 pounds.

DELL Leader Formula

Ask many fly fishers if they ever make their own leaders and the majority will tell you that they don't bother. Why? Leader formulas are confusing and difficult to remember. I usually rely on three separate sizes and strengths for my leaders. For wet fly fishing and using the tandem I usually use a 10-foot leader. For dry flies up to a size 16 I often use a 9-12-foot leader; and for small dry fly fishing like the trico I use a 12-15-foot leader. A leader has three distinct parts: the butt section, the middle or tapered section, and the tippet. I use a stiff leader material like Maxima or Mason leader material for the butt section (heavier section connecting the fly line—often from .022 to .013); and softer material like Orvis, Dai-Riki, Rio, Climax, or Umpqua for the middle and the tippet sections (.012 to.005).

You'll find plenty of leader recipes like the 20-50-20 and the 60-20-20 formulas. These numbers refer to the percent of the leader that is included in the butt, middle and taper sections. For example in the second formula, 60-20-20, the butt is 60 percent of the leader; the middle section, 20 and the taper 20. The tippet is that last and finest piece of leader. The butt in this latter formula should be slightly longer than the taper and tippet combined (60 per cent butt to 40 per cent for the taper and tippet.). In the first leader formula below you'll see that the butt section is 64 inches (56 per cent) long (.019 through .013). The taper and tippet sections in that same formula are 51 inches long (44 percent). Here are my leader formulas using Mason or Maxima leaders for the butt and Orvis or Rio for the front end of the leader. These leader formulas work well with a 5-weight line. If you're using a 7-weight line or heavier I suggest you start with a .022 butt section. If you have a 1-3-weight line you might want to start with .018.

4-6 weight lines—10-foot plus leader formula—wet flies and the tandem

.019—19 inches—Mason or Maxima
.017—17 inches—Mason or Maxima
.015—15 inches—Mason or Maxima
.013—13 inches—Mason or Maxima
.011—11 inches—Orvis or Rio
.009—9 inches—Orvis or Rio
.007—7 inches—Orvis or Rio
.006—24inches—Orvis, Rio or Climax fluorocarbon
Total length—10'3"

7-9-weight lines —10-foot leader—dry flies

.021—21 inches—Mason or Maxima
.019—19 inches—Mason or Maxima
.017—17 inches—Mason or Maxima
.015—15 inches—Mason or Maxima
.013—13 inches—Mason or Maxima
.011—11 inches—Orvis or Rio
.009—9 inches— Orvis or Rio
007—7 inches—Orvis, Rio or Climax
.006—28 inches— Orvis, Rio or Climax fluorocarbon
Total length—9' 11"

1-3 weight lines—8-9-foot leader
.018—18 inches—Mason or Maxima
.015—15 inches—Mason or Maxima
.013—13 inches—Mason or Maxima
.012—12 inches—Orvis, Rio or Climax
.010—10 inches—Orvis, Rio or Climax
.008—8 inches—Orvis Rio or Climax
.007—28 inches— Orvis, Rio or Climax fluorocarbon
Total length—8' 8"

7-9-weight lines—Low Water——13-foot leader—dry flies
.022—22 inches—Mason or Maxima
.020—20 inches—Mason or Maxima
.018—18 inches—Mason or Maxima
.015—15 inches—Mason or Maxima
.013—13 inches—Orvis, Rio or Climax
.011—11 inches—Orvis, Rio or Climax
.009—9 inches— Orvis, Rio or Climax
.008—8 inches— Orvis, Rio or Climax
.007—7 inches—Orvis, Rio or Climax
.005—35 inches— Orvis, Rio or Climax fluorocarbon
Total length—13"4"

Look at the DELL leader formulas. I originated the name DELL. It's an acronym for Diameter Equals Leader Length. These leaders couldn't be easier to remember and tie. I don't know who first came up with this idea to make the leader so simple. Whatever diameter is you use convert that to inches and tie that length on for the leader. For example, if you use a .020 diameter leader you add 20 inches and so on. When you get to the tippet add a piece that's at least two to three feet long. That'll allow for longer drag free floats.

The longer the tippet (the last piece of the leader) usually the longer the float you'll get without drag. We examine drag and what causes it in Chapter 6. When you tie your own leader remember not to drop down too quickly in diameter from one section to another. As a rule you should not go down more than .002 from one piece of leader to the next. This will make for a much smoother tapered leader and one that is definitely better to cast. (There is at least one leader formula, the 35-percent down formula, defies that old adage and drops by .003 to .006" per segment.) It's often difficult to find leader material that drops .019, .017, .015, and .013 and so on. More often you'll find leaders like .020, .018, .015, and .012. Don't ask me why manufacturers do this, but it's a common practice.

Try the DELL leader formula. You'll find it simple to remember and extremely effective.

You should always try to match the tippet with the size fly you're using. To determine the diameter tippet you need divide the size of the dry fly by 3. If you're using a size 24 fly you'd normally use an 8X tippet (24 divided by 3=8). *However, when you use fluorocarbons you don't have to use as small a diameter tippet. In other words you can use a 6X or 7X fluorocarbon for a size 24.*

If I'm in a hurry I often buy my leaders. I often select a knotted one because it has a better feeling to me. If you plan to fish water with a lot of algae or weeds you might prefer to use a knot less tapered leader. The knotted one will pick up debris in the water more quickly. I often buy leaders with a 2X or 3X tippet so I can add my own tippet.

Knots

There are three basic knots you'll need to know to connect the various parts of your equipment. You need to use knots when you connect the following:

1. Backing to reel—improved clinch knot
2. Backing to fly line—nail knot
3. Fly line to leader—nail knot
4. Leader to leader—surgeons knot
5. Leader to fly—improved clinch knot
6. Fly to fly (when using the tandem)—hand tied improved clinch knot

On the stream you'll use the improved clinch knot quite a few times in an average day, especially on those frustrating trips when you're constantly changing fly patterns. On the other hand you might not need to tie a nail knot more than once or twice a season. But, when you need that knot it becomes extremely important to know how to tie it. A couple times a year I have had to tie a nail knot for someone who wants to replace an entire leader. I always carry a small diameter straw with me to tie it. Use one of those small mixing straws rather than a larger drinking straw. In a pinch on the stream I've looked for and found a hollow stem of a dead piece of grass. I use a 2-inch piece of this stem to form the nail knot. Try it some time on the stream—it really works. More recently many fly fishers use the Zap-a-Gap method to fasten the butt of the leader to the fly

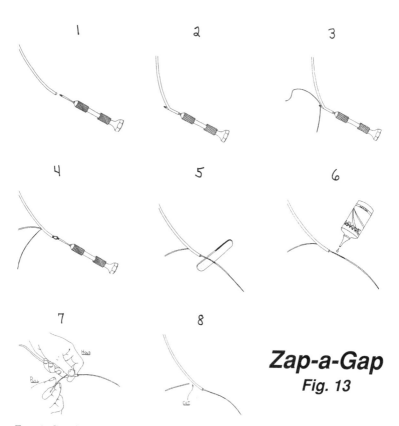

Zap-a-Gap

Fig. 13

Zap-A-Gap is a good method of connecting the leader to the line without using any knots.

line. Use a bodkin and force it up through the middle of the fly line. Bring the bodkin out of the fly line about an inch above where it entered. Place the roughened butt of the leader up through the hole and out the opening. Apply Zap-a-Gap to the roughened section of the butt and pull it into the line. Cut off the excess and you have a great connection without a knot.

  I like using the surgeons knot for leader to leader connections because I have a decided handicap. While I was finishing *Pennsylvania Trout Streams and Their Hatches,* and sitting at my computer, I lost part of my finger on a folding chair. Since that incident in 1988 I have been unable to tie a blood knot so I've resorted to connecting leader to leader with a surgeon's knot. Both knots have about the same strength, but the surgeon's knot has one distinct disadvantage. If you're replacing a middle piece of your leader, and the fly is still attached to the tippet, you have to bring the

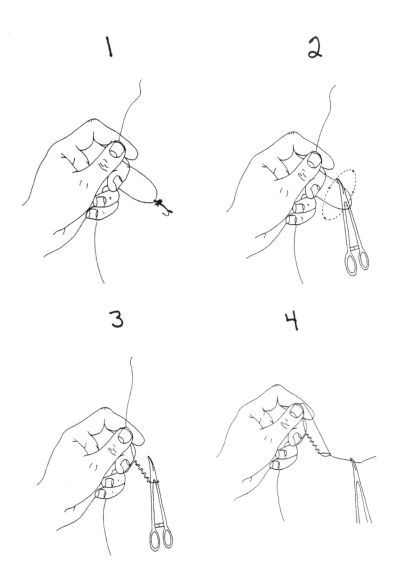

Improved Clinch Knot
Fig. 14

Tying the improved clinch knot—use the improved clinch knot to connect leader to fly and fly to fly (tandem). To tie the improved clinch knot, twist the leader five times with a hemostat (Fig. 14-2 & 14-3) Grab the loose end with the hemostat and pull it through the loop (Fig. 14-4). Finally, pull the leader back through the loop you've just created.

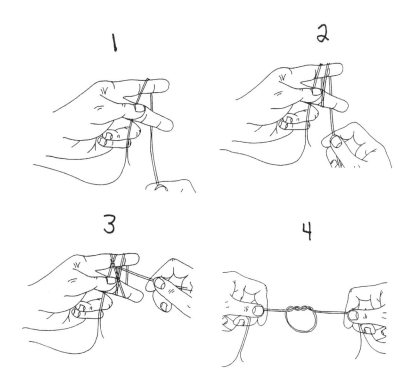

Surgeon's Knot
(Meck Style)
Fig. 15

leader and *the fly* through the opening twice. You don't have to do that with a blood knot.

The improved clinch knot is easy to tie. To connect the leader to the fly, first put the leader tippet through the eye of the hook. With the shorter piece of leader though the eye make five turns around the tippet; put the end of the tippet through the opening you've created, then place the tippet back through the second opening you've just created. To connect the second improved clinch knot from fly to fly when you're using the tandem, use your forefinger as the eye of the hook. When you're finished tying this improved clinch knot secure it to the bend of the hook of the dry fly.

The surgeon's knot is also simple to tie. Overlap by three or four inches the two leader pieces. Make a loop in the two and bring both leaders through the loop two times. Gary Borger came up with an easier

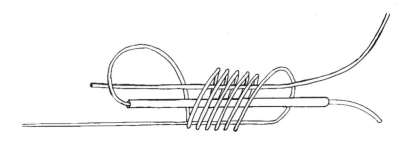

Nail Knot
Fig. 16

way to tie this knot. I've dubbed it "One, Two, and Pull It Through."
Overlap the two leaders by a few inches, then wrap the two around your
forefinger two times, and put them through the opening.

Do you want to catch more trout? You've already selected a
pattern that has worked for you many times before. If that pattern didn't
catch trout you varied the depth of it. Now you're considering leaders.
*Remember, what you use to connect that fly can be as important or even
more important as the pattern you choose.*

– 6 –
PREVENT DRAG ON THAT PATTERN

Rule 1. ***Understand that in most cases trout prefer a pattern that floats drag free.***

Rule 2. ***During some hatches and egg laying events such as caddis and white flies, if a drag free drift doesn't work, move the fly.***

Rule 3. ***If you're having trouble with drag, make certain you follow something on the surface near your fly.***

I often spend Wednesdays experimenting. On that day I often test new patterns, different techniques, and new equipment. I must admit that I've tried some terrible patterns on that day—some, no many of them that never caught a trout. I also experiment with techniques and tactics on that day. Again, I've tested some wild ideas—some that never helped me one bit! On one recent summer day I spent an entire Wednesday morning watching some angling friends cast to trout in the same pool and riffle section of a spring creek in the East. I had fished this section frequently over the past year so I knew it held quite a few trout.

All of these fly fishers used the same pattern, a Dark Olive Bead Head Caddis, trailing behind a size 12 Patriot dry fly. I consider all of them fairly skilled fly fishers. One angler caught a half dozen trout in the section I watched; while for the other two, success ranged from no trout to one trout. And the person who caught the six trout was not the first to fish that section of the stream, but the last. From my excellent vantage point I watched all of them cast, then I followed the dry fly drift through the riffle and pool below. After a half day of watching these three anglers fish, I have become more convinced than ever that there was one thing

The Salt River
near Phoenix,
Arizona. Here a
drag free drift is
important.

that generated success or failure that day—*micro drag*. What is micro drag? What is drag? I consider drag as the uneven or unnatural drift of the fly with current—the fly floats either slower or faster than the stream flow. Micro drag is an almost imperceptible abnormal, either slower or faster, movement of the fly.

This type of drag occurs on almost every drift. How can you detect micro drag? I often follow a leaf or bubble or other free-floating object on the surface close to my fly. When a hatch is on I follow the imitation with the drift of naturals. I watch how my pattern floats in conjunction with them. By watching an object floating freely nearby you can easily

Abrams Creek in Tennessee has many currents requiring skill to produce a drag free float.

A drag free float is important to catch large trout on heavily fished waters.

detect micro drag with your fly.

What about an area where you have three or four different velocities of water? Here's where drag occurs very quickly. How many times have you seen trout feed in these areas? They seem to select these because they can readily detect drag from an unnatural drift

How can you prevent micro drag? There are several ways—a slack leader cast; a longer, finer tippet; mending your line; changing your location and fishing downstream; using one of several special casts—all will help. George Harvey's slack leader cast is one of the most important things you can do to prevent drag—yet few anglers do it. I have unconsciously done it for years. On my final cast I aim the dry fly about three feet above the surface and stop the cast short. What does that do? It brings the fly line up short and makes curves in your leader. The

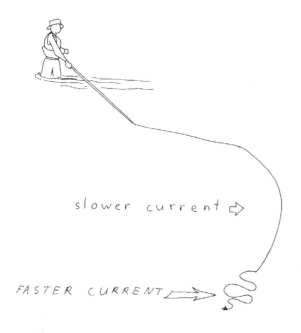

slower current ⇨

FASTER CURRENT →

**Figure 16.
Mending the
fly line
downstream
helps when the
water is slower
near you than
it is at the fly.**

more curves the longer the drag free float. Remember that you want the curves in the leader. On some occasions I aim 10 to 15 feet high, stop the cast abruptly, and let the line and leader settle to the surface. With either of these two techniques you should get plenty of s-curves in your leader.

Another way to help prevent drag is to mend your line. If you have two currents—a slower one on the far shore and a faster one on the near shore—then mend the line upstream by lifting the rod and making an arc in the fly line. If the current is faster near the far shore than it is near you, then make the arc downstream. I often make many small mends in the line—this allows for a much longer drag free drift. As the fly floats downstream I'm constantly making small mends—maybe 10 to 20 of them. Too many anglers I've watched make one large mend when the fly first settles on the surface. That big mend often yanks the dry fly out of the water and scares any trout nearby. Be careful—if you make too exaggerated a mend at the beginning of a drift it will also take all the s-curves out of your leader. So the secret is to make mends—but don't try to disturb the s-curves in the leader nor the fly floating.

A third way you can prevent micro drag is to attach a longer, finer leader to your line. A finer and longer tippet will make more curves and allow for a longer drag free drift. Try increasing your tippet length. If you're using a two-foot tippet increase it by a half-foot or more. If lengthening the leader doesn't work, then go to a smaller diameter tippet—

Figure 17. Mending the fly line upstream helps prevent drag when the water is faster near you than it is at the fly.

FASTER CURRENT ⟹

slower current ⟹

maybe from 4X to 5X or 6X. In Chapter 5 I suggest you start off with a 5X tippet on cloudy days when the stream is low and clear. On bright, sunny days try a 6X. I usually try using a 32-inch tippet if I'm casting just a dry fly and a 24 to 27-inch tippet when I use the tandem.

There's another method I often use when I have a long, fairly slow pool, and when I can walk along the stream bank unobstructed. I cast the fly, make a mend or two, then I walk the fly downstream. I call the tactic "walking the dog." By using this method you can often float your pattern, drag free, for a hundred feet or more.

I mentioned earlier changing location as another way of preventing drag. I know one particular section of one of my favorite Arizona streams—Big Bonito Creek in the White Mountains—where I fished a section across stream and I got a poor float with a dry fly. I moved downstream below the pool and cast up to it. Guess what? I caught three trout from that more favorable location. Had I not moved I wouldn't have caught a trout because of micro drag. By fishing the section from a different location I prevented that.

There are other important methods of preventing drag like using one of several special casts. Both a reach cast to the right or left and a wiggle cast will help with drag problems. To use a reach cast: On the final cast, just before the fly lands, and as you're lowering the fly rod, move the rod to the right or left. Moving the rod to the right will make a bend, arc or mend in the fly line to the right. If you want the mend to the left move the fly as your dropping the fly rod to your side rod to the left. To make a wiggle cast shake the fly rod from side to side on the final cast. The wiggle cast puts several curves in the fly line. Watch when using the wiggle cast—if you're not careful it can pull out all of the s-curves in the leader and cause more drag.

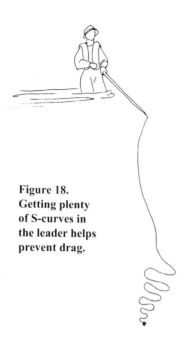

**Figure 18.
Getting plenty
of S-curves in
the leader helps
prevent drag.**

There are other ways to help prevent micro drag. I fished a cream cahill spinner fall several years ago on the Colorado River near Kremmling, Colorado. Just at dusk thousands of spent females floated past me, and more than a dozen trout fed freely on them. For more than 15 minutes I cast an almost exact copy of the spinner over these rising trout and all of them refused it. I then tried a different tactic—I fished the spinner downstream. I got directly above the risers, cast above one of them a couple feet, stopped the leader short so I'd have plenty of slack, and let the fly float downstream. A heavy rainbow trout took the fly on the very first cast. I caught several more trout that evening before I left the river.

All things being equal, the longer you have that correct fly on the water, with a good leader, the more trout you'll catch. Yet, I often see anglers who are constantly casting and only occasionally drop the fly on the water. I sometimes get the feeling that they're enthralled with their casting ability. Why do they do this? In one word: drag. They see that the pattern isn't drifting with the current so they cast and try again. Keep that fly on or in the surface as long as possible—of course without drag.

Multiple currents really present a problem with drag and especially micro drag. There are sections of some of my favorite streams that I often avoid because it's almost impossible to get a drag free float. Do these areas hold trout? You bet they do. (See Heavily Fished Trout Streams in Chapter 8.)

Remember the old way that fly fishers wished each other success? They'd say, "tight lines." That brings up the subject of drag versus setting the hook. There's a fine line between drag and the ability to set the hook on a strike. If you have no bends or curves in your leader or line it's easy to set the hook. But, too tight a line and leader causes drag. Conversely, too much slack line and you can't set the hook properly. Remember how much line your fly rod can take up when you lift it for a strike and fish accordingly. You can test it with your fly rod when you begin fishing.

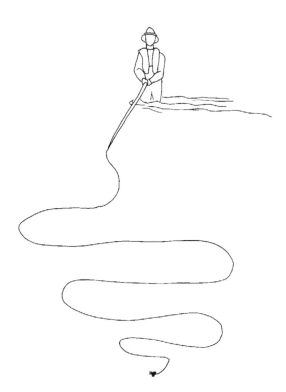

Figure 19. The Wiggle Cast. One problem using this type of cast is that you often curves in your line but not in your leader.

That's why I prefer using a nine-foot fly rod on most occasions. Shorter rods don't give you the luxury of having as much slack line as you might need to prevent drag.

When to Use Drag on a Dry Fly

Can a fly fisher use drag to his or her advantage? I'll never forget those many times I've fished over grannom and other caddisflies returning back to the surface to lay eggs, and nothing seemed to work. Finally, in desperation, I dragged the floating caddis pattern just in front of a rising trout. That worked one afternoon and I caught trout on that tactic.

I conducted an experiment recently while a green caddis hatch appeared on the surface. I carried a counter with me so I could record the number of strikes I had that morning. I made one cast with a Green Caddis wet fly drifting with the current, drag free, and the second cast where I purposely imparted action to the imitation. That morning I caught twice as many trout on the wet fly that I purposely moved than on the one drifting with the current. *With caddis patterns it's often important to move them.*

Dragging a White Fly often works when you hit the hatch of these mayfly naturals *(Ephoron leukon)* in late August. Several years back Bob Budd and I fished a heavy white fly hatch. We moved upriver to see if trout were rising to the hatch and I carried my rod back over my shoulder like a soldier would carry his gun in a parade. The White Fly on the end of my leader dragged across the surface as I waded upriver. Soon a trout struck that dragging fly. Can you imagine trying to bring in a trout over your shoulder? I did and I released the 12-inch brown trout. I've often resorted to dragging my pattern unnaturally during the white fly hatch. But, on most occasions, especially when no caddisfly or white fly hatch is apparent, use a drag free float or drift.

Wet Flies and Drag

Even if you plan to use a wet fly, drift can be important. When do trout hit a wet fly? Often when it is drifting with the current or on its arc or swing. Why do most strikes occur then? I think there are two reasons. First, the pattern is drifting downstream, then makes a move across stream. This movement might get trout to hit the wet fly. Second, and I think most important, trout strike when the wet fly makes its swing and begins rising towards the surface. This latter movement effectively imitates a nymph emerging.

To get the proper drift of a wet fly I often connect it to a dry fly on a tandem rig. The tandem rig has the wet fly connected to a dry fly at the bend of the hook secured by an improved clinch knot. If the dry fly is floating drag free on the surface then often the wet fly underneath is drifting correctly (not always, however). Often I think it's important to fish wet flies on a drag free drift. I most often use this method when no hatch appears.

If a drag free float hasn't worked try dragging the dry fly or twitching the wet fly. Eastern Washington's Yakima River holds a great Mother's day grannom caddisfly hatch. Dave Engerbrettson and I fly fished while Craig Shuman and Jack Mitchell drifted us down a series of rapids. Al Novotny accompanied us videotaping the entire event. He produced the tape as part of a Kodak outdoor series. One of the first words out of the director's mouth was "catch a trout." Dave and I floated past and cast to many risers without even one look. I used a size 14 Black Caddis with a size 16 Black Caddis emerging pupa trailing just behind it. I'd cast the tandem just in front of risers and move it. Soon one hit, then another, and most of them hit the wet fly. Just imparting motion that day saved our director and us from a frustrating float trip.

Fred Brauberger of Scottsdale, Arizona, is one of those skilled fly fishers. I mentioned in *Arizona Trout Streams* that if you hand him a fly rod and one of several wet fly patterns Fred will catch trout. Recently Fred and I used the same weighted Green Weenie pattern. I fished mine behind a Patriot dry fly on a tandem and Fred fished his solo. I let mine drift with the current and just off the bottom. Fred twitched his Green Weenie on the bottom. Dozens of trout followed and took his pattern while few followed mine.

The same often goes for streamer patterns: Impart motion on some occasions and you'll get strikes. I'll never forget that trip to the X-Diamond Ranch on the Little Colorado in Arizona. For an hour Craig Joshepson and I had little success. Then I tried a bead head Wooly Bugger and twitched the pattern. For the next three hours Craig and I landed a couple dozen heavy brown and rainbow trout on that Wooly Bugger. I'm certain imparting motion to the fly helped.

I've learned a lot by sitting back and watching while others fly fish. I look at trout feeding, insects emerging and anglers fishing. I've learned four things that really make a difference: pattern selection; where you fish that pattern; what you use to connect that pattern; and how that pattern floats on the surface or drifts underneath. All four are extremely important, but I consider drag as one of the top tactics. How that pattern drifts or floats can make the difference between a trip full of excitement or one filled with frustration.

Now that you've learned about patterns, leaders, drag and depth it's important to see how a strike indicator can help you catch more trout.

– 7 –
USE A STRIKE INDICATOR

Rule 1. Use a strike indicator to detect even the subtlest of strikes

Rule 2. Vary the depth of your strike indicator

Rule 3. If you don't use wet flies you've got to start if you want to catch more trout.

Rule 4. On heavily fished streams the smaller the indicator the better your chances of hooking a trout.

As a kid I used a bobber all of the time. When I was a kid we didn't have plastic ones so we used cork. That bobber gave me a couple advantages. First, I could see any bite immediately. Second, the bobber kept the bait off the bottom where a fish could see it. Guess what? Some strike indicators work in a similar way.

When I began fly-fishing—and for many years after that I used only dry flies. I covered it all in *Meeting and Fishing the Hatches* published in 1977 and in 1992. I said, "enticing a trout to the surface with a lifelike dry fly is much more enjoyable, rewarding, and challenging than any other type of fishing." Boy, have I changed my tune in the past 10 years! I've finally seen the light. I now realize that if I want to catch more trout I'll most often catch them underneath—yes underneath—not on the surface. Richie Montella first helped me stray from dry flies when he guided my son, Bryan, and me on the Bighorn River in southeastern Montana. Richie handed me a rig and asked me to tie it onto my tippet. The "rig" consisted of a large attractor dry fly and a wet fly trailing behind it. The wet fly was attached a two foot piece of 4X tippet and was attached to the bend of the hook of the dry fly. Richie explained that while the dry

A tandem using a dry fly as a strike indicator.

fly floated the wet fly would sink beneath the surface a foot or more. He added that all I had to watch was the dry fly. If it went under the surface I probably had and strike and I should set the hook. He called the dry fly on the tandem a "strike indicator with an attitude." If trout hit the dry fly indicator they'd get hooked. I agreed to try this new tactic since the dry fly I had used for several hours netted only one trout. It didn't take long to get "hooked" on this setup new to me. I caught more than a dozen trout on that tandem setup that day.

I can still remember coming back from my trip to the Bighorn anxious to try the tandem in the East. At the time—a decade ago—few anglers used that combination on Eastern or Midwestern waters. The tandem became so successful that all my friends began using the same setup. Five years after I began using the tandem I wrote a book about using it entitled. *Patterns Hatches, Tactics, and Trout.*

I'll never forget that trip to the Blue River in central Colorado back in 1976 when I prepared the manuscript for *Meeting and Fishing the Hatches*. The high altitude on this river made me dizzy and I had to rest for an hour. As I sat back on the bank and relaxed another angler tried his luck in a huge riffle in front of me. He had an unusual setup—a spinning rod and reel with a wet fly attached, and a large clear plastic bubble. He placed the plastic bubble about 5 to 6 feet above a weighted wet fly. He'd cast that darn contraption into the heavy riffle and let it float down the entire length of that fast water. It often didn't make it very far. The bubble would go under, he'd set the hook, and bring in a heavy rainbow. I sat back in amazement and awe the way that angler caught trout. Here

I was trying to catch trout on a dry fly in that heavy water. The only good time to use a dry fly there would be during a hatch. But, little did I know that that clear plastic bubble that that angler used would be a harbinger of things to come for fly fishers.

Strike indicators come in a variety of shapes, sizes, colors, and materials. Some anglers use just a brightly colored dot, mark, or piece of plastic on their leader or line. Others use a bobberlike contraption made of plastic or wood. Still others use a type of floating putty that's easy to place on the line. And some others use a dry fly as their strike indicator. Recent strike indicators come in a plastic or rubber that are self-sealing around the leader, and some now come with a combination of plastic and poly. All have several things in common—they usually float and they're bright in color. I say usually float because many of the smaller devices sink under the surface especially in fast water. Many are easy to put on and take off and some are fastened with a rubber band.

Many fly fishers in recent years have added a piece of poly to the leader as a strike indicator. This poly floats well even on fast water rivers like the Colorado at Lee's Ferry in Arizona or the Gallatin in Montana. You can now buy braided poly that fits easily over the leader and can be moved at a moment's notice. On extremely fast, deep water I prefer using a poly indicator—on all other waters I use the tandem with a wet and dry fly. The dry fly floats while the wet fly behind it sinks under the surface. If a trout strikes the wet fly, the dry fly, floating on the surface, sinks. Anglers can attach the wet fly to the dry fly "strike indicator" by using an improved clinch knot (See Chapter 5 for knots) and attaching the leader from the wet fly to the dry fly at the bend of the hook of the dry fly.

What are the advantages of each? First and foremost if you use the tandem—a wet fly and a dry fly—you can catch trout on either. How many times have you had a trout strike your strike indicator? I've seen trout strike brightly-colored indicators many times. Earlier I said that I often refer to the dry fly on the tandem a strike indicator with an attitude. On several occasions I've landed two trout—one on the dry fly and one on the wet fly. On many trips I've averaged up to thirty per cent of the trout caught on the dry fly—especially during the summer. Second, the dry fly will show you even the subtlest of strikes. If trout are striking quickly or short the tandem should be the indicator of choice. Third, the dry fly will float all day under most conditions. As I indicated earlier, however, under extremely fast water conditions like those on many Western waters the dry fly often sinks and the better choice would be a poly or plastic strike indicator.

As with everything there are disadvantages to using the tandem. First and foremost it's easy to tangle the line with the tandem. I'll never forget

The tandem does get tangled up from time to time.

the first time Don Whitesell used the tandem. Don's a great artist. He drew illustrations for my recent book, *Pennsylvania Trout Streams and Their Hatches*. He's an excellent fly fisher—but had never tried using the tandem before. He had a mess on his first cast. It took him a good 15 minutes to get his line untangled. But, he wanted to try casting the tandem a second time. On the second cast he hooked and released a five-pound brown. Five casts later Don landed another brown just a few inches shorter than the first one. Does the tandem work? You bet it does. Just ask Don Whitesell.

Strike indicators made of putty, and self sealing foam or rubber are some of the easiest to apply. The small stick-on foam dots seal around the leader and stay put for hours of fishing. However, they don't hold the wet fly up, and in deep water they're sometimes difficult to follow. Furthermore, they're often difficult to take off when you want to change the location on the leader. Paul Weamer of the West Brach Anglers Shop on the Delaware River uses these stick-on foam dots frequently. When he wants to take them off the leader or line he first clips some of the foam off with a scissors then pulls them off. Putty works well and is easy to take off the leader. Putty lasts for up to a half-hour before you have to replace it. It has a tendency to sink or to fall off the line. Poly strike indicators usually float high above the surface even in extremely fast water. Add a bit of floatant and rub them on a Velcro patch and they will ride for

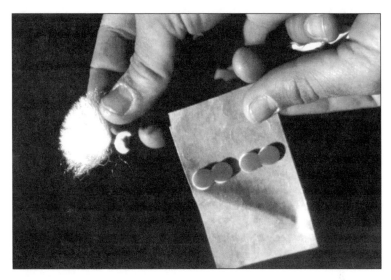

Two types of strike indicators include the poly loop (left) and stick-on-foam (right).

a long time.

Plastic bubbles or bobbers come in a variety of sizes. They're usually brightly colored and easy to see on most waters. Some are, however, difficult to move on the leader.

I mention in Chapter 4 that where you place that fly is often as important as what pattern you're using. *If you're not catching trout at the depth you're fishing then change the strike indicator so that the pattern can go deeper or shallower.* By varying the placement of many strike indicators you can regulate the depth of the wet fly.

I know I should be an intense fly fisher if I want to be a good one—especially when I use wet flies or nymphs. I should spend every second carefully following that line or leader on its drift downstream to see when I have a strike and set the hook quickly. But, I'm not intense and I don't do that. If I see a mayfly take off I check to see what it is. I look for trout rising—my eyes are always going from the fly line to something else. There's where a larger strike indicator comes in handy. I've had some experts laugh at me when I used any but the most subtle of strike indicators. These so-called experts think that all anglers should use only a maker on the line or leader—and follow that marker or the fly line every second. But, they miss the whole point—*strike indicators can and do make even the neophyte a good wet fly fisher. Strike indicators give the angler the earliest possible alert that a trout has struck the wet fly.*

Table 16. Strike Indicators and Advantages and Disadvantages of Each

Advantages	Tandem	Poly Loop	Poly	Plastic Bubble	Plastic Bubble/poly	Self-sealing rubber, plastic circle or stick-on foam	Wooden Bobber	Putty	Line Marker
Easy to see	x	x	x	x	x	x	x	x	
Easy to move		x	x	x	x		x	x	
Easy to apply		x	x	x	x	x	x	x	x
Inexpensive	x	x	x			x	x		x
Can catch trout on indicator	x								
Permanent	x					x			x
Fish different depths	x	x	x	x	x		x	x	x
Easy to change				x			x		
Disadvantages									
Doesn't float well						x		x	x
Not easy to see									x
Doesn't hold up well			x		x			x	
Difficult to move	x					x			
Gets line tangled	x								

Look at some of the advantages and disadvantages to the strike indicators in Table 16. For me the indicator has to float well and be easy to see. If it doesn't have these two qualities I don't want to use it. Look at the one advantage that I've mentioned earlier that the tandem and only the tandem has: You can catch trout on the strike indicator.

I've often mentioned before the four important tactics necessary to become a better fly fisher—to catch more trout. The four are pattern selection, where you fish that pattern, what leader you use to connect that pattern, and how naturally you drift that pattern. Probably the most important of the four is how you drift the pattern. I always tell fly fishers to follow a nearby bubble or other object on the surface and have their pattern float in synchrony with that. By using the tandem or other floating device not only can you have the dry float drag free, but also you can have the sunken fly drifting freely underneath.

I've found over the years that wet flies far out-produce dry flies in an average fishing season. I can remember those first 30 years I fly fished, when I used dry flies almost exclusively, how many times I came home with little or no success. When I began using bead heads my rate of success jumped algorithmically. Sometimes I catch nine or ten trout on the wet fly with the bead for every trout I catch on the dry fly. *If you don't use wet flies you've got to start if you want to catch more trout.*

The reason I didn't use wet flies was because I had a devil of a time detecting strikes with underwater patterns. Strike indicators have negated that problem. As I stated before I've seen some so-called experts decry the use of strike indicators suggesting that you rely on a marker on the leader or line. Hogwash! Use any indicator short of a bobber that makes you feel confident when fishing wet flies. I said earlier that my two selections are the tandem for slow and moderate water and the poly loop for fast water.

What are the disadvantages of just about all strike indicators? Most make casting a bit more difficult; some tend to get the line tangled; and trout that strike tend to let go faster when they feel the indicator. With these disadvantages in mind the one main advantage of strike indicators totally outweighs any possible disadvantage: *strike indicators detect strikes easily and quickly even for the beginner.*

One thing I haven't listed in the table and that I think is extremely important is how quickly trout detect the strike indicator. With large plastic bubbles I often feel that trout let go more quickly because they feel that indicator. With the tandem or a mark on the line they feel it less quickly and consequently give you more time to set the hook.

In Chapter 8 I talk about fishing on heavily fished streams and rivers. I can always tell when a stream is heavily fished by how quickly trout let go of a pattern. On streams with little pressure you get a fairly long window of opportunity to set the hook. Not so on water with plenty of angling pressure. Here's where small indicators come in handy. *On heavily fished streams the smaller the indicator the better your chances of hooking a trout.*

Do you want to catch more trout? First, use wet flies. Then carry a variety of strike indicators with you—and above all don't be afraid to use them.

– 8 –
FISH SMARTER, NOT HARDER

Rule 1. *Know what hatches prefer what sections of a stream and position yourself accordingly for that hatch.*

Rule 2. *When fishing spinner falls realize that most of the spinners fall over fast sections or riffles so position yourself just below these sections.*

Rule 3. *Fish those miserable dreary days in the summer. Hatches, especially little blue-winged olives seem to prefer those overcast days.*

Rule 4. *Try something different. If your spinner pattern doesn't work, sink it.*

Rule 5. *The longer a hatch appears in the season the more selective trout become, especially on heavily fished streams.*

Rule 6. *Fish the hatch shortly after it first begins for the season.*

Rule 7. *Trout in heavily fished streams reject a pattern quicker than those in less heavily fished waters.*

Rule 8. *Try smaller patterns when matching hatches on heavily fished streams.*

Rule 9. *Take time and read the water.*

Rule 10. *Fish when the trout are feeding.*

Reading Water

Wow! Now you've learned how to select the best pattern, choose the right leader, and fish that fly at the right depth and with the proper drift. You've even learned the value of strike indicators and how they help you catch trout. You've learned it all! What else do you have to do to catch more trout? Your casting skill and your ability to read the water and several other important considerations will complete your quest for more trout.

Fly-casting is a skill you learn best by actually doing, not reading books. I know a great fly caster who teaches classes in casting. He casts rings around me. He can outdistance me by 20 feet. His dry fly lands precisely on the water at 90 feet. But, he has difficulty reading the water. His accurate precise casts often fall on barren stretches.

I can usually tell how long someone has fly fished by where they cast their pattern. If trout aren't rising it's important to try to figure out where trout are holding so you can cover them. When a hatch appears trout show you where they are. When there is no hatch you've got to figure out where these trout lay. This aspect, reading the water, is extremely important.

How do you read the water? Look for hiding places for trout. Are there boulders nearby? Then cast to them—above, behind, and on either side. What about the stream bank? Is it deep and undercut? Then cast that pattern so it covers trout hiding under that bank. What about that riffle just upstream from you? Is it deep? Cover it thoroughly. How about that food line in that riffle? Do you see a line of small bubbles and flotsam drifting down the stream? Make certain you fish this area fully. Look for these telltale signs of locations where you'll find trout and where you should be casting.

Don't overlook deep pools. If you're fishing in cold weather trout often hold in the deepest part of these pools. In low water trout also often stay in these deep pools.

As I sit back and watch my friends fish I often find myself suggesting to them where they should cast. Reading the water is fishing smarter, not harder.

Sometimes you'll hit warm water. What do you do when you encounter this? Look for a spring or a cool tributary. I remember the time Nick Nicholas, Jerry Meck, and I fished the Firehole River in Yellowstone National Park. It was late June and the water temperature registered 78 degrees where we fished. Nick took us upriver a couple miles where a cool tributary fed by snowmelt entered the main stem.

Here the temperature was eight degrees lower and we caught trout. I've often hit warm water on other western waters like the Portneuf River near Pocatello, Idaho, in midsummer.

It's been almost a decade ago that Jim Ravasio, Bob Budd and I fished on a hot August day. The temperature rose well into the nineties and every stream we hit was too warm to fish. By early afternoon the three of us had arrived at the Little Juniata River in central Pennsylvania. From Tyrone to Spruce Creek the Little Juniata River holds dozens of limestone springs that cool the main stem considerably. Some of these are fairly large. We positioned ourselves just below one of the larger springs on that river that afternoon and had a great time catching trout.

There are plenty of things you can do to catch more trout other than pattern selection, leaders, drag, depth, and strike indicators and reading the water. The reason I enjoy fly-fishing is it's an extremely challenging sport. You've always got to be thinking. Where will I find fish? What's the best time to fish? Where can I find trout on a heavily fished stream and how should I change my tactics? You should be asking yourself these questions—and others in your quest to catch more trout.

The first ingredient to fishing smarter not harder is to take time and read the water.

Fish when Trout Are Feeding

I still remember those fishing trips I took more than 20 years ago. We headed for the stream at 5: 00 A.M. We began fishing as soon as we arrived and continued to fish until dark. Those are pretty much a thing of the past. I can't do those all day trips anymore. Now I usually limit my fishing to three or four hours at a time. During the summer it's often useless to fly fish in the afternoon. I often limit my time on the stream to an hour or two in the morning and an hour at dusk. Occasionally, anglers will still insist on fishing an entire day and there's no way to convince them differently. How many times have you fished all day during the summer and saw relatively little activity until just at dusk?

So the second way to fish smarter, not harder, is to fish the stream at the proper time. What is the proper time? Think of times when insects emerge on streams and you'll know when the best time occurs. During the spring and late fall you'll see insects emerging mainly in the afternoon. You'll encounter hatches like the blue quill, little blue-winged olive dun, quill gordon, and hendrickson appearing in the afternoon. One of the greatest hatches I've ever hit was the western march brown on the

McKenzie River near Eugene, Oregon in early April. That hatch appears on that and many other western rivers from late February until early May—and it emerges in the afternoon.

But, things change in the East and Midwest with the advent of the sulphur hatch, which usually occurs in mid May. For the first day or two of this hatch it often emerges in the afternoon. But, after that short burst the sulphur appears just at dusk. *For much of the summer insect activity is relegated to early morning and late evening. Your fishing should do the same.*

Of course if you're on vacation and fishing a Western river you'll probably fish the entire day. Some of the best hatches I've encountered on Henry's Fork in Idaho have occurred on those hot western afternoons. You'll often see little blue-wings and midges appearing all afternoon. Add to that hatches like the blue quill and little brown dun and you'll see why fishing in the afternoon in the West can be rewarding.

Fish when the trout are feeding—I devoted 188 pages to just this theory in *Meeting and Fishing the Hatches*. I specified four rules in that book that anglers should follow. I suggested that if you followed those four rules you'd catch more trout. Those four rules are:

1. Select a common and fishable hatch.
2. Choose a probable date the hatch emerges.
3. Look for the hatch on a good stream.
4. Fish at the proper time for a specific hatch.

All four rules are important, but rule number 4 stands out to me as the most important.

So the second rule of fishing smarter, not harder is fish when the trout are feeding. This often is also the time when the hatches appear.

Location, Location, Location

A third rule to fishing smarter not harder is to remember to fish at the right location for a hatch or spinner fall. How many times have you heard when buying real estate it's location, location, location? The very same can be said when fishing the hatches. Let me explain with an event that occurred recently.

John Gierach, A.K. Best, Mike Clark, Walt Carpenter, Jim Black, Carl Roszkowski, Bob Budd and I make a three-day annual trek to some of Pennsylvania's finest trout streams. John, A.K., and Mike fly in from

Location can be everything—Penns Creek in central Pennsylvania.

Colorado to join us. We usually select different streams each year so these western anglers can experience a variety of eastern waters. They usually arrive in mid May—just in time for the famed sulphur hatch.

On their last trip back East the seven of us decided to spend a day on Penns Creek. Anybody who's fly-fished even for a short period of time has heard of this great limestone trout stream. It's one of the most fertile in the East with plenty of hatches throughout the season. Since the Pennsylvania Boat and Fish Commission recently decided not to plant trout in the lower 15 miles, wild brown trout have thrived here. Below the town of Coburn, Penns ranges from 60 to 100 feet wide and holds plenty of productive riffles, and deep long pools. Water temperatures in the upper end, from Coburn downstream to Engleby, remain cool throughout the summer because of one of Penns' major tributaries, Elk Creek.

We parked our car in the crowded parking lot at the old railroad tunnel just below Coburn and hiked downstream on the abandoned railroad tracks. As soon as we arrived we caught a good number of trout on bead head Pheasant Tail patterns. But, in the afternoon—as it often is in mid and later season—action slowed considerably and all of us sat around the bank of this holy river to chat and talk about what hatches and spinner falls we'd see and planned our strategy for the evening hatch.

About 7:00 P.M. the seven of us spread out along a half mile of this placid limestone stream ready to meet the evening hatch. Bob Budd and Mike Clark headed downstream a couple hundred feet to the middle of a long pool. A.K. headed upstream a few feet to the head of a riffle. John, Jim, and Walt waded a couple hundred feet upstream to a productive looking glide. I forgot my prescription glasses and headed back to the car to get them. Sulphurs didn't appear until 8:30 that evening and when they did appear they did so only in shallow riffles. I said earlier that A.K. had placed himself just below a productive 2-to 3-foot deep riffle. He swears he literally had more than 200 trout rising in front of him. Bob and Mike, fishing in the slow water of the pool just below A.K., said they had only a couple trout rise in front of them during the half hour that the hatch and spinner fall occurred. Upstream two miles I selected a riffle near the car. I had dozens of trout rising to a combination of sulphur spinners, sulphur duns, and March brown spinners.

What does all of this prove? Sulphurs prefer shallow riffles to emerge, so position yourself where you should see the hatch in its heaviest intensity. Where you place yourself for the hatch (location) will often decide what kind of a fly fishing experience you'll have. Trout realize when the hatch will come off and congregate to that section of the stream. With the sulphur, which prefers riffles, A.K. Best positioned himself just correctly to get the most out of the hatch.

Location can also be important when fishing spinner falls. When I fish New York's Beaverkill I always position myself on a long riffle near dusk. Why? Most of the spinners congregate over that riffle and fall. Trout sense this and also assemble in this same location.

How many times have you talked to someone who has had a good evening matching the hatch and you've had just the reverse? I'll never forget that day on Little Pine Creek in early spring. I had a so-so evening with few trout rising in front of me. I headed back to the car at dark, headed downstream to a restaurant, and chatted with a few other fly fishers. These anglers had fished several miles downstream from me and you would have sworn they fished a different stream. They boasted about the great caddis hatch they had experienced and all the trout they had caught. Just a couple miles downstream they had a spectacular evening while upstream I saw only a couple trout rise.

Of course you often might see a hatch or spinner fall with few trout rising. What to do? Move upstream or downstream. How about the great hendrickson hatches in the East and Midwest? How many times have I moved from one section of a stream to another while the hatch was in full force in search of rising trout?

I'll never, ever forget that first trip on a Western river more than 30 years ago. I had a deadline. I had to complete the western half of the

Table 17. Where Nymphs or Larvae are Found for Various Hatches

Common Name	Found in the East (E); Midwest (M); or West (W)	Emergence Date	Scientific Name	Emergence Time	Nymph Burrows in silt or gravel (B); Clings to rocks (R); or Swims freely (F)	Nymph is found in Fast (F); Medium (M); Slow (S); or All (A) Water
Little Black Stonefly	E, M, W	Feb 1	*Capnia vernalis*	Afternoon	R	M, F
Western March Brown	W	Feb 25	*Rhithrogena morrisoni*	Afternoon	R	M, F
Little Blue-winged Olive Dun	E, M, W	Jan* to Dec	*Beatis intercalaris*	Afternoon	F	M, F
Little Golden Stonefly (s)	W	Apr 1	*Skawala parallela*	Afternoon	R	F
Little Blue-winged Olive Dun	E, M, W	Apr 1	*Baetis tricaudatus*	Afternoon	F	M, F
Quill Gordon	W	April, May, early June	*Epeorus longimanus*	Afternoon	R	M, F
Early Brown (S)	E, M	April 10	*Strophopteryx faciata*	Afternoon	R	M, F
(M) Blue Quill	E, M	April 15	*Paralepto-phlebia adaptiva*	Afternoon	F	A
Quill Gordon	E	April 15	*Epeorus pleruralis*	Afternoon	R	F
Blue Quill	W	April 15	*Paralepto-phlebia memorialis*	Morning	F	A
Dark Quill Gordon	E, M	April 18	*Ameletus ludens*	Afternoon	F	M, F
Little Black Caddis (C)	E, M	April 20	*Chimarra atterima*	Afternoon	R	F

Table 17. Where Nymphs or Larvae are Found for Various Hatches *(continued)*

Common Name	Found in the East (E); Midwest (M); or West (W)	Emergence Date	Scientific Name	Emergence Time	Nymph Burrows in silt or gravel (B); Clings to rocks (R); or Swims freely (F)	Nymph is found in Fast (F); Medium (M); Slow (S); or All (A) Water
Male Dun: Red Quill Female *Dun:* Hendrick-son	E, M	April 20	*Ephemerella subvaria*	Afternoon	F	A
Black Quill	E, M	April 22	*Leptophlebia cupida*	Afternoon	F	S
Grannom (C)	E, M	April 22	*Brachy-centrus fulliginosis*	Afternoon	Wooden, derrick-like case	S, M
Grannom (C)	E	April 22	*Brachy-centrus numerosis*	Afternoon	Wooden, derrick-like case	S, M
Grannom (C)	W	May 1	*Brachy-centrus occidentalis*	Evening	Wooden, derrick-like case	S, M
Light Stonefly (S)	E	May 8	*Isoperla signata*	Afternoon	R	F
Sulphur	E, M	May 8	*Ephemerella rotunda*	Evening	F	M, F
Green Caddis (C)	E, M	May 8	*Rhyacophilia lobifera*	Afternoon	F	F
Little Blue-winged Olive Dun	W	May 10	*Baetis brunneicolor*	Afternoon	F	A
Western Green Drake	W	May 20	*Drunella grandis*	Morning	F	M
Little Blue-winged Olive Dun	W	May 20	*Baetis bicaudatus*	Afternoon	F	A

Table 17. Where Nymphs or Larvae are Found for Various Hatches *(continued)*

Common Name	Found in the East (E); Midwest (M); or West (W)	Emergence Date	Scientific Name	Emergence Time	Nymph Burrows in silt or gravel (B); Clings to rocks (R); or Swims freely (F)	Nymph is found in Fast (F); Medium (M); Slow (S); or All (A) Water
Salmon Fly (S)	W	May 20	*Pteronarcys californica*	Morning	R	F
Pale Morning Dun	W	May 20	*Ephemerella inermis*	Morning, afternoon, or evening	F	A
Gray Fox*	E, M	May 15	*Stenonema fuscum*	Afternoon, evening	R	F, M
Pale Evening Dun	E, M	May 18	*Ephemerella septentrionalis*	Evening	F	F, M
Pale Morning Dun	W	May 20	*Ephemerella infrequens*	Morning	F	M
American March Brown*	E, M	May 20	*Stenonema vicarium*	Afternoon	R	F, M
Pale Evening Dun	E	May 20	*Leucrota aphrodite*	Evening	R	F
Sulphur	E, M	May 20	*Ephemerella invaria*	Evening	F	M, F
Chocolate Dun	E, M	May 22	*Eurylophella bicolor*	*Dun:* Afternoon *Spinner:* Evening	F	M
Spotted Sedge (C)	E, M	May 23	*Hydropsyche slossanae*	Afternoon	R	M, F
Light Cahill	E	May 25	*Stenonema ithaca*	Evening	R	M, F
Slate Drake	E, M	May 25	*Isonychia bicolor*	Evening	F	M, F

* The March Brown and Gray Fox are now listed as one. I see enough difference physically that I've listed them separately.

Table 17. Where Nymphs or Larvae are Found for Various Hatches (continued)

Common Name	Found in the East (E); Midwest (M); or West (W)	Emergence Date	Scientific Name	Emergence Time	Nymph Burrows in silt or gravel (B); Clings to rocks (R); or Swims freely (F)	Nymph is found in Fast (F); Medium (M); Slow (S); or All (A) Water
Female: Pink Cahill *Male:* Lt. Cahill	E, M	May 25	*Epeorus vitreus*	Evening	R	M, F
Light Cahill	E, M	May 25	*Stenacron inter-punctatum*	Evening	R	M, F
Dark Green Drake	E, M	May 25	*Litobrancha Recruvata*	*Dun:* Afternoon *Spinner:* Evening	B	S
Brown Drake	E, M, W	May 25	*Ephemera simulans*	Evening	B	S, M
Green Drake	E	May 25	*Ephemera guttulata*	Evening	B	S, M
Gray Drake	E, M	May 25	*Siphlonurus quebecensis*	*Dun:* Day *Spinner:* Evening	F	S
Blue-winged Olive Dun	E, M	May 25	*Drunella cornuta*	*Dun:* Morning *Spinner:* Evening	F	A
Blue Quill	E, M	May 26	*Paralepto-phlebia mollis*	Morning	F	A
Female: Olive Sulphur *Male:* Chocolate Dun	E, M	May 30	*Ephemerella needhami*	*Dun:* Morning *Spinner:* Evening	F	M
Pale Evening Dun	E, M	May 31	*Ephemerella dorothea*	Evening	F	M

Table 17. Where Nymphs or Larvae are Found for Various Hatches *(continued)*

Common Name	Found in the East (E); Midwest (M); or West (W)	Emergence Date	Scientific Name	Emergence Time	Nymph Burrows in silt or gravel (B); Clings to rocks (R); or Swims freely (F)	Nymph is found in Fast (F); Medium (M); Slow (S); or All (A) Water
Dark Blue Sedge (C)		June 1	*Psilotreta frontalis*	Evening		
Blue-winged Olive Dun	E, M	June 10	*Drunella cornutella*	*Dun:* Morning *Spinner:* Evening	F	M
Yellow Drake	E, M	June 15	*Hexagenia rigida*	Evening	B	S
Pale Evening Dun	W	June 15	*Heptagenia elegantula*	Evening	R	S, M
Blue-winged Olive Dun	W	June 15	*Drunella flavilinea*	Morning	F	M, F
Blue-winged Olive Dun	E, M	June 15	*Danella simplex*	*Dun:* Morning *Spinner:* Evening	F	M
Light Cahill	E, M	June 15	*Heptagenia marginalis*	Evening	R	M, F
Cream Cahill		June 15	*Stenonema pulchellum*	Evening	R	M, F
Yellow Drake	E, M	June 15	*Ephemera varia*	Evening	B	S, M
Pale Evening Dun	E, M	June 22	*Leucrocuta hebe*	Evening	R	M, F
Blue Quill	E, M	June 25	*Paralepto-phlebia guttata*	Morning	F	A

Table 17. Where Nymphs or Larvae are Found for Various Hatches (continued)

Common Name	Found in the East (E); Midwest (M); or West (W)	Emergence Date	Scientific Name	Emergence Time	Nymph Burrows in silt or gravel (B); Clings to rocks (R); or Swims freely (F)	Nymph is found in Fast (F); Medium (M); Slow (S); or All (A) Water
Golden Drake		June 25	Anthopota-manthus distincus	Evening	B	S, M
Little Olive Dun	E, M	July 1	Tricorythodes allectus (attratus)	Morning	F	S
Gray Drake	W	July 1	Siphlonurus occidentalis	Afternoon	F	S
Cream Cahill		August 1	Stenonema modestum	Evening	R	M, F
White Fly	E, M	August 12	Ephoron leukon	Evening	B	M
Big Slate Drake	E, M	August 15	Hexagenia atrocaudata	Evening	B	S
Little Blue-winged Olive Dun	E, M, W	Sept. 1	Baetis tricaudatus	Dun: Afternoon Spinner: Afternoon & Evening	F	A
Slate Drake	E, M	Sept. 1	Isonychia bicolor	Afternoon, Evening	F	F
Autumn Sedge (C)	E, M	Sept. 15	Neophylax species	Afternoon	R	F

manuscript on *Meeting and Fishing the Hatches* in another two months. I had no guide—the angler from Missoula, Montana, who was to accompany me canceled out. My first stop on that late June trip was the Bitterroot River near Victor. I arrived on the river near the end of June just before noon. I hiked a half-mile down river without seeing one insect or any rising trout. Then I came to a heavy riffle, still running high from snowmelt from the nearby Kootenai Mountains, and I saw a half dozen trout rising. A good hatch of Western green drakes continued for a couple hours and the trout went crazy. The knowledge I had of the green drake—that it appears near the end of June and in early July late in the morning and where I could find it—saved the day.

So, when fishing a hatch or when you expect a hatch, remember that location is everything. You can be on the right stream at the right time, but in the wrong location. Remember if you're uncertain move to a productive looking riffle just before dusk. If a hatch is emerging and you don't see trout rising walk up or downstream and look for risers. Table 17 should help you locate the hatch. Use this table to help you position yourself where the hatch appears. If you know the hatch to expect, all you have to do is to decide where that nymph is found and look for the hatch in slow, moderate or fast water.

Fish When Conditions are Terrible

That Fourth of July day on Penns Creek that occurred more than two decades ago will remain with me forever. That day I couldn't do anything wrong! I selected the right pattern, a size 16 Blue-winged Olive Dun, and I fished it on the surface where the trout were rising. I wrote about that memorable day in *Pennsylvania Trout Streams* and discussed it in Chapter 2 of this book. What made the incident on Penns Creek memorable? The blue-winged olive dun appeared under less than ideal conditions. Normally this mayfly takes off quickly from the surface once it emerges. The cold air and drizzle that day slowed the takeoff of these mayflies and made them easy prey for feeding trout.

What about other mayfly hatches? Do they also slow their takeoff when conditions are less than favorable? Some of the greatest matching-the-hatch episodes I've ever experienced in my more than 50 years of fly fishing have occurred when blue quills (*Paraleptophlebia adoptiva*) emerged. If you've ever encountered this small but extremely important April hatch on Eastern and Midwestern waters then you already know how important it can be.

But, this phenomenon doesn't just occur in the East and Midwest. I've hit great hatches on lousy days throughout the West. Even on the Salt River just outside Phoenix, Arizona, on several January days I've seen trout rise to tricos unable to fly because of the inclement weather. Oregon and Washington coastal and near coastal rivers are noted for their dreary days in late winter and early spring. On many of these you can fish over the Western March brown for three months. Several float trips down the

Oregon's Metolius River holds great hatches and rising trout—especially on dreary overcast day.

McKenzie River near Eugene, Oregon, proved the merits of fishing the Western March brown on a lousy day. We fished that same hatch for several dreary days and saw hundreds of trout rises to laggard mayflies.

In *Great Rivers—Great Hatches* I devoted an entire chapter to fishing on those "lousy days." Some hatches seem almost to enjoy appearing on those rainy inclement days. A partial list of those hatches that seem to appear on inclement days is on Table 18 on the facing page.

The winner by far for the hatch that appears on the dreariest days— in all parts of the country—is the *Baetis* or little blue-winged olive dun. I have seen prolonged, aborted hatches of these mayflies in Oregon, Washington, Arizona, New Mexico, Maryland, New York, Pennsylvania, and Michigan. One of the heaviest I've ever experienced occurred on the Metolius River in central Oregon. Jay Kapolka and I had fly fished this river in late May and had little to show for a day of intense fly-fishing. We returned a few days later to give the river a second chance. This time we encountered an overcast, cold, rainy central Oregon day. We no sooner arrived a few miles down river from the Camp Sherman store when we saw trout rising in every pool, eddy, and riffle for a hundred yards. I quickly collected a few of the insects on the surface and tied on a size 20 Little Blue-winged Olive pattern. For more than four hours that early afternoon and evening Jay and I had trout rising in front of us. For the first part of that time the trout eagerly took little blue wings. But, about

Table 18. Hatches that Appear on Overcast Days

Common Name	Scientific Name	Size	Time of Day	Time of Year	Location
Blue-winged Olive Dun	*Baetis tricaudatus*	20	Morning & Afternoon	Year round	East, Midwest, West
Blue-winged Olive Dun	*Baetis intercalaris*	20	Morning & Afternoon	Year round	West
Western March Brown	*Rhithrogena morrisoni*	14	Morning & Afternoon	March to May	West
Quill Gordon	*Epeorus pleuralis*	14	Afternoon	April & May	East
Hendrickson	*Ephemerella subvaria*	14	Afternoon	April & May	East, Midwest
Blue Quill	*Paraleptophlebia adoptiva*	18	Morning & Afternoon	April & May	East, Midwest
Western Green Drake	*Drunella grandis*	12	Morning & Afternoon	May, June & July	West
Blue-winged Olive Dun	*Drunella flavilinea*	14	Morning & Evening	May, June & July	West
Pale Morning Dun	*Ephemerella inermis*	16	Morning & Evening	May, June, July & Aug.	West
Blue Quill	*Paraleptophlebia memorialis*	18	Morning	May, June & July	West
Sulphur	*Ephemerella rotunda* & *invaria*	16	Afternoon & Evening	May & June	East, Midwest
Female: Olive Sulphur *Male:* Dark Brown Dun	*Ephemerella needhami*	16	Afternoon & Evening	June	East
Blue-winged Olive Dun	*Drunella cornuta*	14	Morning & Afternoon	June & July	East, Midwest
Blue-winged Olive Dun	*Drunella cornutella*	16	Morning & Afternoon		East, Midwest
Blue Quill	*Paraleptophlebia guttata*	18	Morning & Afternoon	June, July & August	East, Midwest
Dark Blue-winged Olive	*Seratella deficiens*	18-20	Afternoon	June	East, Midwest

an hour later, pale morning duns and Western green drakes became the dominant food for the rainbows of the Metolius River. We changed patterns and caught trout on all three hatches. The same type of event has occurred on the San Juan River in New Mexico and Oak Creek in Arizona—multiple hatches on an inclement day.

Why are overcast dreary days so productive? Trout like to feed on cloudy, not sunny days. Some insects (Table 17) emerge for an expanded time on those dreary days. I still remember that drizzly overcast day Vince Gigliotti, Bryan Meck, and I spent on a small limestone stream in the East. We saw sulphurs emerging and trout rising from 10:00 a.m. until 5:00 p.m. How's that for fishing an extended hatch?

Special Tactics for Fishing Heavily Fished Waters

I've fly fished for more than 50 years. When I first began I could go fishing for days and never encounter another fly fisher. To see another angler fly fisher was indeed the exception and not the rule. But, times have changed. Within the past 10 years fly fishing pressure on many of our streams has become immense and almost intolerable. It's not unusual during a well-known hatch to share a river with hundreds of other fly fishers. What's a person to do?

You wouldn't expect to see crowded conditions in the West, but you do. I will always remember those great hatches of the West! I will long remember that first trip to New Mexico's banner river, the San Juan. For more than four hours that morning and afternoon I had rising trout in front of me. Trout began the morning feeding on midges in the flats just below the Navajo Dam. A few hundred yards below the flats, and in the afternoon, trout fed on little blue-winged olive duns. Throughout that entire day I could look up and down the river and see as many as 20 other anglers in full view. And this angling pressure occurs on this river almost every day of the year!

I can say the same about that trip to the South Platte River just below Elevenmile Reservoir in Colorado. Phil Camera and I fished over trout feeding on tricos for more than three hours. Dozens of other anglers fished nearby. What about that first time I fished at Lee's Ferry, Arizona's premier blue ribbon trout river? My brother, Jerry, and I fished this great river shortly after an article about this prolific fishery had appeared in *Fly Fisherman* magazine. We fished over trout feeding on midges for more than six hours. Scanning a mile of water, in mid March, we saw 20 to 30 other fly fishers.

What about the great hatches on Henry's Fork? We can't omit the great hatches on this famous, fabled Idaho river. Talk about heavily fished waters—Henry's Fork is the epitome of angling crowds. On Oregon's Metolius River I mentioned earlier that I experienced a triple hatch of little blue-winged olives, blue-winged olives, and western green drake appearing simultaneously. I also witnessed something else—heavy angling pressure.

But, I've also had my share of great hatches and angling crowds in the East and Midwest. Sulphurs on Spring Creek and green drakes on Penns Creek, both in Pennsylvania, remain indelible events in my list of great matching-the-hatch episodes. The angling pressure during those two hatches can become immense. Great hendrickson appearances on New

New Mexico's San Juan River can be classified as one of those heavily fished waters.

York's Beaverkill and Delaware Rivers will always bring rising trout and angling crowds. Michigan's Au Sable provided me with plenty of great trico hatches well into September. Even that late in the season I had to contend with other anglers.

And the problem exits outside the United States. Even when I fished the Grand River in Ontario, Canada in late August I saw dozens of anglers fishing during the early morning trico spinner fall. As I cast to a couple risers one morning I saw eight anglers fishing within a hundred yards of me. One morning we got up at 5:00 a.m. so we could beat the crowd to a particular hot spot.

Usually within a half an hour of fishing a stream or river—even if I'm the only angler on the stream—I can tell if that water gets excessive angling pressure. How? Catch one of the trout and you'll often see a mouth red from getting hooked many times before. But, the way I often determine if a stream is heavily fished is how quickly trout spit out a fly when they strike. Let me cite an example.

Tony Gehman and Dave Eshenower own the Tulpehocken Creek Outfitters in West Lawn near Reading, Pennsylvania. Tony and Dave are both exceptional fly fishers. I asked them to take me on a morning trip to

Canada's Grand River holds great hatches, rising trout, and plenty of angling pressure.

Heavily fished Oak Creek in Arizona.

see the trico on the Tulpehocken Creek. We met at a parking lot and waded upstream a half mile to get away from some of the anglers. Wading on this stream in most places is relatively easy so we headed upstream far enough so we couldn't hear the roar of engines or cars crossing the open iron bridge. Dave and I decided to fish a three-foot deep riffle while Tony headed to a faster section upstream where he saw some rising trout. Spent female trico spinners already fell on the surface as we began casting to rising trout. The three of us cast over riser after riser without as much as a refusal. Finally I tied on a sunken trico spinner and connected to the Patriot dry fly in a tandem setup. In the next half-hour I had more than a dozen strikes with that setup, but did not manage to hook many trout. We ended the morning landing a dozen trout and missing three times that

Even Montana's Ruby River gets some angling pressure. Want to overcome the pressure? Offering the trout a smaller sized hook of the selected pattern can be part of the answer.

many.

The size of the pattern you use on any heavily fished stream can be important. Dick Henry, a great writer and fly fisher recently commented about the trico hatch on the Tulpehocken Creek. He's an acute observer about hatches and how to match them. Here's what he had to say about the trico hatch on the Tulpehocken:

"Here's another observation, for whatever it's worth. Trout that are under heavy fishing pressure can almost become impossible to catch. I remember your writing about (Vince) Marinaro's complaint that the trout in Falling Springs had become annoyingly selective to trico imitations. Despite a few great days of fishing tricos below Blue March Dam [on the Tulpehocken] late last season, frustrating times were more common. I remember when netting 15-20 trout on a day was reasonably common, but no more. Typically, if they come easy, it comes early in the rise. After that they look and turn away, or if they appear to take the fly they don't get hooked. Ten years ago I took them easily on a size 22 imitation, but now I'm using 26's and feeling that perhaps my flies aren't small enough.

Mark Fortuna, I believe, may have the right idea. Tie a size 28 fly on a 26 hook, open the gap slightly and bend the point to either side. And tighten quickly when a fish takes your fly. He believes a fish can eject a fly quickly enough to avoid being hooked if the angler's response is even slightly delayed."

I agree totally with Dick's observations. *When fishing heavily fished waters during a hatch try offering rising trout a smaller pattern.*

Over my 50 years of fly-fishing I have come to some other conclusions about patterns and sizes, especially on heavily fished waters. I now strongly recommend parachute or comparadun type patterns over the classic or Catskill pattern. Why? The parachute and comparadun ride flush on the surface while the Catskill rides higher (See Chapter 2). I'm convinced that this lower profile is extremely important. So important that if trout refuse my classic pattern I'll often cut the hackle off the bottom so the pattern rides lower in the water.

The secret to a successful day on the Tulpehocken or on any other stream and river throughout the United States with excessive fishing pressure is a fine tippet, the right pattern and size, and a drag free drift.

Tippet

The tippet you use on those heavily fished streams and rivers can make all the difference in the world. Always use the smallest leader possible to land trout when you see plenty of anglers.

I recalled that trip to the abandoned gold dredging ponds near Alder, Montana, in Chapter 5. That day will always remain a bright, memorable one in my list of great fly fishing experiences. I also recounted the experiment I conducted on a heavily fish trout stream in Chapter 5. The 6X tippet caught many more trout than did the 4X one. All of these personal experiences lead up to one point: use the lightest leader you think is possible. We looked at tippets and leaders in Chapter 5. You might want to review that important information.

But, there's more you can do to ensure a successful day on those heavily fished streams. Here are some suggestions and alternatives.

Fishing Early in the Hatch

Try fishing the hatch when it first appears. Whether it's sulphur, pale morning dun, or a trico, fish the hatch the first few days it emerges in the season. It usually takes a day or two for the trout to acclimate to a new hatch, but once they do, they feed voraciously on it. If a hatch like the trico appears for three months I like to fish it the first week it appears. After the first week you'll often notice a distinct selectivity set in.

I mentioned earlier in this chapter about the trip to Elevenmile Reservoir in Colorado. Phil Camera took me to show me the South Platte River and its hatches. Almost from the minute we arrived on that fertile river we saw heavy rainbows feeding within feet of us on trico emergers, duns, and spinners. Trout fed constantly for the next two hours. But, catching these huge rainbows was another story. Evidently these fish saw so many anglers that they fed undisturbed next to us, many times just a few feet away.

I casted conventional patterns for the first hour and had only one 16-inch rainbow to show for my frustration. Phil had fished the same stretch just a couple weeks before, when the hatch first appeared for the year, and he had done exceptionally well. But, this day, two weeks later, proved to be a frustrating experience.

Look for Streams Not Heavily Fished

Pennsylvania has more than 80 trout streams that hold good green drake hatches. Back in 1995 I wrote a book entitled *Mid-Atlantic Trout Streams and Their Hatches*. That book included a lot of Pennsylvania and New York trout streams virtually overlooked by many anglers. Many of these streams hold good green drake hatches but lack one ingredient often associated with that hatch: angling pressure. It often takes some time to find some of these overlooked gems, but it's well worth it.

I never in my lifetime thought I'd talk about angling pressure in Montana, but I am. I've already discussed that trip to southwestern Montana a few years ago with Ken Rictor, Lynn Rotz, and my son, Bryan. When we landed at the Bozeman Airport I saw hundreds of passengers carrying fly rod cases. It was the exception rather than the rule to see someone without one of these cases. As we crossed the Madison on our way to the Ruby River we saw dozens of anglers fishing the river. How times had changed in just a decade!

We fished that week out of the Upper Creek Canyon Lodge just outside Alder, Montana. Even in this isolated stretch of Big Sky Country we saw plenty of anglers fishing the Ruby River. One day all of us decided we'd take a horseback trip to the East Branch of the Ruby River. Jake and Donna McDonald, owners of the Upper Canyon Lodge, assured us that we were probably the first anglers to fish the upper reaches of this river that year. We mounted our horses and headed over a mountain range and into some extremely picturesque, wild country. Now I said, "mounted our horses" rather casually since I had never seen the back of a horse

Looking for streams not heavily fished is one of the most obvious solutions to overcoming heavy fishing pressure.

close-up before. Besides, I had just recently been under the knife for a hemorrhoid operation. Just the thought of riding that horse for several hours brought pain to my backside. I certainly wasn't looking forward to the eight-mile trek into the river, but if the others were willing to do it I decided to give it a try.

We finally arrived at the East Branch and not a moment too soon. My back ached—my rear end ached—my whole body ached. Those horses have no springs or shock absorbers. Besides, on the trip into the river we had to travel on trails only a couple feet wide. On the right and left sides of the horse were 300 to 400 foot cliffs. I just closed my eyes and let the horse do the worrying.

All of us grabbed our gear and headed to the 15-20 foot wide stream called a "river." Just about every cast on this tiny river produced a strike. No matter what pattern we used, we caught trout. On attractor patterns and small trico patterns we caught trout. We quit three hours later after we caught dozens of eager trout.

Now we had to head back to our trucks—8 miles away. As we crossed over one of the high rises we were suddenly confronted with one of those quickly appearing summer thunderstorms. As I looked to my front I saw lighting hit a mile away several times. I finally closed my eyes and let the trained horses follow the narrow, treacherous trail back to our trucks. After three hours of rain, lightning, and difficult trails we arrived back at

The lower Kootenai, below Libby, Montana, has great hatches and rising trout—especially on dreary overcast days.

our modern transportation. But, that trip was worth all the effort and turmoil. We caught trout, and plenty of them, because we fished a stream not heavily fished.

Add to pattern selection, leader, drag, depth and strike indicators another important ingredient for catching more trout: fishing smarter, not harder. Yes, I still remember those 12 to 15 hours fishing days when I was younger. I still remember that much of the day on those trips was barren. I now fish less time, but have more success because I think about location, fishing on lousy days, fishing at the best times of day and coping with angling pressure. You should do the same.

– 9 –
TIE YOUR OWN PATTERNS

Rule 1. *Tying your own patterns should help you catch more trout.*

Rule 2. *Patterns like the Quill Gordon, Light Cahill, Blue Quill and many others copying hatches often work well even when no hatch is evident.*

Why Tie Flies?

I recently gave a talk to a group of fly fishers. Before I even got started one of the older anglers got up and ask why he should tie flies. He said he had been fly-fishing for more than 30 years and had gotten away without tying one pattern. He went on to ask why should he start now. Why is it important to tie your own patterns? The bottom line and the question you want to ask yourself is *how will it help me catch more trout.*

Tying your own patterns will help you in several ways to catch more trout. First, you can tie a pattern that you want quickly. That trip to the South Island of New Zealand showed me how valuable fly tying was and how it is linked to my success. Mike Manfredo of Fort Collins, Colorado, and I spent a month on the South Island—most of it hundreds of miles away from the largest city, Christchurch. That also meant that many times we were many miles away from the nearest fly fishing shop. I remember the time we fished the Oreti River and hit an unbelievable quill gordon spinner fall one morning. I lost my last dark spinner pattern so I had to quit early—even while other large trout fed nearby.

We had brought a full complement of fly tying material into the country. Some of our necks were confiscated at the customs office. Thankfully we had material with to us to copy those dark spent spinners.

Mike and I headed back to our small motel room and spent the rest of the day tying Quill Gordon Spinners. Armed with a couple dozen patterns we arrived early the next morning. The spinner fall occurred around 8:30 A.M. and Mike and I were prepared. Lunker brown trout fed on these dark gray spinners throughout a heavy riffle. Those patterns we had tied the day before caught a dozen heavy trout that morning before the spinner fall ended.

On that same trip to that great country, I brought two dozen Patriot dry flies with me. Within a week after we had arrived in New Zealand Mike and I ran out of these attractor patterns. What would we do now? I mentioned earlier in the book that we tore a blue knapsack apart to get the blue material for the body. We tied enough patterns for another week of fishing. I also mentioned earlier that the Patriot dry fly caught 12 of the 13 largest trout we caught on that month long trip.

So, the first reason you should tie your own patterns is the rapid turnaround you can achieve. I've found myself tying a pattern more than a dozen times at streamside on Henry's Fork in Idaho. Henry's Fork is an insect factory. You'll see a hatch just about every day, and almost every minute of every day. Several times I hit hatches for which I had no match. By tying patterns streamside I had immediate success. Talk about catching more trout—tying patterns by the bank on Henry's Fork proved the point.

A second reason relates to the first one: You can match unusual hatches. Several years ago, in early June, I saw quite a few sulphurs appear on a cloudy afternoon. As evening approached the hatch grew heavier and heavier. I tied on size 16 Sulphur and began casting just above risers in a heavy riffle. I cast 20, 30 and 40 times before I caught a trout. Now I became frustrated with the hatch and my ineptness at catching any trout. I leaned over and examined a few mayflies resting on the surface. With its wings of pale gray and legs and tail of pale cream it looked like sulphur. But when I turned the dun over to look at the belly I saw a bright green olive body—not the yellowish orange body of normal sulphurs. I vowed to come back the next evening with the correct pattern. I went home that evening and tied a half dozen patterns I called the Olive Sulphur. These patterns really caught trout that next evening. I picked up 20 trout on that new pattern. Now where would I have gotten a pattern like that one overnight?

A third reason you should think of tying flies is to test new patterns. I've mentioned several times before that on Wednesdays I experiment. I

Table 19. Patterns Suggested When There is No Hatch

Wet Flies	Dry Flies	Streamers
Green Weenie Sizes 10 to 12	Adams Sizes 12 to 18	Bead Head Wooly Bugger Sizes 10 to 12
Bead Head Pheasant Tail Sizes 12 to 18	Trout Fin Sizes 12 to 18	Muddler Minnow Sizes 10 to 12
Bead Head Olive Caddis Sizes 12 to 18	Patriot Sizes 12 to 18	Pink Ugly Sizes 10-12
Flashback Nymyph Sizes 12 to 18	Wulff Royal Coachman Sizes 12 to 18	Clouser Minnow Sizes 10 to 12
Bead Head Tan Caddis Sizes 12 to 18		Marabou Mickey Finn Sizes 10 to 12
Glo Bug (Egg color) Sizes 12 to 16		Lady Ghost Sizes 10 to 12
		Peacock Lady Sizes 10 to 12

said before that I test new patterns, new techniques and test new equipment on that day. If I didn't tie flies, how would I have developed the Patriot dry fly? Dozens of people who don't tie flies keep ask me where they can buy Patriots.

A fourth reason to tie is to get the shape, color, size and subtleties you want. Do you want to add an egg sac to some patterns? If you tie your own flies you can go ahead and do it. To catch more trout you should begin tying your own flies.

Recommended Patterns

Let's review the top patterns we covered in Chapters 2 and 3. In Chapter 2, we listed patterns that I've found extremely effective when there's no hatch on the stream. In Chapter 3, I suggested patterns to match many of the more common hatches. In this chapter you'll find recipes for most of these recommended patterns. A complete listing of the recommended flies are found on Table 19 above and Table 20 on the following page.

Table 20. Patterns Suggested When There is a Hatch

Common Mayfly Duns	Common Mayfly Spinners	Stoneflies and Caddisflies	Midges	Terrestrials
SPRING				
Little Blue-winged Olive Dun Sizes 16 to 22	Red Quill Spinner Sizes 14 to 16	Grannom Sizes 12 to 16	Griffith's Gnat Sizes 20 to 24	Poly Ant Sizes 14 to 22
Quill Gordon Sizes 12 to 16	Dark Brown Spinner Sizes 16 to 18	Cream Caddis Sizes 14 to 16	Black Midge Sizes 20 to 26	Poly Beetle Sizes 14 to 20
Blue Quill Sizes 16 to 20	Rusty Spinner Sizes 18 to 22	Tan Caddis Sizes 12 to 16	Gray Midge Sizes 20 to 24	Ken's Hopper Sizes 10 to 16
Hendrickson Sizes 14 to 16		Green Caddis Sizes 12 to 16	Cream Midge Sizes 20 to 24	Caterpillar Sizes 10 to 14
			Zebra Midge Sizes 16 to 20	LeTort Cricket Sizes 12 to 16
MIDSEASON				
Light Cahill Sizes 10 to 20	Sulphur and Pale Morning Spinner Sizes 16 to 18	Dark Blue Sedge Sizes 12 to 16		
Sulphur or Pale Morning Dun Sizes 14 to 20	Dark Brown Spinner Sizes 12 to 18	Tan Caddis Sizes 12 to 16		
Slate Drake Sizes 12 to 16	Brown Drake Spinner Sizes 10 to 14			
Blue-winged Olive Dun Sizes 12 to 16	White-gloved Howdy Sizes 12 to 14			
	Quill Gordon Spinner Sizes 12 to 14			

Table 20. Patterns Suggested When There is a Hatch *(continued)*

Common Mayfly Duns	Common Mayfly Spinners	Stoneflies and Caddisflies	Midges	Terrestrials
MIDSEASON *(continued)*				
	Dark Olive Spinner Sizes 14 to 16			
	Trico Spinner Sizes 22 to 26			
	White Fly Sizes 14 to 16			
FALL				
Little Blue-winged Olive Dun Sizes 16 to 22	Rusty Spinner Sizes 18 to 22	Amber Caddis Sizes 10 to 16		
Slate Drake Sizes 12 to 16	White-gloved Howdy Sizes 14 to 16	October Caddis Sizes 10 to 14		
Cream Cahill Sizes 12 to 18	Cream Cahill Spinner Sizes 12 to 18			

The Green Weenie.

Tables 19 and 20 suggest patterns you can use for every occasion. Don't overlook the patterns in Table 20 even when there is no hatch. Patterns like the Quill Gordon, Light Cahill, Blue Quill and many others copying hatches often work well even when no hatch is evident.

Tying Patterns for the Hatches

The patterns we use to catch trout fall into several categories. Some copy no insect, but contain bright colors designed to irritate trout into striking. Anglers call these attractors. Most other patterns copy various phases of a mayfly's, caddisfly's, or stonefly's life cycle. Still others, like streamers, copy minnows in the stream. Another group of patterns, terrestrials, copy insects usually found on the land.

The nymph copies the larval stage. Wet flies and emergers often copy the emerging stage of the insect; and the dry fly copies the dun or spinner stages. We looked at the life cycle of mayflies in Chapter 3. It might be a good idea to review that life cycle.

Mayfly Spinners and the Patterns that Copy Them

The female mayfly spinner, or mature adult (scientists call the spinner an imago), mates with the male spinner, usually over fast stretches of a stream and most often in the evening. The male appears over the stream first, waiting for the female spinner. The female, after mating, deposits her fertilized eggs. Some imitations copy even the egg sac found on spinners and caddisflies.The Beaverkill dry fly represents the female Hendrickson spinner. I'm convinced that during a sulphur spinner fall an angler could catch trout if he or she used a pattern copying just the small yellow egg sac. Try it sometime. Often Grannom patterns have a turn or two of peacock wound at the rear to imitate the egg sac of this early-season caddisfly.

After the egg laying is completed, many females fall onto the water, usually with wings spent (flat on the surface). When female spinners fall in great numbers on the surface it is both a blessing and a curse to many anglers. Often furious surface feeding occurs at this time. Moreover, this feeding frenzy often occurs around dusk. It's imperative that you know what spinners might fall that evening and be prepared with appropriate spinner imitations. You might want to follow how I prepare for the spinner

Quill Gordon

Red Quill

A parachute-style Hendrickson.

A parachute-style Little Blue-winged Olive.

falls in Figure 3 of Chapter 3. Not all duns are equal in importance and neither are spinner falls. (See Chapter 3, Tables 5 through 8 for the most important.) Some spinners never take on the importance of their dun stage. In all my years of fly-fishing the Western green drake I have never seen a legitimate spinner fall with plenty of feeding trout.

Most spinner imitations copy the spent-winged variety. These spinner patterns usually contain a tail, body and wings of poly yarn. These spent winged patterns float flush with the surface and are often difficult to locate. I often tie smaller spent spinners like the Trico behind a lead fly on the tandem rig. Don't forget what we discussed in Chapter 4: Sink that pattern if trout refuse it on the surface.

It's important to include imitations of some species with divided, upright poly yarn wings. Some sulphur species, for example, lay their egg sac and remain on the surface with wings upright.Copies of spinners with these upright wings are much easier to locate on the surface at dusk.

Nymphs and the Patterns that Copy Them

Nymphs hatch from the fertilized eggs in a couple of weeks to as long as several months later. The nymph spends approximately a year (there are many exceptions) in slow, medium, or fast stretches on rocky or muddy bottoms—many species are specific in their habitat. After almost a year of growing and shedding its outer covering many times (instars), the nymph is ready to emerge.

It amazes me that most anglers use only one size to copy a particular nymph. The size they most often use is the size of the nymph when it hatches. But, let's say you want to use a Light Cahill in April. It would be considerably smaller in size than when it emerges a month or two later. A size 16 pattern might be used to copy the nymph in April. Remember to tie some of the nymphs in sizes smaller than suggested in the recipes.

As the nymph lives and feeds for almost a year underwater it is naturally a source of food for feeding fish. Since the nymph is the longest phase of the life cycle, trout have an opportunity to feed on this stage more often than any other stage. Imitations of nymphs work well most of the year because trout feed on this stage almost daily.

Since the advent of Sparkle Yarn and Krystal Flash some fly tiers add these materials to their nymphal imitations as part of the wing pad. You'll see a recipe for the Flashback Nymph included in this chapter. I'm convinced that this sparkle or flash brings trout to the pattern.

Emergers and Patterns that Copy Them

After a year or so the nymph moves toward the surface. Here it sheds its nymphal skin dorsally (a few do this on the bottom of the stream), and becomes a dun. Skilled anglers realize that trout forage on emerging nymphs and imitate that stage with an emerger that is a hybrid between the nymph and the dun. Often the nymph works well just as the hatch begins. The emerger works well throughout. Tie several patterns to copy the various stages of the emerger. Review Chapter 3 for a discussion of emergers.

How many times have I been frustrated with a hatch? Many times what I thought were rises to hatches were in reality trout feeding on the emergers. The two largest trout I have caught on imitations in the United States both happened when I sank a Green Drake fly and fished this floating pattern just a few inches under the surface. What does this tell you?

Trout often feed on nymphs in the process of transforming into duns. Don't overlook this important phase of fly-fishing. And don't forget to add a nymphal shuck to some of your patterns copying the dun. The change from nymph to dun is a gradual one. While the mayfly is shedding it nymphal shuck it is at its most vulnerable stage. Trout sense this and often take a stage of the emerger readily (See Chapter 3). Adding a shuck to your pattern copying the nymph often proves to be the deciding feature whether or not a trout will take a pattern.

Nymphs change to air-breathing mayflies in a series of deliberate steps. Most often the nymph moves towards the surface and rests, or rides in surface film for a time while it splits its nymphal skin dorsally. Slowly the dun evolves out of what was the outer skin of the nymph. First the wings appear, then the rest of the dun appears out of the nymphal skin. While this whole process is evolving the nymph, emerger, and dun are vulnerable. What anglers often think is a rise to the dun is in reality a rise to the emerger or nymph.

There are many ways to tie an emerger pattern. Here are just a couple. To tie one type of emerger, use the tail fibers listed below. Use the same hook for emergers that you would use for the dry fly. Tie in a short wing of hen hackle or deer hair. Slant the wing back at a 45-degree angle over the body. Whether you use deer hair or hackle tips make certain the wings are one-half to three-fourths the length of the body. If you want the emerger to float rather high in the film use some floatant. If you plan to fish the emerger behind a dry fly copying the dun you might want to add a couple wraps of lead to the body. Place the emerger about a foot behind the dry fly. The added body weight will keep it just beneath the surface.

Here's a second way to tie an effective emerger pattern. Let's look at a Sulphur Emerger as an example. Tie in a dark brown tail, dub in an olive brown body of opposum halfway up the shank. Next, tie in, at the middle of the shank, about 15 barbules of a very long dark gray hackle. Tie these barbules in by the butt section. Finish the body with the olive brown dubbing you used in the back half of the body. Next, pull the 15-hackle barbules up over top of the front half of the body. Tie in half of the hackle to the right side and the other half to the left side. This hackle represents the legs and the other part of the hackle copies the bulging wing pad.

There are many other ways to tie an emerger pattern. You can add a loop at the wing to represent the dun emerging. You can also make the emerger pattern bicolor. The back half copies the nymph and the front half the color of the dun.

Duns and Patterns that Copy Them

The nymph appears on the surface as an air-breathing dun. Many of these duns ride the surface for some distance before taking flight. Mayflies that appear early or late in the season, and those that emerge under poor weather conditions tend to spend more time on the surface before taking flight. These duns are especially important to imitate with dry fly patterns. Patterns like the Hendrickson, Western Green Drake, Green Drake, and many others have gained notoriety because they match insects that normally take off slowly from the surface. I said before that trout sense that the most vulnerable part of this entire process of changing from a nymph to a dun is when the nymph is near the surface and in the process of ridding itself of its shuck. You'll note that I've included shucks as optional for many of the dry fly patterns.

When the dun finally becomes airborne, it usually heads for a nearby tree or bush close to the stream. Duns emerging early in the season sometimes rest on sun-warmed rocks or debris next to the water to protect themselves from early-season freezes.

Although a few mayflies change from dun to spinner in an hour or less, and a few never change, in most the transformation requires one or two days. With a final molt, the dun shucks its outer covering and reappears over the water as a more brightly colored mayfly with clear glassy wings. These spinners then meet and mate to complete the life cycle.

With this abbreviated look at the life cycle you can readily see that all phases of the insect become important sources of food. While larva of aquatic insects are available every day of the year to trout, adults become available from March through November.

Caddisflies and stoneflies are similar in their life cycles. Neither has a spinner stage that mayflies have. Caddisflies have a complete life cycle and contain a resting or pupal stage. Stoneflies and mayflies lack this stage. Caddisflies go into the pupal stage prior to emergence on the surface. Soft-hackled wet flies often copy this emerging pupa.

Downwings, Midges and Terrestrials

I suggested in Chapter 3 that you carry plenty of downwing patterns with you. In Figure 3 in that chapter, I showed how I stock my Wheatley box for downwings. I seldom use a Henryville pattern. I usually tie in a body of poly, a deer or elk hair wing, and I tie a couple turns of hackle for

A caddis with a trailing shuck.

fast water patterns. I often omit the hackle on patterns I plan to use on slower water. If you prefer tying the pattern Henryville style then add a hackle to the body and palmer it up to the wing.

Caddisflies have no tail, but I often feel that a tail helps balance the pattern, so I add a shuck. Are shucks important on caddis patterns? Just ask Bryan Meck, Pat Elam or Mike Bay. Pat and Mike guided us on the Missouri near Wolf Creek, Montana, more than a decade ago. On our trip we saw dozens of trout feeding on a black caddis, but few even looked at out patterns. I tied on a size 16 Black Caddis with a tan Z-lon shuck for Bryan. He cast the pattern over one of the risers and the surface exploded. He finally landed a 24-inch brown trout on that caddis pattern with a shuck. Soon the four of us fished downwing patterns with shucks and we all began catching trout.

Tying the Patterns

R ecently I spoke to the Cleveland Museum of Natural History Trout Club. This club is one of the most impressive trout organizations in the United States. They not only invite some of the fly fishers of note to speak to their club, they also have some of the best dinners I've ever attended. It's the best of the best. At the end of the speech one of the members of the club asked why I preferred classic fly and parachute patterns over no-hackle, comparadun, and thorax dun patterns. He felt that the body of no-hackle type patterns more closely resembles the natural. Comparaduns and parachute-type flies come in contact with the water. In the classic pattern the body tends to ride much higher. I agreed with the man asking the question and feel that a parachute tie or a comparadun will usually out-fish a conventional high riding one. I often prefer a low riding parachute pattern to one of the classic high riding Catskill types, especially for highly selective trout during a hatch (See Chapter 2.).

In the following two sections you'll see directions for patterns copying mayflies, caddisflies, and stoneflies. Each description can be used for tying either a wet or dry fly. If you prefer using wet flies substitute a heavier steel hook, less buoyant body material, and hen hackle for the tail and legs. Rather than use a body made of dubbed poly you might substitute fur, or any other material which tends to sink more rapidly to tie the wet fly. When the wings of the dun are dark gray and the dry fly calls for dark gray hackle tips, use instead mallard quill sections for the wet fly. Don't forget to add some weight to the body of some of your spinner and dun patterns to make them sink when a floating one doesn't work.

If you prefer to tie no-hackle type patterns they might not float as well on fast Western waters, but they work. If you prefer tying a comparadun, then omit the hackle and use brown deer hair for the wings and spread them in a semicircle.

Try tying some of your smaller patterns (size 16 and smaller) with a vernille body. Vernille is a much finer type of chenille. Ask Brian Williams of Gilbert, Arizona, if the vernille-bodied Little Blue-winged Olive Dun works. I fished with Brian on Silver Creek near Show Low, Arizona. That morning we hit an unbelievable hatch of little blue-wing olives. Maybe 50 trout rose in front of Brian in a small pool not wider than 20 feet and no longer than 100 feet. I handed Brian a pattern someone had given me earlier. Brian tied on that size 20 parachute Little Blue-winged Olive and on the first 10 casts he had 10 strikes. Yes, he was 10 for 10. What pattern caught so many trout? The parachute pattern was tied with a fine vernille body. That vernille was extended out over the bend of the hook. Use a lighter or match to get a smooth rear end. There's no need to tie any tail on this pattern. Make several turns with your tying thread from the rear to the eye to hold the vernille on the hook. Make certain that the thread you use is the same color as the vernille. Tie in an appropriate hackle, parachute style and you have an effective dry fly pattern. Don't tie any of these patterns on hooks larger than 16. On larger patterns the vernille sinks the fly.

A Pale Morning Dun with a vernille body.

New Tying Techniques

I doubt if there are any new tying techniques left. I'm certain others use the same shortcuts I use. I think, however, they're important enough to mention here. I've used these tying tricks at many of the fly fishing symposia conducted by Chuck Furimsky and Barry Serviente. Anglers watching me at those featured fly tier events have asked me to incorporate some of these tying techniques in this book. I've even received several e-mails from people attending these programs urging me to include these tying techniques in an article or book.

I've been tying flies since 1949. George Harvey first taught me at a Junior Conservation Camp conducted by Penn State University. I classify myself as a lazy tier and if I find productive shortcuts I eagerly use them. There are several methods I use in fly tying that I have found extremely effective. The first is an effective method for tying wings on a dry fly. The second has a duel purpose: it prevents the body from moving back over the tail and also prevents the hackle on a parachute style fly from moving up over the post. A third tying trick I use is use with beads.

Dividing Dry Fly Wings

Plenty of fly tiers have trouble with dry fly wings. Whether they're tied from deer hair, calf hair, or a duck flank feather the method I use separates the wings quickly and holds them in one position permanently. Here's the simple method.

I also use this technique when I'm tying the Patriot. Tie in the white calf body hair on the shank about third of the way back from the eye of the hook. You want the wings to be as long as the shank of the hook. Make plenty of wraps over the butt section of the calf hair to firmly secure the wings. Now lift the calf hair up and make about a dozen turns with the tying thread just in front of the wings. Next, tie in a six-inch piece of tying thread just behind the wings. Take that new piece of tying thread and divide the wings in half with it. Now take the new thread completely around the left wing and back to the shank. Then make a couple turns with your regular tying thread to secure the short piece. Next, use the added tying thread and wrap it the right wing. Tie this piece also on the shank just behind the wing. This thread first divides the wing in half—then it pulls back and keeps the wings apart. This technique is quick, easy and simple.

Preventing Body Material from Moving Back over the Tail

If you use Krystal Flash or other synthetic as body material you'll find that it often moves back over the bend of the hook and renders the fly useless. There's an easy tying method to prevent the material from moving back over the tail and bend of the hook. Here's how you do it when tying the Patriot. Tie in five 6-inch pieces of smolt blue Krystal Flash just in front of the tail. Keep one of these pieces to the rear and wind the other four around the shank about half way up the shank. Now take the fifth piece of Krystal Flash that you left behind and pull it up over the body you've just wound and tie it in where you just tied the others in. This method prevents the body from moving back.

You can use the same principle with the wings or post on a parachute type dry fly to prevent the hackle from creeping up the post. Tie in a piece of thread with the post. Then wrap the hackle around the post and the piece of thread. After you've made a half dozen turns with the hackle tie it off just behind the eye. Now pull the piece of thread front over the hackle and tie off at the eye. This piece of thread will prevent the hackle from creeping up the post.

Using Beads

When you use beads do you lose a lot of them on the floor? I've seen all kinds of gadgets to prevent this. A very easy method is to use a tube of tying wax and dip the tube into a bag of beads. Keep the beads on the wax until you're ready to use them. Position the beads so the hook goes through the smaller opening first.

HOOKS

Instead of suggesting a hook for each pattern in this chapter I've listed some of the more common hooks and their purpose in Table 21.

Table 21. Some of the More Common Hooks and Their Purpose

Hook Type and Number	Wire	Eye	Length	Purpose
DRY FLY				
Daiichi 1170	1x Standard	Down	Standard	Standard Dry Fly
Daiichi 1180	1x Fine	Down	Standard	Small Barb
Daiichi 1190	1x Fine	Down	Standard	Barbless
Daiichi 1310	1x Fine	Down	Short Shank	Tricos and other small flies
Daiichi 1480	1x Fine	Straight	2x Short	Midges
Orvis 1523	2x Fine	Down	Standard	Extra Fine
Orvis 1877	1x Fine	Down	Standard	Traditional Dry Fly
Orvis 4864	1x Fine	Down —oversized	Standard	Oversized down eye for people who have difficulty threading a dry fly
Mustad 94831	2x Fine	Down	2x Long	Used for larger patterns like the Hex and Green Drake

Table 21. Some of the More Common Hooks and Their Purpose (continued)

Hook Type and Number	Wire	Eye	Length	Purpose
DRY FLY (continued)				
Mustad 94833	3x Fine	Down	Standard	Very light hook for dry flies
Mustad 94840	1x Standard	Down	Standard	Standard dry fly hook
Mustad 94842	Standard	Turned-up eye	Standard	Dry fly, turned-up eye
Mustad 94845	Standard	Down	Standard	Barbless
TMC 100	1x Fine	Down	Standard	Wide gap
Fenwick DSE	1x Fine	Straight eye	Standard	Dry fly, mini barb
WET FLY				
Mustad 9671	1x Stout	Down	2x Long	Long wet fly; Green Weenie
Mustad 9672	1x Stout	Down	3x Long	Muddlers
Mustad 3908	2x Stout	Down	Standard	Heavy wet fly
Mustad 3906	1x Stout	Down	Standard	Standard wet fly
Tiemco (TMC) 8526	1x Stout	Down	Standard	Standard wet fly
NYMPH				
Daiichi 1273	1x Strong	Straight	3x Long	Curved shank nymph hook
Daiichi 1560	1x Stout	Downn	1x Long	Nymph
Mustad 3906B	1x Stout	Down	1x Long	Standard nymph hook
Mustad 9672	1x Stout	Down	3x Long	Long nymphs and small
Tiemco (TMC) 8527	1x Stout	Down	x Long	Nymphs

Table 21. Some of the More Common Hooks and Their Purpose (continued)

Hook Type and Number	Wire	Eye	Length	Purpose
EMERGING PUPA / SCUD / BEAD HEAD				
Daiichi 1150	1x Stout	Up	1x Short	Bead Heads, scuds, emerging pupa
Orvis J8891	1x Fine	Down	1x Short	Bead Heads, scuds, emerging pupa
Mustad 80200BR	1x Stout	Down	1x Short	Bead Heads, scuds, emerging pupa
Tiemco (TMC)	2x Heavy	Down	2x Short	Bead Heads, scuds, emerging pupa
Tiemco (TMC) 2487	1x Fine	Down	2x Short	Caddis pupae, emergers
Fenwick BS1XS	1x Stout	Down	1x Short	Bead Heads, scuds, emerging pupa
STREAMER				
Daiichi 2220	Standard	Down		
Mustad 9672	Standard	Down	3x Long	Small streamer
Mustad 79580	Standard	Down	4x Long	Medium streamer
Mustad 3665A	Standard	Down	6x Long	Large streamer
Mustad 94720	Standard	Down	8x Long	Extra-long streamer
Tiemco (TMC) 300	Standard	Down	4x Long	Medium streamer
Tiemco (TMC) 5262	Standard	Down	2x Long	Muddler
Tiemco (TMC) 5263	Standard	Down	3x Long	Small streamer

There are so many hooks available that it's difficult to keep abreast of all of them. Several years ago Dave Hughes presented a concise description of the various uses of the different hooks in an article in *Flyfishing* magazine.

Another helpful document is Dick Steward's *The Hook Book* (Northland Press, Intervale, NH, 1986). It covers Eagle Claw, Kamasan, Mustad, Partridge, Tiemco, and VMC hooks. For each hook the author includes diagrams, uses, possible substitutions, and vital statistics. This fine book is a must for all fly-tiers.

"Wire" in the hook table refers to the weight or strength of the hook. There are essentially three weights: fine, standard, and stout. A 2x fine hook contains the same wire found in a hook two sizes smaller. A Mustad hook 94831 in size 12 contains the same wire as a standard, size 16 hook. Conversely, a stout wire rating indicates that the hook is heavier than normal. For instance, a size 12 hook in model 3908 is 2x stout. This hook has the same wire as a size 8 standard. Hooks with fine wire float better but have less strength than standard or stout hooks.

Hook lengths vary from short to standard to extra large. Remember, only the length of the shank is reduced as length decreases, not the gap (the distance between the point and the shank). Look at an extra large, size 12 hook, Mustad 9671 (2XL). This hook contains the same gap as a standard, size 12 hook but has the length of a standard, size 8 hook.

Note in the chart that Mustad 94845 hooks are barbless. Barbless are usually more expensive than barbed hooks. Make your hooks barbless before you start tying; then if the point breaks before you tie, you can throw them away. I always use barbless hooks. If you use the tandem and the lead dry fly is tied on a barbless hook you can slip the rig with the leader and wet fly back over the hook easily.

Tie some of your streamer patterns for small streams on 9672 hooks. This hook works well with the Muddler Minnow, Green Weenie and the Lady Ghost. You'll see the recipes for these patterns next.

Patterns to Tie when there's No Hatch to Match

L et's face it—you'll often fish trout streams across the United States when there's little hatching activity. What pattern do you use then? Over the past decade or two I've experimented with the tandem on streams all across the country and it has proved to be extremely productive. I usually use an attractor pattern like the Patriot for the dry fly and a bead head or Green Weenie for the wet fly. This combination has proved deadly on most streams and rivers across the United States. Tie the Patriot in sizes 12 and 14 to float the wet fly. That doesn't mean that you can't use a pattern like the Light Cahill as the lead fly when there's no hatch.

For the wet fly half of the tandem I use a Tan Bead Head Caddis, an Olive Bead Head Caddis, a bead head Pheasant Tail Nymph, Glo Bug, or the Green Weenie. I tie the bead head patterns in sizes 12 to 16 and the Green Weenie in a size 12. I add weight to the body of all the patterns so they sink quickly. To the size 12 and 14 bead heads I wrap 10 winds of .010 lead and to the size 16, 10 wraps of .005. This extra weight, in addition to the bead, gets the wet fly deep quickly. By using a size 12 dry fly like the Patriot with plenty of hackle the dry fly acts as a strike indicator with an attitude—trout hit the indicator and are hooked.

Note: Those patterns listed on the following pages with the pattern name in all CAPITALS are part of the required patterns listed in Chapters 2 and 3, and earlier in this chapter in Tables 19 and 20.

PATRIOT

Thread: Red
Tail: Brown hackle fibers
Body: Smolt blue Krystal Flash wound around the shank. Wind some of the red thread in the middle of the shank, similar to the Royal Coachman.
Wings: White calf body hair, divided
Hackle: Brown
Hook: Mustad 94833, sizes 10-18

The Patriot   **The Royal Coachman**

TROUT FIN

Thread: Orange
Tail: Brown hackle
Body: Orange floss
Wings: White calf body hair, divided
Hackle: Brown hackle
Hook: Mustad 94833, sizes 10-18

ADAMS

Thread: Gray or yellow
Tail: Half brown and half grizzly
Body: Gray, or yellow poly dubbed
Wings: Grizzly hen hackle tips
Hackle: One brown and one grizzly
Hook: Mustad 94833, sizes 10-18

WULFF ROYAL COACHMAN

Thread: Red
Tail: Brown hackle
Body: Peacock with a red floss midrib
Wings: White calf body hair
Hackle: Brown
Hook: Mustad 94833, sizes 10-18

The Bead Head Pheasant Tail

BEAD HEAD PHEASANT TAIL

Thread: Dark Brown
Tail: Five or six fibers from a ringneck pheasant tail
Body: Continue winding the pheasant tail fibers used to tie in the tail up to the bead, and tie in
Thorax: Copper bead
Hackle: Ten pheasant tail fibers
Head: Copper bead
Hook: Tiemco 2457, sizes 12-16

BEAD HEAD OLIVE CADDIS

Thread: Olive
Body: Dubbed with a heavy amount of dark olive opossum fur, ribbed with fine gold wire. I tie several shades of this pattern.
Head: Copper bead
Hook: Tiemco 2457, sizes 12-16

The Bead Head Olive Caddis

GREEN WEENIE

Body: Cut off a 5-inch piece of small or medium chartreuse chenille. Form a small loop with the chenille extending out over the bend of the hook, then wrap the chenille around the shank of the hook up to the eye.

Hook: Mustad 9672, sizes 10 or 12

Tying Notes: I include a loop as the tail of the Green Weenie. I feel this loop makes the pattern move as it drifts downstream. I often add weight to the body. I add 10, 15, 20, and 25 wraps of .015 lead, then color code the patterns. For 25 wraps I use orange thread, for 20 wraps I use a chartreuse thread, etc.

BEAD HEAD GLO BUG

Thread: Red

Body. Two large strands of Glo Bug material in one of many yellow, cream, pale orange, or orange colors. I prefer the color they call "egg." Tie on either side of hook, tie in with thread, pull tight and tie just behind the bead.

Head: Copper bead

Hook: Tiemco 2457, sizes 12 to 18.

FLASHBACK NYMPH

Thread: Brown or gray

Tail: Dark brown hackles

Body: Tie some with a dark brown, black and gray angora so you have a variety.

Thorax: Twenty to thirty strands of bright silver Krystal Flash or Flashabou tied in one third of the way back from the eye. Pull the strands up over the eye and tie in. Make certain the strands cover the entire thorax, top and bottom.

Hook: Mustad 3906B, sizes 12 to 18

BEAD HEAD WOOLY BUGGER

Thread: Black

Tail: A mixture of black marabou and six strands of silver flashabou

Body: Dark olive, gray, or black chenille palmered with a black saddle hackle

Head: Copper bead

Hook: Mustad 3665A, sizes 10 and 12

Streamers for Eastern, Midwestern and Western Waters

I'll never forget that first day I fly-fished on Sunrise Lake in Arizona. While Craig Josephson, Bob David, and Josh David used Peacock Lady patterns I used the infamous Green Weenie. In the first hour the three of them caught more than a dozen trout while I caught none. After refusing to try the Peacock Lady I finally succumbed. Within an hour I caught eight trout on that pattern.

There's another pattern that works especially well on Arizona streams and rivers. I fished the Little Colorado River at the X-Diamond Ranch several years ago and I experienced high water. Snow melt in late March pushed the small river two feet above its normal level. Nothing I used seemed to work—until I tied on a Biggety Eyed Chook. Preston Mauk of Altoona, Pennsylvania, first tied that particular streamer. If you ever meet Preston, and ask him about the pattern, he'll immediately hand you one and ask you to try it. In a fit of frustration I tied on the Biggety Eyed Chook on the Little Colorado's high water. The heavy pattern sank to the bottom quickly and on the first cast I had a strike. If you want to fish an excellent pattern near the bottom—even in high water—use the Biggety Eyed Chook. In an hour fishing that awkward pattern I caught half dozen trout. The pattern is difficult to cast but really works—across the United States, especially in heavy water conditions.

PEACOCK LADY

Thread: Black

Body: Two or three strands of peacock wound up to the eye

Hackle: Wind a small grizzly hackle at the bend of the hook. The barbules of the hackle should be as long as the gap of the hook. Wind a brown hackle with barbules about twice as long as the grizzly hackle just behind the eye.

Hook: Mustad 79580, size 10

Tying Notes: Tie some of the Peacock Ladies with lead wire. If I plan to fish heavy water, I use twenty-five wraps of .015 wire. Also try a bead head on some patterns. The weight and the bead head allow you to get deeper quicker.

Biggety-Eyed Chook

Thread: Black

Eye: Lead eyes

Tail: 10 strands of Smolt Blue Krystal Flash

Body: Peacock

Hook: Mustad 3665A, size 6

MUDDLER MINNOW

Thread: Brown

Tail: Mottled turkey quill sections with several strands of Flashabou

Body: Flashabou wrapped around shank

Wings: Mottled turkey quill sections, and several black deer hairs, and several strands of Flashabou

Hackle: Thirty to forty pieces of deer hair with the tips back toward the tail and the butts tied in forward. Trim off the butts to form a rounded head.

Hook: Mustad 79580, size 10

LADY GHOST

Thread: Black
Body: Flashabou wrapped around the shank
Wings: Four badger saddle hackles under four peacock herls
Throat: Yellow deer hair underneath and white deer hair on top
Cheeks: Small reddish brown feathers with a darker tip from a ring-necked pheasant
Hook: Mustad 3665A, size 10

MARABOU MICKEY FINN

Thread: Black
Tail: Five or six strands of smolt blue Krystal Flash
Body: Silver Flashabou ribbed with oval silver
Wings: Yellow marabou, then red marabou, then yellow marabou on top. Add 10 strands of smolt blue Krystal Flash underneath the three layers of marabou
Hook: Mustad 3665A, size 10

CLOUSER MINNOW—GOLDEN SHINER

Thread: Tan
Eye: Lead eyes, painted dark red
Wing: Three separate layers: On the bottom tie in 10 pieces of gold or smolt blue Krystal Flask; on top of that tie in 10 tan bucktail fibers; on top of that tie in 10 white bucktail fibers. Make certain the wing is sparsely tied.
Hook: Tiemco 811S, sizes 6 and 8

PINK UGLY

Thread: Pink
Eye: Lead eyes
Body: Silver tinsel
Wing: Pink marabou mixed with smolt blue Krystal
Flash
Hook: Mustad 3665A, size 8 or 10

Eastern and Midwestern Mayfly, Caddisfly, and Stonefly Imitations

Note: Use the hook chart found earlier in this chapter for specific hooks. If you want a standard dry fly hook you might want to use a Mustad 94840. If you'd like a lighter hook you might want to try Mustad 94833. For wet flies use a hook similar to Mustad 3906, and for nymphs use one comparable to Mustad 3906B. All dry fly recipes can be converted to wet fly patterns.

MAYFLY IMITATIONS

LITTLE BLUE-WINGED OLIVE DUN

Copies *Baetis tricaudatus*, and other *Baetis*
species
Thread: Dark gray
Tail: Medium to dark gray hackle fibers
Body: Gray muskrat or medium gray poly,
dubbed; for the Little Blue-Winged Olive
use olive-gray poly
Wings: On smaller sizes (20) use dark gray
mallard quills; on larger sizes use dark
gray hackle tips.
Hackle: Blue dun
Shuck (optional): Brownish black Z-lon
Hook: sizes 18 and 20

RUSTY SPINNER

Thread: Dark brown
Tail: Dark grayish brown hackle fibers
Body: Grayish brown poly, dubbed and ribbed
        with fine tan thread
Wings: Pale gray poly yarn, tied spent
Hook: Same as above

Little Blue-winged Olive Nymph

Thread: Dark olive
Tail: Wood duck fibers, dyed dark olive
Body: Dark olive brown opossum
Wings: Dark gray mallard quill section
Hackle: Cree or ginger variant hackle, dyed
        dark olive
Hook: size 18

•••

BLUE QUILL

Copies all *Paraleptophlebia* species
Thread: Dark gray
Tail: Medium to dark gray hackle fibers
Body: Eyed peacock herl, stripped, or dark gray
        poly, dubbed
Wings: Dark gray hackle tips
Hackle: Light to medium blue dun
Shuck (optional): Dark brownish black Z-lon
Hook: sizes 18 and 20

DARK BROWN SPINNER

Thread: Dark brown
Tail: Dark brown hackle fibers
Body: Dark brown poly, dubbed
Wings: Pale gray poly yarn, tied spent
Hook: Same as above

Blue Quill Nymph

Thread: Dark brown
Tail: Mallard flank feather, dyed dark brown
Body: Dark brown angora, dubbed
Wings: One dark gray mallard quill tied down
Hackle: Dark gray
Hook: sizes 16 and 18

•••

BLUE-WINGED OLIVE DUN

Copies many *Drunella* (*Ephemerella*) species and *Dannella* (*Ephemerella*) like *cornuta, longicornus, attenuata, cornutella, lata, simplex, walkeri,* and others
Thread: Olive
Tail: Grayish olive hackle fibers
Body: Light to medium olive poly, dubbed
Wings: Dark gray hackle tips
Hackle: Medium creamish olive
Shuck (optional): Dark olive black Z-lon
Hook: sizes 14 to 20

DARK OLIVE SPINNER

Thread: Dark olive or black
Tail: Moose mane (dark brown)
Body: Dark olive poly (almost black with an olive cast)
Wings: Pale gray poly yarn, tied spent
Hook: Same as above

Blue-winged Olive Nymph

Thread: Olive
Tail: Wood duck
Body: Dark brown angora tied over dubbed in olive opossum
Wings: Brown turkey
Hackle: Ginger variant, dyed olive
Hook: sizes 14 to 18

•••

QUILL GORDON

Copies species like *Epeorus pleuralis, Ameletus ludens* and some *Rhithrogena* species

Thread: Dark gray
Tail: Dark gray hackle fibers
Body: Eyed peacock herl, stripped and lacquered
Wings: Wood duck or imitation wood duck, divided; or dark gray hackle tips
Hackle: Dark gray hackle
Shuck (optional): Black Z-lon
Hook: size 14

Red Quill Spinner

Use same pattern as spinner listed under Hendrickson

Quill Gordon Nymph

Thread: Dark brown
Tail: Fibers from a mallard flank feather, dyed dark amber
Body: Dark brown fur or angora, mixed with a bit of lighter brown or amber
Wings: Mottled brown turkey, tied down over thorax
Hackle: Cree or ginger variant hackle (dark and amber mixed)
Hook: size 14

•••

The Light
Cahill

LIGHT CAHILL

Copies diverse species like *Stenonema ithaca,
Stenacron interpunctatum, Heptagenia
marginalis,* and many others

Thread: Cream or tan
Tail: Cream hackle fibers
Body: Cream poly, fox fur, or angora, dubbed
(for the female of *S. interpunctatum* the
body should be creamish orange)
Wings: Mallard flank feather, dyed pale yellow,
divided
Hackle: Cream hackle
Shuck (optional): Dark brownish black
Hook: size 14

Light Cahill Spinner

Same as dun except omit hackle and add pale
yellow poly yarn for wings. Tie them
spent.

Light Cahill Nymph

Thread: Brown
Tail: Fibers from a mallard flank feather, dyed
brown
Body: Dark brown angora yarn on top and pale
amber belly, dubbed
Wings: Dark brown turkey
Hackle: Dark cree
Hook: size 12

•••

SLATE DRAKE

Copies all *Isonychia* species
Thread: Black
Tail: Dark gray hackle fibers
Body: Peacock herl (not from eye), stripped; or
dark gray poly, or muskrat, dubbed
Wings: Dark gray hackle tips
Hackle: One cream hackle tied in behind and
one dark brown hackle tied in front
Shuck (optional): Black Z-lon
Hook: sizes 12 and 14

WHITE-GLOVED HOWDY

Thread: Dark brown or maroon
Tail: Medium gray hackle fibers
Body: Dark mahogany poly, dubbed
Wings: Pale gray poly yarn
Hook: Same as above

Isonychia Nymph

Thread: Dark brown
Tail: Three dark brown hackle with one side cut
off
Body: Dark brown angora or opossum
Wings: Dark gray mallard quill section, tied
down over thorax
Hackle: Cree hackle, dyed pale olive
Hook: sizes 10 and 12

•••

A Sulphur Dun

SULPHUR DUN

Copies *Ephemerella rotunda, invaria, septentrionalis*, and to a lesser degree *dorothea*

Thread: Yellow

Tail: Cream hackle fibers

Body: Usually pale yellow poly with an orange (and sometimes olive-orange) cast (*E. septentrionalis* and *E. dorothea* the body has more yellow than orange)

Wings: Pale gray hackle tips

Hackle: Cream hackle

Shuck (optional): Medium to dark brown Z-lon

Hook: sizes 16 and 18

SULPHUR SPINNER

Thread: Tan

Tail: Tan deer hair

Body: Female with eggs—yellowish tan poly; female without eggs—tan poly; male—bright red hackle stem, stripped and wound around hook

Wings: Pale gray poly yarn, tied spent (also tie some upright)

Hook: Same as above

Sulphur Nymph

Thread: Grayish brown
Tail: Brown pheasant-tail fibers
Body: Brown (ground color) fur
Wings: Dark gray mallard quill section, tied down over thorax
Hackle: Cree hackle
Hook: sizes 14, 16 and 18

•••

HENDRICKSON AND RED QUILL

Red Quill copies the male and the Hendrickson the female of *Ephemerella subvaria* and several closely related subspecies. In addition the Red Quill effectively imitates many spinners like *Ephemerella subvaria, Epeorus pleuralis,* and the male spinner of *Ephemerella invaria* and *rotunda.*

Thread: Brown
Tail: Medium gray hackle fibers
Body: Red Quill—reddish brown hackle fiber stripped of its barbules and wound from the bed of the hook to the wings. Hendrickson—tan poly, dubbed
Wings: Wood duck, divided. Optional on Hendrickson are gray hackle tips.
Hackle: Medium gray hackle
Shuck (optional): Brownish black Z-lon
Hook: sizes 14 and 16

RED QUILL SPINNER

Thread: Brown
Tail: Bronze dun hackle fibers
Body: Dark tannish brown poly, dubbed and ribbed finely with tan thread
Wings: Pale gray poly yarn, tied spent
Hook: Same as above

Hendrickson Nymph

Thread: Dark brown
Tail: Fibers from a mallard flank feather, dyed brown
Body: Dark brown angora, mixed with a bit of amber
Wings: Mottled-brown turkey, tied down over thorax
Hackle: Cree hackle
Hook: sizes 12 and 14

•••

Yellow Drake

Copies *Ephemera varia* and *Hexagenia rigida*
Thread: Yellow
Tail: Tan deer hair
Body: Pale yellow poly, dubbed
Wings: Mallard flank feather dyed pale yellow, divided
Hackle: Pale yellow with a turn or two of grizzly in front
Shuck (optional): Pale tannish gray Z-lon
Hook: size 12

Yellow Drake Spinner

Thread: Yellow
Tail: Dark brown deer hair
Body: Same as above
Wings: Gray poly yarn, tied spent
Hook: Same as above

Yellow Drake Nymph

Thread: Tan
Tail: Pale gray, trimmed
Body: Amber-colored angora or opossum
Wings: Medium to light brown turkey
Hackle: Ginger
Hook: sizes 10 and 12

•••

The Green Drake

Green Drake

Copies *Ephemera guttulata*
Thread: Cream
Tail: Moose mane
Body: Cream poly, dubbed
Wings: Mallard flank dyed yellowish green,
        divided
Hackle: Rear—cream hackle; front—dark brown
        hackle
Shuck (optional): Pale grayish Z-lon
Hook: sizes 8 and 10

Coffin Fly

Thread: White
Tail: Light tan deer hair
Body: White poly, dubbed
Wings: Grayish yellow poly yarn, tied spent
Hook: Same as above

Green Drake Nymph

Thread: Tan
Tail: Three medium brown hackle, trimmed
Body: Pale tan angora
Wings: Dark brown turkey, tied down and over
        thorax
Hackle: Cree
Hook: sizes 8 to 12

•••

Brown Drake

Copies *Ephemera simulans*
Thread: Dark brown
Tail: Moose mane
Body: Yellowish brown poly, dubbed
Wings: Mallard flank feather, dyed yellowish brown, divided
Hackle: Rear—cream; front—dark brown
Shuck (optional): Tannish gray Z-lon
Hook: sizes 10 and 12

Brown Drake Spinner

Thread: Dark brown
Tail: Brown hackle fibers
Body: Yellowish brown poly, dubbed
Wings: Gray poly yarn, tied spent
Hook: Same as above

Brown Drake Nymph

Thread: Brown
Tail: Three light brown hackle, trimmed and tied in
Body: Tan angora or opossum
Wings: Brown turkey, tied down and over thorax
Hackle: Dark cree
Hook: sizes 10 and 12

•••

March Brown

Copies *Stenonema vicarium (*now combined with *S. fuscum)*
Thread: Yellow
Tail: Dark brown hackle fibers
Body: Tan poly, dubbed and ribbed with dark brown thread
Wings: Mallard flank feather, dyed yellowish brown and divided
Hackle: One cream and one dark brown, mixed
Shuck (optional): Dark brown
Hook: size 12

Great Red Spinner

Thread: Dark brown
Tail: Dark brown hackle fibers
Body: Dark reddish brown poly, dubbed
Wings: Pale gray poly yarn, tied spent
Hackle: Dark brown with a turn or two of pale
        ginger, mixed
Hook: Same as above

March Brown Nymph

Thread: Brown
Tail: Fibers from a mallard flank feather, dyed
        brown
Body: Same as Gray Fox below
Wings: Dark brown turkey, tied down over
        thorax
Hackle: Dark cree
Hook: size 12

•••

Gray Fox

Copies *Stenonema ithaca*, and lighter
        Stenonema vicarium naturals
Thread: Cream
Tail: Tan deer hair
Body: Cream poly, dubbed
Wings: Mallard flank feather, dyed pale
        yellowish tan, divided
Hackle: Cree hackle or one brown and one
        cream, mixed
Shuck (optional): Dark brown
Hook: sizes 12 and 14

Ginger Quill Spinner

Thread: Brown
Tail: Dark brown hackle fibers
Body: Eyed peacock herl, dyed tan and stripped, or grayish brown poly, ribbed with brown thread
Wings: Gray hackle tips (conventional); or pale gray poly, tied spent
Hackle: Dark ginger (conventional); or none with poly wings
Hook: Same as above

Gray Fox Nymph

Thread: Brown
Tail: Fibers from a mallard flank feather, dyed brown
Body: Brown angora yarn, tied on top over cream. Tie in brown at tail, and dub in cream so that top (*tergites*) of body is brown and the belly (*sternites*) is cream.
Wings: Dark brown turkey, tied down over thorax
Hackle: Dark cree
Hook: size 12

•••

CREAM CAHILL

Copies species like *Stenonema pulchellum* and *Stenonema modestum*
Thread: Cream
Tail: Cream hackle fibers
Body: Very pale cream (almost white) poly, dubbed
Wings: Mallard flank feather dyed pale yellow, divided
Hackle: Cream
Shuck (optional): Brownish black
Hook: sizes 14 and 16

Cream Cahill Spinner

Thread: White
Tail: Pale cream hackle fibers
Body: White poly, dubbed
Wings: Pale poly yarn, tied spent
Hook: Same as above

Cream Cahill Nymph

Thread: Olive brown
Tail: Light brown hackle fibers
Body: Dub pale creamish gray on the hook, then tie pale brownish olive yarn in at bend and bring over top to wing case and tie in
Wings: Dark brown turkey
Hackle: Dark olive brown
Hook: sizes 14 and 16

•••

WHITE MAYFLY *(dun and spinner)*

(Since the female dun never changes to a spinner, I've listed one pattern for both phases.)

Copies *Ephoron leukon* and *album* and other similar species

Thread: White
Tail: White hackle fibers
Body: Female dun—creamish white poly, dubbed; male spinner—a couple turns of dark reddish brown poly at the rear, then white poly for the rest of the body, dubbed
Wings: Pale gray hackle tips
Hackle: Cream (a turn or two of dark brown for the male spinner)
Shuck (optional): Pale tannish gray
Hook: sizes 14 and 16

White Mayfly Nymph

Thread: Gray
Tail: Tannish gray hackle fibers
Body: Pale gray angora or opossum, dubbed heavily
Wings: Pale gray mallard quill sections
Hackle: Cream ginger
Hook: sizes 14 and 16

•••

Chocolate Dun

Copies species like *Ephemerella needhami* (male dun only)and *Eurylophella* (*Ephemerella*) *bicolor*
Thread: Brown
Tail: Medium gray
Body: Chocolate brown poly, finely ribbed with lighter brown thread
Wings: Dark gray hackle tips
Shuck (optional): Dark brown
Hackle: Tan hackle
Hook: size 16

Chocolate Spinner

Thread: Dark brown
Tail: Tannish gray hackle fibers
Body: Dark rusty brown poly, dubbed
Wings: Pale gray poly yarn, tied spent
Hook: Same as above

Chocolate Dun Nymph

Thread: Brown
Tail: Light brown mallard flank feather fibers
Body: Light brown poly nymph dubbing
Wings: Dark gray mallard quill
Hackle: Brown hackle
Hook: size 16

•••

Olive Sulphur

Copies *Ephemerella needhami*
Thread: Olive
Body: Medium olive poly, dubbed for the
female; dark brown poly, dubbed for the
male
Wings: Cream hen hackle tips
Hackle: Cream
Shuck (optional): Dark olive brown
Hook: size 16

Olive Sulphur Spinner *(female)*

Thread: Dark olive
Tail: Cream
Body: Dark olive poly, dubbed
Wings: White poly yarn, tied spent

Olive Sulphur Nymph

Same as regular Sulphur.

•••

Dark Green Drake

Copies species like *Litobrancha recurvata*
Thread: Dark gray
Tail: Dark brown moose mane
Body: Dark slate poly, dubbed and ribbed with
yellow thread
Wings: Mallard flank, heavily barred and dyed
dark green
Hackle: Rear—tannish brown hackle; front—
dark brown hackle
Shuck (optional): Tannish brown
Hook: sizes 8 and 10

Brown Drake Spinner

Thread: Brown
Tail: Brown hackle fibers
Body: Reddish brown poly, dubbed and ribbed
with yellow thread
Wings: Pale gray poly yarn, tied spent
Hackle: Dark brown
Hook: Same as above

Dark Green Drake Nymph

Thread: Light brown
Tail: Three dark bronze hackles, trimmed and
tied in
Body: Tan with a grayish cast angora, or
opossum
Wings: Dark brown turkey
Hackle: Dark cree
Hook: sizes 8 and 10

•••

Trico Dun

Copies all *Tricorythodes* species
Thread: Pale olive
Tail: Cream hackle fibers
Body: Pale olive-green poly, dubbed; male—dark
brown poly
Wings: Pale gray hackle tips
Hackle: Cream hackle
Shuck (optional): Olive brown
Hook: sizes 20 to 24

**A Trico
Spinner**

Trico Spinner

Thread: Dark brown
Tail: Female—short cream hackle fibers; male—
     long dark brown moose mane
Body: Female—rear one-third is cream poly,
     dubbed, and front two-thirds is dark
     brown poly, dubbed; male—dark brown
     poly, dubbed, and ribbed with a fine light
     tan thread
Wings: White poly yarn, tied spent
Hook: sizes 20 to 24

Trico Nymph

Thread: Black
Tail: Dark brown hackle fibers
Body: Dark brownish black fur
Wings: Dark gray mallard quill section
Hackle: Dark reddish brown
Hook: size 22

•••

Pale Evening Dun

Copies species like *Ephemerella dorothea, E. septentrionalis,* and many *Heptagenia* species like *H. walshi, aphrodite,* and others

Thread: Pale yellow
Tail: Cream hackle fibers
Body: Pale yellowish cream poly, dubbed
Wings: Pale yellow hackle tips
Hackle: Cream
Shuck (optional): Dark olive brown
Hook: sizes 16 to 20

Pale Evening Spinner

Thread: Cream
Tail: Cream hackle fibers
Body: Pale yellowish cream poly, dubbed
Wings: Pale gray poly yarn, tied spent
Hook: Same as above

Pale Evening Nymph

Thread: Brown
Tail: Dark brown pheasant tail fibers
Body: Dark tan opossum dubbing
Wings: Gray mallard quill section
Hackle: Cree
Hook: sizes 16 and 18

•••

Pink Cahill

Copies female of *Epeorus vitreus*. Male dun is
 copied with the Light Cahill, size 16
Thread: Cream
Tail: Gray hackle fibers
Body: Pinkish cream poly for female and pale
 yellow poly for male, dubbed
Wings: Mallard flank feather, dyed pale yellow
Hackle: Cream ginger hackle
Shuck (optional)**:** Dark brownish black
Hook: size 16

Salmon Spinner

Thread: Pink
Tail: Cream ginger hackle fibers
Body: Pinkish red poly, dubbed
Wings: Pale gray poly yarn, tied spent
Hook: Same as above

Pink Cahill Nymph

Thread: Tan
Tail: Dark brown fibers from a pheasant tail
Body: Dub amber on the entire shank, tie in a
 dark brown yarn at the bend of the hook
 and bring up and over and tie in at
 where you tie in the wings.
Wings: Brown turkey section
Hackle: Several turns of a ginger hackle
Hook: size 14

A Green Caddis with a Z-lon shuck.

GREEN CADDIS

Copies many members of the genus
 Rhyacophila
Deer-Head Green Caddis
Thread: Brown
Body: Medium olive-green poly with a gray cast,
 dubbed
Wings: Medium brown deer hair tied in with
 butts pointing toward the bend of the
 hook and the tips of the deer hair
 extending out over the eye of the hook.
 Tie in hair securely near the eye of the
 hook, then wind thread one-fourth of the
 way back towards the bend. Bend deer
 hair back and tie in.
Hackle: If you prefer the regular fluttering
 caddis, you can tie as above and add a
 ginger hackle where you tie in the hair.
 Place a drop of lacquer on thread and
 finished head.
Hook: sizes 14 and 16

Spotted Sedge

Copies *Symphitopsyche slossanae*
Thread: Tan
Body: Grayish tan poly, dubbed
Wings: Medium brown deer hair
Hackle: Ginger
Hook: sizes 14 and 16

DARK BLUE SEDGE

Copies *Psilotreta frontalis*
Thread: Dark gray
Body: Dark gray poly, dubbed
Wings: Dark grayish brown deer hair
Hackle: Dark brownish black
Hook: size 12

GRANNOM

Copies many species of the genus
Brachycentrus
Thread: Black
Body: Dark brownish black to black poly (with olive reflections), dubbed
Wings: Dark brown deer hair
Hackle: Dark brown
Hook: sizes 12 and 14

Little Black Caddis

Copies *Chimarra atterima*
Thread: Black
Body: Black poly, dubbed
Wings: Deer hair dyed dark gray
Hackle: Dark brown
Hook: size 16

CREAM CADDIS

Copies some *Hydropsyche* species
Thread: Tan
Body: Creamish tan poly, dubbed
Wings: Medium brown deer hair
Hackle: Ginger
Hook: size 14

AMBER CADDIS

Copies some *Neophylax* species
Thread: Tan
Body: Tannish poly with an amber hue, dubbed
Wings: Dark brown elk hair
Hackle: Dark brown
Hook: sizes 14 to 18

Dark Brown Caddis

Copies *Deplectrona modesta* and many other
caddis species
Thread: Dark brown
Body: Dark brown poly
Wings: Dark brown deer hair
Hackle: Dark reddish brown
Hook: size 12

Caddis Larvae
Caddis Larva

Thread: Appropriate color (most often dark brown or black)

Tail: Olive, green, brown, yellow, black, or tan fur dubbed and ribbed with fine wire, or use a rubber band of the appropriate color and tie in at the bend of the hook and spiral to the eye

Thorax: Dark brown fur, dubbed; or an ostrich herl, dyed dark brown wound around the hook several times

Hook: sizes 12 to 18

Emerging Caddis Pupa

Thread: Same color as the body color you select

Body: Olive, green, brown, yellow, black, or tan fur or poly nymph-dubbing material

Wings: Dark mallard quill sections, shorter than normal and tied in on both sides of the fly, not on top

Legs: Dark brown grouse or woodcock neck feather wound around the hook two or three times

Hook: 37160, sizes 12 to 18

Early Brown Stonefly

Copies species like *Strophopteryx fasciata*
<u>Adult</u>
Thread: Yellow
Tail: Short dark brown hackle fibers
Body: Dark grayish brown poly, dubbed; or
peacock herl, stripped
Wings: Dark brown deer hair
Hackle: Dark brown
Hook: sizes 12 and 14

<u>Nymph</u>
Thread: Brown
Tail: Fibers from a brown pheasant tail
Body: Reddish brown opossum dubbing
Wings: Brown turkey
Hackle: Brown
Hook: size 12

•••

Light Stonefly

Copies species like *Isoperla signata*
<u>Adult</u>
Thread: Pale yellow
Tail: Short ginger hackle fibers
Body: Pale yellow poly, dubbed and ribbed with
tan thread
Wings: Light tan to cream deer hair
Hackle: Ginger
Hook: sizes 12 and 14

Thread: Tan
Tail: Fibers from a mallard flank feather, dyed
brown
Body: Tan fox fur or nymph dubbing
Wings: Light brown turkey
Hackle: Cree
Hook: size 12

•••

Little Green Stonefly

Copies species like *Alloperla imbecilla*
Adult
Thread: Green
Tail: Short pale cream hackle fibers
Body: Medium green poly, dubbed
Wings: Pale gray hackle tips, tied downwing
Hackle: Pale creamish green hackle
Hook: size 16

Yellow Sally

Copies species like *Isoperla bilineata*
Adult
Thread: Yellow
Tail: Short cream hackle fibers
Body: Pale yellow poly, dubbed
Wings: Cream hackle tips, tied downwing
Hackle: Cree hackle
Hook: sizes 14 and 16

•••

Great Brown Stonefly

Copies species similar to *Acroneuria lycorias*
Adult
Thread: Dark brown
Tail: Short dark brown hackle fibers
Body: Dark brownish gray poly, dubbed and
ribbed with yellow thread
Wings: Dark gray deer hair
Hackle: Dark brown
Hook: sizes 10 and 12

Nymph
Thread: Brown
Tail: Light brown hackle fibers
Body: Light brown fur or nymph dubbing
Wings: Brown turkey
Hackle: Light brown
Hook: size 10

•••

Acroneuria Nymph

Copies many species like *Acroneuria arida,*
abnormis, and *carolinensis*
Thread: Dark brown
Tail: Light brown hackle fibers
Body: Dark olive-brown yarn, laid over top of
pale yellow dubbing fur
Wings: Dark brown turkey
Hackle: Cree
Hook: sizes 10 and 12

•••

Great Stonefly Nymph

Copies many species like the common
Phasganophora capitata

Thread: Tan
Tail: Soft ginger hackle fibers
Body: Dark cream below with darker brown on top
Wings: Mottled turkey quill
Hackle: Cree
Hook: sizes 8 and 10

TERRESTRIALS

POLY BEETLE

The Poly Beetle is tied exactly like the Crowe Beetle, using black poly yarn, however, rather than black deer hair. On a size-16 beetle use three strands of the yarn (about three matchsticks thick). Tie in the poly securely below the bend of the hook. If you wish, tie in a peacock herl at the bend of the hook to imitate the Japanese Beetle. Wind the tying thread up to the eye of the hook, and wind the peacock. Pull the poly up over the shank of the hook and tie in securely just behind the eye. Cut off the excess poly, but leave some to imitate the head. You'll really like this excellent pattern. It's simple, realistic, and takes less than a minute to tie. Tie on hook sizes 12 to 20.

POLY ANT

Body: Black poly, dubbed into two humps on the hook with the rear hump being a bit larger than the front

Hackle: Add a black hackle after you complete the rear hump and before you start the front

KEN'S HOPPER

Body: Yellowish olive, olive, or yellow poly, dubbed heavily.

Head and wings: Use deer body hair dyed yellow and tie in just behind the eye as you would with the Muddler. Clip the butts also as in the Muddler

Hook: sizes 10 to16

LETORT CRICKET

Body: Black poly, heavily dubbed

Wings: Black dyed goose quill sections, tied downwing

Hackle: Deer body hair, dyed black and tied in similar to the Muddler

Hook: sizes 12 to 16

CHERNOBYL CRICKET

Body: Polycelon cut underneath with a slit and placed over the shank of the hook. Extend the body out past the bend a half inch. Add a drop or two of quick drying cement to hold the body to the hook.

Wings: Tie in 10 strands of deer hair, 5 strands of Krystal Flash, and a small piece of orange poly

Hackle: Three black rubber legs on either side.

Hook: size 10

CATERPILLAR

Thread: Black

Body: Black polycelon cut on the bottom and placed on the hook. Add quick dry cement to hold to the shank.

Hackle: Tie in a grizzly saddle hackle at the bend of the hook and palmer up to the eye.

Hook: size 10 or 12

Western Patterns

I'll never forget the first time I planned to fly fish Western waters more than 30 years ago. I called a well-known writer in Montana and asked him what kind of hatches I could expect to see on my first trip to the great trout waters of the West. And I'll never forget his reply.

"You won't see any hatches on most streams and lakes in the West. A few of them hold some stoneflies—but, other than that, you won't see much," that famous writer explained.

How wrong that forecast proved to be.

Patterns When No Hatch Appears

Bead-head patterns have evolved as important wet fly patterns within the past decade. They work extremely well on lakes, rivers, and streams from Arizona and New Mexico to Montana. Patterns like the Olive Bead-head, Tan Bead-head, Bead-head Pheasant Tail, and the Green Weenie have proved great patterns when no hatch appears. You'll find these patterns listed earlier in this chapter..

Patterns to Match the Western Hatches

MAYFLY IMITATIONS

BLUE QUILL

Copies all *Paraleptophlebia* species including
debilis, heteronea, memorialis, gregalis,
and *bicornuta.*
Thread: Dark gray-brown
Tail: Medium gray hackle fibers
Body: Eyed peacock herl, stripped
Wings: Dark gray hackle tips
Hackle (optional)**:** Medium gray or dun
Shuck (optional): Dark brown
Hook: size 18

Blue Quill Spinner

Thread: Dark brown
Tail: Dark brown hackle fibers
Body: Dark brown poly, dubbed
Wings: Pale gray poly yarn, tied spent
Hook: size 18

Para Nymph

Thread: Dark brown
Tail: Mallard flank feather, dyed dark brown
Body: Dark brown angora, dubbed
Wings: One dark gray mallard quill
Hackle: Dark gray
Hook: sizes 16 and 18

•••

Blue Dun or LITTLE BLUE-WINGED OLIVE DUN

Copies *Baetis bicaudatus, tricaudatus, intermedius,* and others.

Thread: Dark gray

Tail: Medium to dark gray hackle fibers

Body: Gray muskrat or medium gray poly with a slight olive cast, dubbed (the body of *Baetis bicaudatus* is more olive than the others)

Wings: On smaller sizes (20) use dark gray mallard quills; on larger sizes use dark gray hackle tips

Shuck (optional)**:** Dark olive brown Z-lon

Hackle: Blue dun

Hook: sizes 18 and 20

(Optional pattern tied with vernille)

Thread: Dark olive

Tail: None

Body: Fine medium olive vernille extending back past the bend of the hook an 1/8 of an inch. Tie in body by ribbing.

Wings: Gray Turkey

Hackle: Gray

Hook: sizes 18 and 20

RUSTY SPINNER

Thread: Dark brown

Tail: Dark grayish brown hackle fibers

Body: Grayish brown poly, dubbed and ribbed with fine tan thread

Wings: Pale gray poly yarn, tied spent

Hook: sizes 18 and 20

Baetis Nymph

Thread: Dark olive

Tail: Wood duck fibers, dyed dark olive
Body: Dark olive brown opossum
Wings: Dark gray mallard quill section
Hackle: Cree, dyed dark olive
Hook: sizes 18 and 20

•••

Trico

Copies all *Tricorythodes* species.
Thread: Pale olive
Tail: Cream hackle fibers
Body: Pale olive poly, dubbed
Wings: Pale gray hackle tips
Hackle: Cream
Shuck (optional): Dark olive gray Z-lon
Hook: sizes 20 to 24

TRICO SPINNER

Thread: Dark brown
Tail: Female: short cream hackle fibers; male:
    long dark brown moose mane
Body: Female: rear third is cream poly dubbed,
    and front two-thirds is dark brown
    dubbed poly. Male: dark brown poly
    dubbed and ribbed with a fine light tan
    thread.
Wings: White poly yarn, tied spent
Hook: sizes 20 to 24

Trico Nymph

Thread: Black
Tail: Dark brown hackle fibers
Body: Dark brownish black fur
Wings: Dark gray mallard quill section
Hackle: Dark reddish brown
Hook: size 22

•••

Pale Evening Dun

Copies species like *Heptagenia elegantula.*
Thread: Pale yellow
Tail: Cream hackle fibers
Body: Pale yellowish-cream poly, dubbed
Wings: Pale yellow hackle tips
Hackle: Cream
Shuck (optional): Dark brown Z-lon
Hook: sizes 16 to 20

Pale Evening Spinner

Thread: Cream
Tail: Cream hackle fibers
Body: Pale yellowish-cream poly, dubbed
Wings: Pale gray poly yarn, tied spent
Hook: Same as dun

Pale Evening Nymph

Thread: Dark brown
Tail: Mallard flank fibers, dyed brown
Body: Dark brown angora loosely dubbed
Wings: Dark mallard section
Hackle: Grouse
Hook: size 14

•••

Pale Morning Dun

Copies species like *Ephemerella inermis,*
infrequens, and *lacustris.*
Thread: Cream
Tail: Cream hackle fibers
Body: Varies from a bright olive to a creamish-yellow. Use poly and dub.
Wings: Pale gray hackle tips
Shuck (optional): Dark brown Z-lon
Hackle: Cream
Hook: sizes 16 and 18

PALE MORNING SPINNER

Thread: Orange
Tail: Tan
Body: Tan
Wings: Pale gray poly yarn
Hook: sizes 16 and 18

Pale Morning Nymph

Thread: Dark brown
Tail: Mallard flank fibers, dyed ginger
Body: Belly is amber angora or nymph dubbing
with a darker brown back
Wings: Brown turkey
Hackle: Cree
Hook: size 16 or 18

•••

Dark Red Quill

Copies species like *Cinygmula par*
Thread: Brown
Tail: Medium dun hackle fibers
Body: Dark reddish-brown hackle stem, stripped
Wings: Dark mallard quills, dark gray calf tail, or
hackle tips
Hackle: Bronze dun
Shuck (optional): Dark gray Z-lon
Hook: size 16

Red Quill Spinner

Thread: Brown
Tail: Pale dun hackle fibers
Body: Reddish-brown hackle stem
Wings: Pale tan polypropylene, tied spend
Hackle: Brown
Hook: size 16 or 18

Red Quill Nymph

Thread: Dark brown
Tail: Mallard flank, dyed amber
Body: Dark grayish-brown furry foam over
      amber angora
Wings: Dark mallard quill
Hackle: Dark grouse or partridge
Hook: size 16

•••

QUILL GORDON

Copies western species like *Epeorus*
      longimanus.and many *Rhitirigena*
      species
Thread: Gray
Tail: Medium dun hackle
Body: Pale to medium gray poly or muskrat fur,
      dubbed
Wings: Dark mallard quills, dark gray calf tail,
      or dark gray hackle tips
Hackle: Pale tannish-gray
Shuck (optional): Dark brown Z-lon
Hook: size 14

QUILL GORDON SPINNER

Thread: Tan
Tail: Moose mane
Body: Pale yellowish-brown poly or dark gray
      peacock herl stripped
Wings: Pale tan polypropylene
Hackle: Ginger with a turn of brown
Hook: size 14

Quill Gordon Nymph

Thread: Dark brown
Tail: Mallard flank dyed amber
Body: Dark brown furry foam over top
Wings: Dark mallard quill
Hackle: Dark grouse or partridge
Hook: size 14

•••

Speckle-Winged Dun

Copies *Callibaetis americanus* and other closely
related species.
Thread: Tan
Tail: Cream ginger hackle fibers
Body: Medium gray polypropylene
Wings: Dark gray mallard flank
Hackle: Pale bronze dun
Shuck (optional): Dark brown Z-*lon*
Hook: sizes 14 and 16

Speckle-winged Spinner

Thread: Gray
Tail: Cream ginger hackle fibers
Body: Pale gray polypropylene
Wings: Mallard flank feather
Hackle: Pale bronze dun
Hook: 14 and 16

Speckle-winged Nymph

Thread: Brown
Tail: Pheasant tail fibers
Body: Medium brown angora
Wings: Dark mallard quill
Hackle: Dark brown grouse
Hook: size 14

•••

Western Green Drake

Copies species like *Drunella grandis.*
Thread: Dark olive
Tail: Moose mane
Body: Olive black polypropylene, ribbed with
pale yellow thread
Wings: Impala, dyed dark gray
Hackle: Grayish black
Shuck (optional): Dark olive brown Z-lon
Hook: size 10 or 12

Great Red Spinner

Thread: Black
Tail: Moose mane
Body: Same as dun
Wings: White polypropylene, tied spent
Hackle: Brownish black
Hook: size 10 or 12

Green Drake Nymph

Thread: Dark brown
Tail: Amber mallard flank feather
Body: Dark olive angora
Wings: Mottled brown turkey
Hackle: Olive brown
Hook: size 12

•••

LIGHT CAHILL

Copies species like *Cinygma dimicki.*
Thread: Yellow
Tail: Ginger hackle fibers
Body: Pale creamish-yellow polypropylene
Wings: Wood duck (or imitation) flank feather
Hackle: Ginger cream
Shuck (optional): Dark brown Z-lon
Hook: size 12

Light Cahill Spinner

Thread: Yellow
Tail: Ginger hackle fibers
Body: Yellowish cream polypropylene
Wings: Pale gray polypropylene
Hackle: Yellowish-cream
Hook: size 12

•••

Pale Brown Dun

Copies species like *Cinygmula reticulata*.
Thread: Tan
Tail: Ginger cream hackle fibers
Body: Pale brown polypropylene
Wings: Yellow mallard flank
Shuck: (optional: Dark brown
Hackle: Ginger cream
Hook: size 12 or 14

Dark Rusty Spinner

Thread: Brown
Tail: Dark brown hackle fibers
Body: Dark brown polypropylene
Wings: Pale yellow polypropylene
Hackle: Dark brown
Hook: size 12 or 14

•••

Pink Lady

Copies species like *Epeorus albertae*.
Thread: Cream
Tail: Cream ginger hackle fibers
Body: Grayish cream polypropylene
Wings: Gray mallard quills or dark gray hackle
tips
Shuck: (optional): Dark brown Z-lon
Hackle: Cream or badger
Hook: size 12

Salmon Spinner

Thread: Cream
Tail: Dark brown moose mane
Body: Female: pinkish-red poly; male: cream gray polypropylene
Wings: Pale gray polypropylene
Hackle: Pale blue dun
Hook: size 12

Pink Lady Nymph

Thread: Brown
Tail: Brown mallard flank
Body: Medium brown furry foam over tan angora
Wings: Light mottled turkey
Hackle: Sandy dun
Hook: size 12

•••

Gray Fox

Copies many species like *Heptagenia solitaria.*
Thread: Tan
Tail: Bronze dun hackle fibers
Body: Yellowish-tan polypropylene
Wings: Pale gray hackle tips
Hackle: Bronze dun
Shuck (optional): Dark brown Z-lon
Hook: size 12

Ginger Quill Spinner

Thread: Tan
Tail: Ginger hackle fibers
Body: Eyed peacock herl, dyed tan and stripped
Wings: Pale gray polypropylene
Hackle: Ginger
Hook: size 12

Gray Fox Nymph

Thread: Brown
Tail: Brown mallard flank
Body: Dark brown furry foam over pale yellow
Wings: Dark mottled turkey
Hackle: Grouse or partridge
Hook: size 14

•••

Pale Brown Dun

Copies *Rhithrogena hageni.*
Thread: Olive
Tail: Cream hackle fibers
Body: Tannish-olive polypropylene
Wings: Gray mallard quills or dark gray hackle
tips
Hackle: Cream ginger
Shuck (optional): Light olive brown Z-lon
Hook: size 12

Dark Tan Spinner

Thread: Tan
Tail: Gray hackle fibers
Body: Pale olive tan polypropylene
Wings: Pale gray polypropylene
Hackle: Cream mixed with dark tan
Hook: size 12

Pale Brown Nymph

Thread: Dark brown
Tail: Wood duck (few fibers)
Body: Greenish brown rabbit with claret hackle
Wings: Dark brown turkey
Hackle: Dark brown
Hook: size 12

•••

Dark Brown Dun

Copies species like *Ameletus veloxi*
Thread: Dark brown
Tail: Dark brown hackle fibers
Body: Dark brown polypropylene
Wings: Teal flank feather
Hackle: Dark brown
Shuck (optional): Dark brown Z-lon
Hook: size 12 or 14

DARK BROWN SPINNER

Thread: Dark brown
Tail: Dark brown hackle fibers
Body: Dark brown polypropylene
Wings: Teal flank feather, dyed yellow
Hackle: Dark brown
Hook: size 12 or 14

Dark Brown Nymph

Thread: Dark brown
Tail: Wood duck (few fibers)
Body: Dark olive brown rabbit with claret hackle
Wings: Dark brown turkey
Hackle: Dark brown
Hook: size 12

•••

Black Quill

Copies *Choroterpes* species
Thread: Dark brown
Tail: Dark bronze dun hackle fibers
Body: Eyed peacock herl, stripped
Wings: Dark gray hackle tips
Hackle: Dark brown hackle with a turn or two of
tan hackle in the rear
Hook: size 14

Early Brown Spinner

Thread: Dark brown
Tail: Dark brown hackle fibers
Body: Dark reddish-brown polyproylene ribbed
with pale yellow thread
Wing: Pale tan polypropylene
Hackle: Dark brown hackle
Hook: size 14

Black Quill Nymph

Thread: Dark brown
Tail: Dark brown hackle fibers
Body: Chocolate brown angora, loosely dubbed
Wings: Dark mallard section
Hackle: Dark brown hackle
Hook: size 12 or 14

•••

Blue Dun

Copies species like *Thraulodes bicornuta.*
Thread: Dark gray-brown
Tail: Medium gray hackle fibers
Body: Dark gray poly
Wings: Dark gray hackle tips
Hackle: Medium gray or dun
Shuck (optional): Dark brown Z-lon
Hook: size 14

Blue Dun Spinner

Thread: Dark brown
Tail: Dark brown hackle fibers
Body: Dark brown poly, dubbed
Wings: Pale gray poly yarn, tied spent
Hook: size 14

CADDISFLY IMITATIONS

GREEN CADDIS

Copies some species in Genus *Rhyacophila* and
        Cheumatopsyche
Thread: Green
Body: Green polypropylene
Wings: Brown deer body hair
Hackle: Tan (optional deer hair)
Hook: sizes 14 and 16

Little Black Caddis

Copies some species in Genus *Chimarra*
Thread: Black
Tail: Optional—add tan Z-lon shuck
Body: Black poly, dubbed; (optional) wind a
        dark brown hackle in at the bend of the
        hook and palmer it to the eye. Clip off
        the barbules on top.
Wings: Dark brown deer or elk hair
Hackle: Optional—dark brown
Shuck (optional): Tan Z-lon
Hook: Size 16

TAN CADDIS

Copies many specie in the Genus *Hydropsyche*
Thread: Tan
Body: Tan Poly, dubbed
Wings: Light brown deer hair
Hackle: Tan
Shuck (optional): Tan Z-lon
Hook: Size 14 or 16

GRANNOM

Copies many species in the Genus
Brachycentrus
Hook: Sizes 12 to 16
Thread: Black or very dark olive green
Body: Black or very dark green poly, dubbed
Wings: Dark deer body hair, tied downwing
Hackle: Optional—Dark brown

OCTOBER CADDIS

Copies several _Dicosmoecus_ species
Thread: Orange
Body: Orange poly
Wings: Dark elk hair
Hackle: Dark brown
Hook: sizes 6 and 8

STONEFLY IMITATIONS

Little Yellow Stonefly

Copies species like _Skwala parallela_
Thread: Yellow
Tail: Short cream hackle fibers
Body: Pale yellow to yellowish olive poly,
dubbed
Wings: Cream hackle tips, tied down-wing
Hackle: Cree hackle
Hook: Size 16

Little Yellow Stonefly Nymph

Thread: Pale yellow
Tail: Pale yellow hackle fibers
Body: Pale yellow angora
Wings: Pale yellow mallard flank
Hackle: Pale yellow hackle
Hook: Size 16

•••

Little Black Stonefly

Copies species like *Encopnopsis brevicanda*
Thread: Black
Tail: Short black hackle fibers
Body: Black poly dubbed
Wings: Pale gray deer hair
Hook: Size 16

•••

Little Brown Stonefly

Copies some species in the Genus
Amphinemura
Thread: Dark brown
Tail: Dark brown moose mane, very short
Body: Dark brown poly
Wings: Gray deer hair
Hook: Sizes 16 and 18

CHIRONOMID OR MIDGE IMITATIONS

Black Midge Pupa

Thread: Black

Body: Black antron (you can tie in other body colors like cream and dark gray)

Ribbing: Fine copper wire. Wing case of white poly of Z-lon tied in like short spinner wings.

Thorax: Black angora, dubbed

Hook: Sizes 18 to 24

Tying Notes: Tie in the white poly and make it extend an eighth- to quarter-inch to the right and left of the shank. Dub a liberal amount of black angora behind, over top of the wing case. After finishing the body and applying the ribbing, tie in a piece of white Z-lon just behind the eye of the hook. Dub the thorax with muskrat, then bring the piece of Z-lon over top of the thorax and tie in at the eye. Let the Z-lon extend over the eye and an eighth inch beyond.

Stillborn Midge

Thread: Black
Body: Black tying thread ribbed with fine copper wire. White Z-lon tied on top and extending over back and front.
Thorax: Black angora, dubbed
Hook: Size 20
Tying Notes: Tie in the Z-lon at the bend of the hook. Let a piece as long as the shank of the hook extend back over the hook. Pull the Z-lon over top of the completed body and secure with the ribbed copper wire. Let the Z-lon extend out over the eye of the hook about half an inch.

GRIFFITH'S GNAT

Thread: Black
Body: Peacock herl
Hackle: Grizzly
Hook: Sizes 20 to 26

GRAY, BLACK AND CREAM MIDGE

Thread: Same as body color
Body: Gray, cream or black
Hackle: Gray, cream or black
Wings: Small pale gray hackle tips
Hackle: Dark gray, black or cream (depending on body color)
Shuck (optional): Pale gray Z-lon
Hook: Sizes 20 to 26

Chad Bayles lands a heavy rainbow on a Zebra Midge at Lee's Ferry on the Colorado River.

ZEBRA MIDGE

Bead: Copper bead (brown body) or brass bead (black body)

Thread: Black or brown

Body: Use tying thread and make a very slim body with it.

Ribbing: Fine copper wire for brown and fine silver wire for black body

– 10 –

REVIEW THE ESSENTIALS

You're fishing with a friend. You both have about the same casting skills, you're both using the same Bead Head Pheasant Tail and you're casting in the same general area. But, he's catching more trout than you are. You've seen plenty of trout come up close to your pattern, but they swim away and refuse it. Why? Look at some of the factors you've read about in this book—the key ingredients to help you catch more trout.

As you've learned throughout the book, pattern selection is only part of the secret to catching more trout. The leader you use to connect that fly, where you fish that fly, and how you float or drift that fly—all blend together to create an angler who will catch more trout. Are you doing any of these differently than your angling friend? I've often seen trout examine a wet or dry fly close up and them refuse it. Often if I add a piece of smaller fluorocarbon tippet material I'll begin to catch more trout.

And don't forget what you use to detect strikes can help you catch more trout. Use a strike indicator to give yourself an edge. Try using the tandem—it gives you the added benefit of fishing at the two depths at the same time.

Finally, in Chapter 8, we looked at some aspects of fly-fishing we often neglect. Remember some of the techniques that you can use on streams that are heavily fished, and how to position yourself for a hatch.

Other anglers might find that pattern selection is their big bugaboo. It is to many anglers. Try a pattern that closely matches the insect on which the trout are feeding. If there is no hatch what do you do? Do you

A trout caught on a bead head.

try a tandem made up of a wet fly and a dry fly? Do you use just a wet fly or a dry fly? Do you resort to a streamer pattern? How do you make your decision? Hopefully, Chapter 2 will help you decide what fly to use and when. If you look closely enough you'll see that the two of you are doing something different.

What will be the outcome if you adhere to the rules that I've set forth? You will indeed become a more skilled fly fisher—one who catches more trout. Once you've progressed with these new skills what should you do? Make certain you return every trout back to the stream—quickly and safely. With the advent of increased angling pressure on many streams we've got to return each and every trout. You will be catching more—you've got to release more.

I know some well-known and skilled fly fishers who continue to kill trout on almost every trip they take. They argue that somebody else will

Irondequiot Creek near Rochester, New York, gets plenty of fishing pressure on the opening day of the trout season.

kill the fish if they don't—or they're planning a large fish fry for friends—or they have a neighbor or relative that wants some fresh fish.

I, too, killed trout—50 years ago. But, I quickly progressed beyond that point. I now believe that each and every trout must be returned back to the stream. Even as a young teenager I learned that I had to release my catch if I wanted to enjoy fully the sport of fly-fishing. My favorite stream in those formative years was Bear Creek in southeastern Pennsylvania. I still remember that pool where I found all the trout one day. Evidently a deputy warden had stocked a section of the stream that normally didn't receive trout. I fished that section one afternoon and landed more than 30 trout on a Yellow Sally pattern. For more than two weeks I came back almost daily to that section and caught trout. Then one day I saw another angler fishing the same section. He had a huge willow creel. I watched him catch his limit, kill them and place them in the creel. This other angler returned just about every day for the next week until he had decimated the trout population in that section. Now the trout that I had enjoyed catching day after day would strike no more. He, too, would never enjoy catching any more trout out of this stretch of stream. They were gone forever.

Fly-fishing has come a long way in the past 55 years. A tremendous change has appeared in the sport. During my first 25 years I rarely saw another fly fisher. If I did that angler most often used wet flies with

The walk-in section of Lee's Ferry on the Colorado is crowded just about any time of the year.

snelled hooks. One other thing predominated in those first 25 years: most anglers killed just about everything they caught.

My first "fly rod" during those two decades was a metal telescoping rod. I had only one reel—a Pflueger—and a level fly line. I finally purchased a Shakespeare fiberglass rod shortly after World War II. Those who could afford them used bamboo fly rods. Shortly after World War II anglers showed up on the streams with bamboo fly rods that were bought in the Far East. I saw my first spinning reel while fishing on a stream near my home in 1946. I can still remember the experience as if it had occurred just yesterday. I watched that spin fisherman cast to areas of that stream that were difficult to reach with a fly rod. I saw that man catch a number of trout and wondered what effect this newfangled reel would have on the sport.

In the next 20 years, from 1969 to 1989, fiberglass and then graphite rods came into wide use. Anglers began thinking about returning trout back to their environs. As this two-decade period progressed, more and more anglers returned trout back so others could also enjoy catching them. Trout Unlimited and other groups began offering fly tying courses and the sport took on another aspect—tying your own fly patterns.

The past 10 years have brought a tremendous change in fly-fishing. Now it is much more common to release that trout so others might enjoy catching it later. The sport grew quickly partly because of the enchantment with the movie *A River Runs through It.* More anglers meant more crowded streams. More fishing pressure meant more highly selective trout. In the past few years I've seen the effects of heavy angling pressure—bloody mouths in trout. I've seen trout strike, then let go so quickly that not even the most adept angler could effectively set the hook.

In these past 10 years fly-fishing has changed in other ways. Even heavier angling pressure, more sophisticated patterns, and better equipment have arrived on the scene. If older anglers haven't changed they'll be left behind.

Even with the added pressure, the future looks fairly bright for fly-fishing and the state of our trout waters. In the past 50 years I've seen plenty of streams once polluted now reclaimed. Streams and rivers that hadn't seen trout for almost a century now boast a good population—some even stream bred fish. As a kid I hiked and trapped along the Schuylkill River in Cressona, Pennsylvania. That river was so dirty that everybody referred to it as the "Black Creek." Just recently many branches of this river, contaminated from the ravages of hard coal mining for almost a century, now boast some trout. In future years this entire resource will hold trout.

I've said several times that the future of fly-fishing—no fishing in general—will be catch and release. I'll never forget the first time I met Craig Hudson. We met during a hatch of blue quills on a stream in northeastern Pennsylvania. Craig didn't have a pattern to match the hatch so I gave him one—on one condition. He had to return every trout back to the stream that he caught on that pattern. He caught a half dozen trout that day and promptly returned every one back to the stream. After that day Craig Hudson never killed a trout.

I can still vividly remember just a couple years back when I handed an angler a Quill Gordon pattern during a hatch and I asked him to return any trout he caught with that pattern. As I walked away I saw the fly fisher hit a trout over the head that he had just caught. Soon he landed and killed another trout. So much for his promise to return the trout.

Just a few expert fly fishers can deplete a stream of trout. I still see plenty of expert anglers killing trout. I can't even kill a trout on a marginal stream. There is no reason strong enough to kill trout. If I hook a trout deeply enough that it bleeds I usually quit for the day. On many occasions in the heat of the summer and when I don't want to put undue stress on the trout, I won't even set the hook when I'm using the tandem. I just record the number of strikes by counting the number of times the dry fly sank.

As you progress in your fly fishing ability you'll find that catching that trout is not as difficult as it was just a few years before. Pattern selection, drag, using the proper leader, depth, and detecting strikes become second nature to you. Hopefully I've instilled another important aspect of fly-fishing—releasing every trout you catch! Want to catch more trout? Then release every one you catch!

INDEX

A

Adams, Ed, 37, 102
Arkansas River, 28, 89, 125
Au Sable, 187

B

Baldacchino, Phil, 26
Bastian, Don, 36
Bay, Mike, 205
Bayles, Chad, 90
Baylor, Don, 31
Bear Creek, 273
Beaverkill River, 181
Best, A. K., 53, 174, 176
Big Bonito Creek, 157
Big Fishing Creek, 108
Bighorn River, 25, 64, 110, 163
Bitterroot River, 52, 63, 86, 182
Black, Jim, 74
Blue River, 13, 164
Bowman Creek, 41
Bradford, Virgil, 37, 102, 113
Brauburger, Fred, 33, 161
Budd, Bob, 35, 132, 173, 174, 176

C

Cache la Poudre, 90, 14, 130
Camera, Phil, 28, 41, 186, 191
Carpenter, Walt, 174
Casselman River, 123
Cave Lake, 90
Clark, Mike, 174, 176
Clouser, Bob, 46
Colorado River, 90, 119, 158, 165

Cramer, Bob, 40

D

David, Bob, 46, 218
David, Josh, 218
Delaware River, 187
Deschutes River, 64, 110
Dorula, Ron, 10

E

Elam, Pat, 205
Engerbrettson, Dave, 87, 160
Eshenower, Dave, 40, 187

F

Falling Spring Run, 120
Finkbiner, Tom, 137
Firehole River, 172
Flowers, Wills, 100
Fortune, Mark, 189
Fryingpan River, 52, 90
Furimsky, Chuck, 207

G

Gallatin River, 165
Gehman , Tony, 40, 187-188
German, Flossie, 46
German, Ron, 46
Gierach, John, 53, 174
Gigliotti, Vince, 186
Glo-Bug, 13, 24, 30, 37, 138, 140, 213
Gordon, Eugene, 123
Grand River, 187